The Peak District in Watercolour

Geoff Kersey

Published by Northern Arts Publications
an imprint of Jeremy Mills Publishing Limited

113 Lidget Street
Lindley
Huddersfield
West Yorkshire
HD3 3JR

www.jeremymillspublishing.co.uk

First published 2012
This revised edition published 2013

ISBN: 978-1-906600-78-5

Contents

Introduction

I have lived in the Derbyshire Dales on the very edge of the Peak District for over twenty years now; but my familiarity and enjoyment of this beautiful area emanates from family outings in a Ford Zephyr from Sheffield during my childhood, when we would visit one of our many favourite picnic spots.

For me, one of the most difficult aspects of working as a professional landscape artist and teacher is finding sufficient fresh and inspiring subjects. Whilst I have travelled throughout the United Kingdom and abroad to satisfy this challenge, I appreciate the wealth of material within walking distance, or a short car journey, from my home. The variety of scenery in the Peak District and Derbyshire Dales is enthralling; from the remnants of its industrial past around Cromford, Matlock and Lathkildale, to the grandeur of Chatsworth, and the ruggedness of the grit-stone edges.

In this book I have included an array of work; from paintings finished a few days prior to the deadline, to others photographed and painted many years ago.

Variation in painting technique and approach is apparent throughout the book; a reflection of my endeavour to improve and develop my skills over the years. For each painting I have commented on the subjects and my approach to painting them, which I hope will help any aspiring artists to make progress themselves. On the other hand you might just enjoy looking through the pictures and hopefully recognize some of your favorite places.

1 *Dovedale*

This is one of the most popular areas of the Peak District with walkers, and over the years has provided me with many painting subjects. Apparently it is one of the most visited natural tourist sites in Britain and was mentioned by George Byron, who wrote in a letter to the poet Thomas Moore: 'I can assure you there are things in Derbyshire as noble as Greece or Switzerland'.

The Dovedale valley is a steep wooded ravine that runs for just over three miles between Thorpe Cloud in the south and Milldale in the north. The rock that forms this valley is the fossilised remains of sea creatures that lived in a shallow sea over the area during the carboniferous period. Evidence of these fossilised creatures can still clearly be seen in the steps that lead up and down the contours of the riverside path; a path that I understand was originally built during the Second World War by Italian prisoners of war.

Our favourite way to do this walk is to start from the car park near Ilam, cross the famous stepping stones – which were much improved in 2010 by raising their height with mortar and limestone slabs – and then with Thorpe Cloud (which is a hill) behind, keeping the river on the left, follow the undulating path right through to the village of Milldale.

This route is rich in a variety of inspiring scenes; and unique limestone spires stick up from the side of the valley, created over millions of years by the river eroding the softer rock and soil around them. These make fascinating subjects for an artist as the hard craggy forms contrast with the surrounding softer appearance of vegetation and foliage. There are many opportunities along the walk to find more painting subjects before crossing over Viator's Bridge (an excellent subject in itself) and entering the tiny village of Milldale.

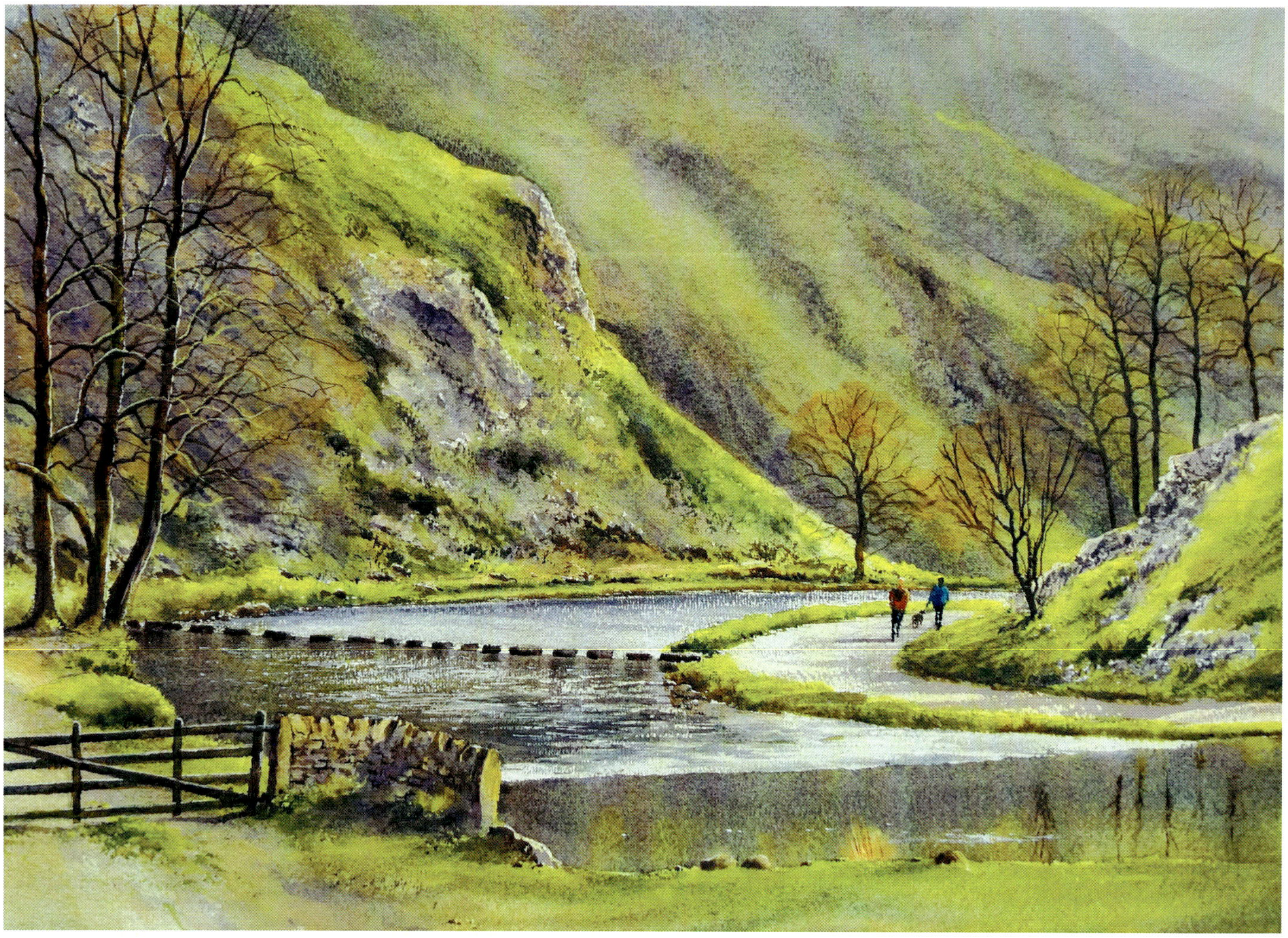

Stepping Stones, Dovedale

This composition was achieved from an elevated view on the bank, to give more of an impression of the curve in the river. The river changed from almost vertical reflections in the slow moving areas, to the more disturbed surface, where the flow of the water sped up just beyond the small waterfall, and then again beyond the stepping stones. To create that vital feeling of distance, the farthest hill was painted using greyer, paler colours, which were then blurred and faded slightly by leaving them to dry before washing over them with clean water and dabbing with tissue. The painting on the opposite page features the same scene but from footpath level.

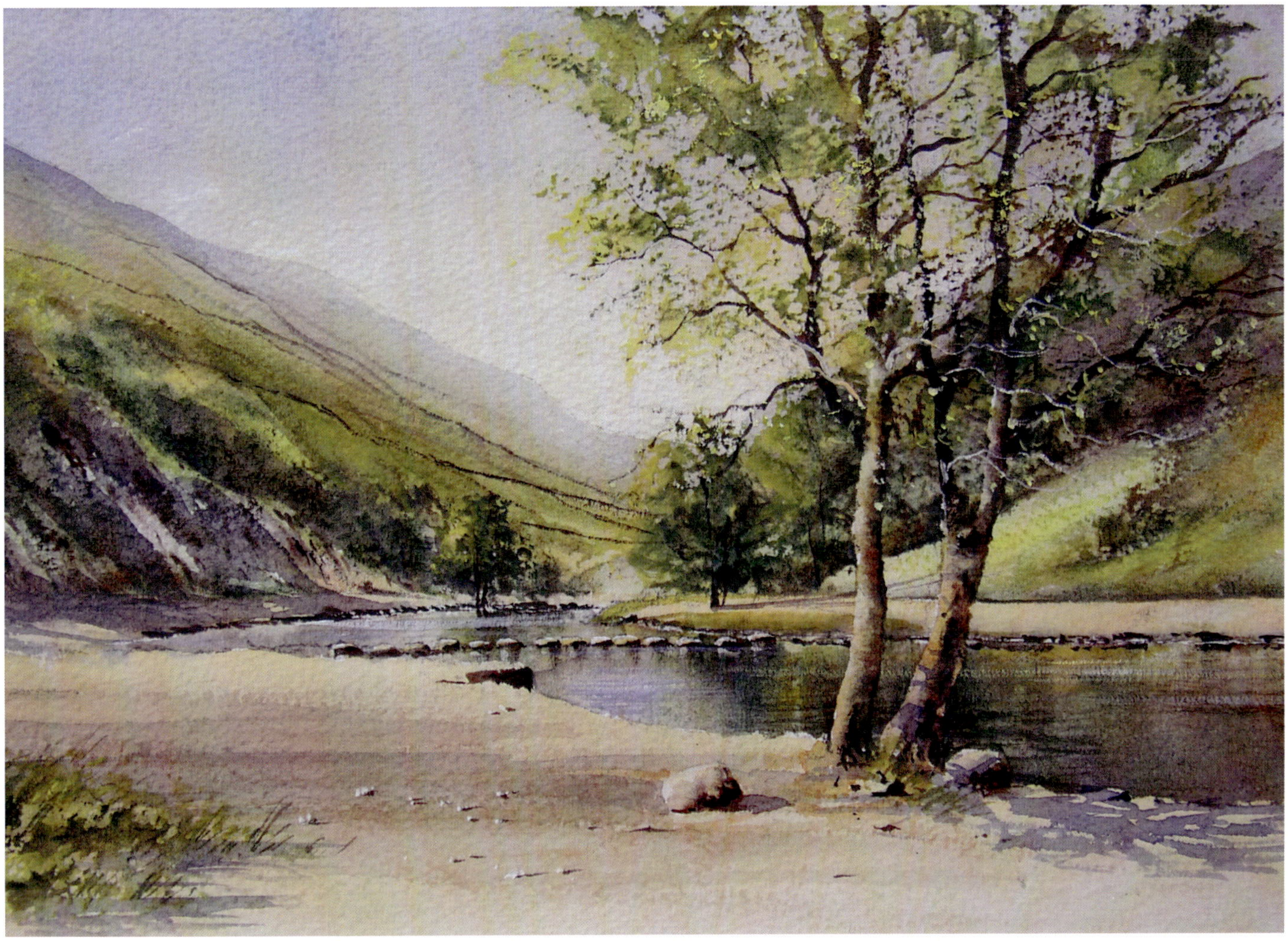

Spring in Dovedale

This view was painted in the spring, just further along from the stepping stones. The low viewpoint highlighted the contrast of the craggy, uneven shapes of the foreground rocks and stones, against the softer shapes of the foliage and slightly blurred reflections in the slow-moving river.

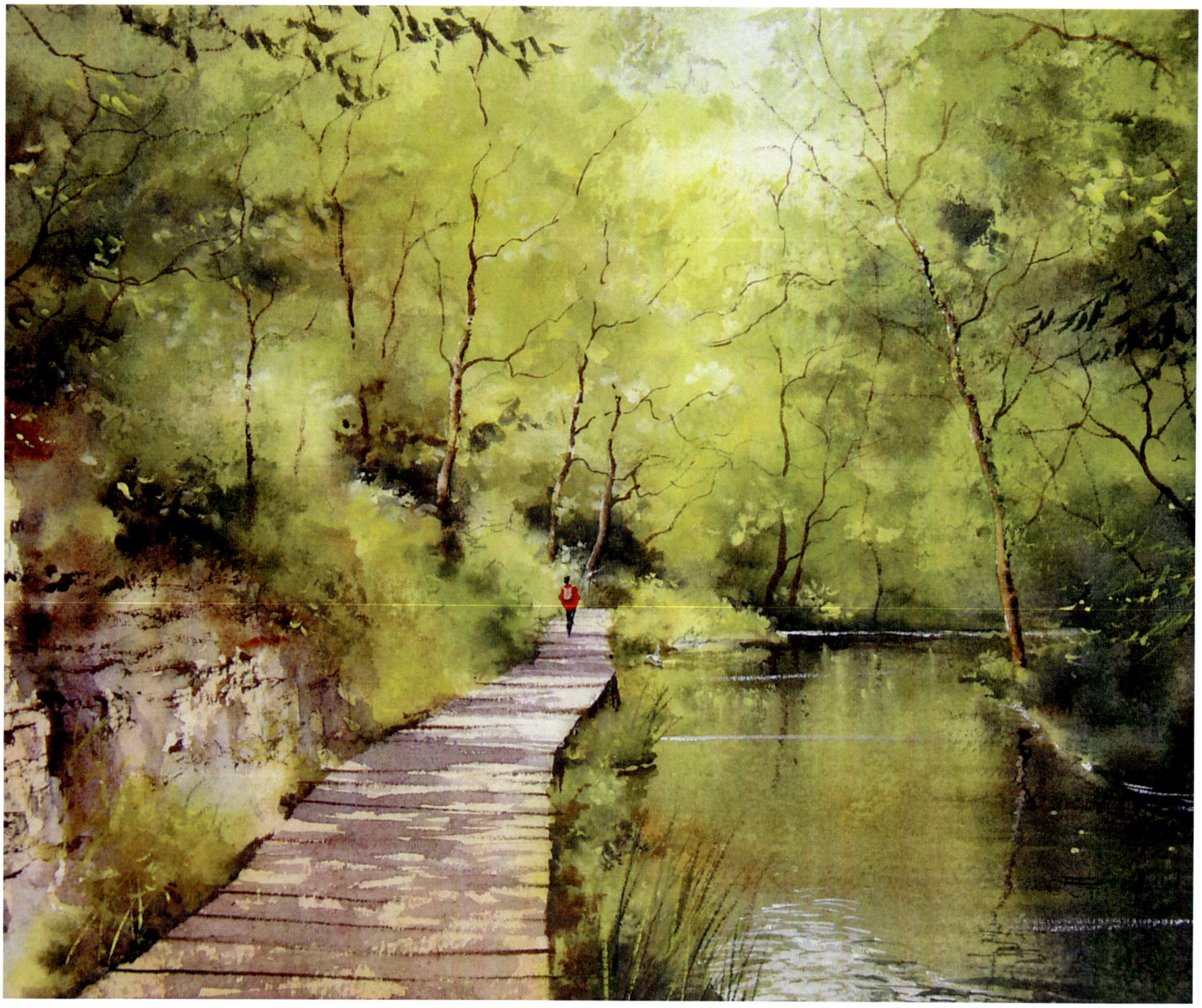

The Boardwalk, Dovedale

A short part of the Dovedale Valley features this wooden boardwalk. It is a favourite subject of mine and over the years I have painted it in the different seasons. The sharp, right-hand edge of the boards gives a sort of 'S' shaped bend which leads into the scene.

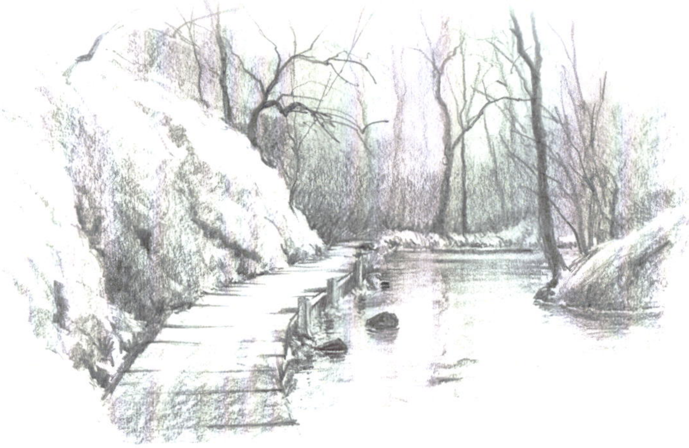

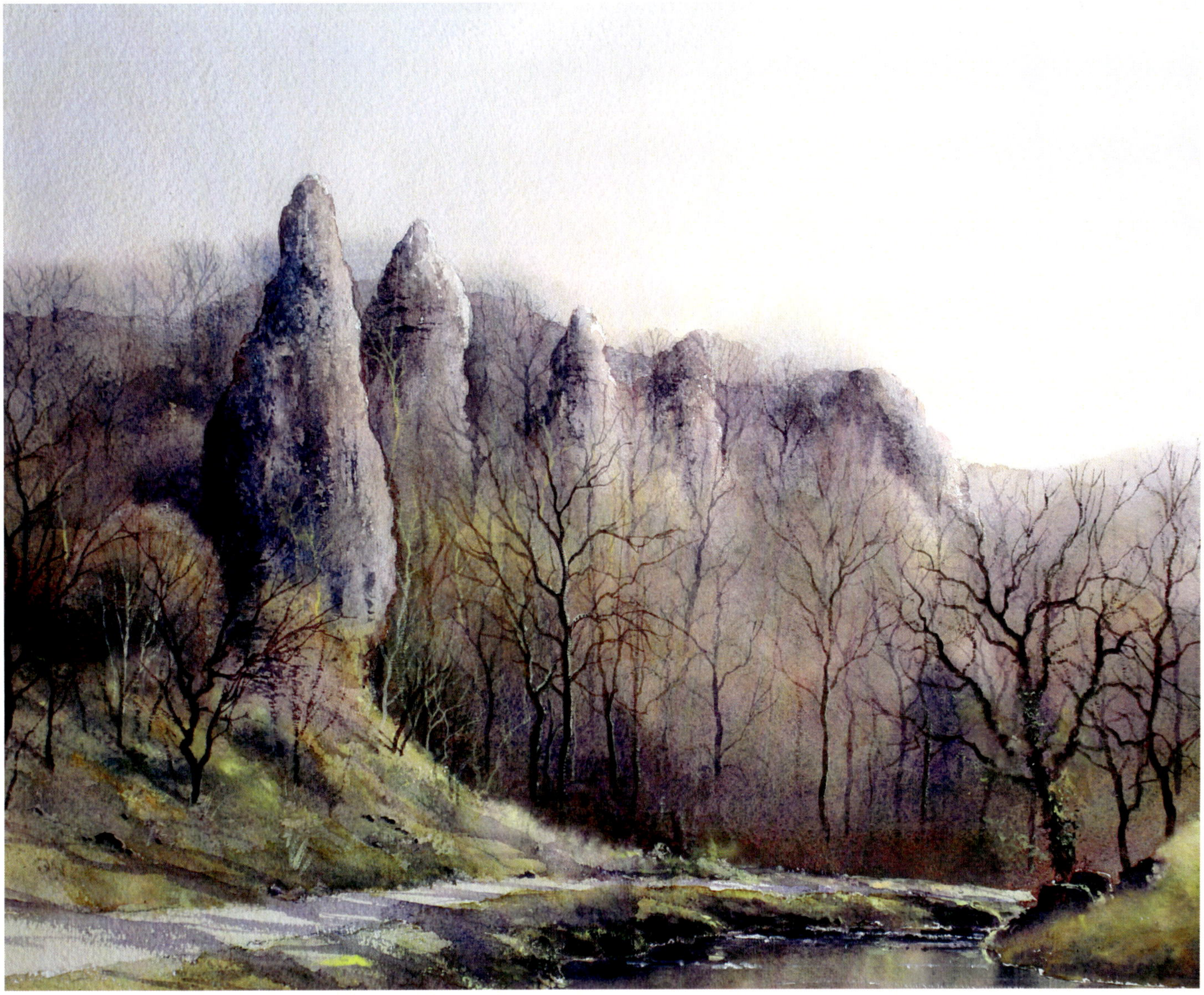

Limestone Spires, Dovedale

This scene is painted from a photograph taken on a bright winter's day in the middle of January. Owing to the depth of the ravine the hours of sunlight can be very short in the winter, and for a time, the sun illuminates these pillars of rock like a floodlight, creating long dark shadows that increase the drama. The colours were deliberately muted here, by using various combinations of grey for the rocks and masses of winter trees. These rich darks are contrasted against bright greens and lemon yellow, with a few splashes of crimson and Naples yellow, to warm the grey in places.

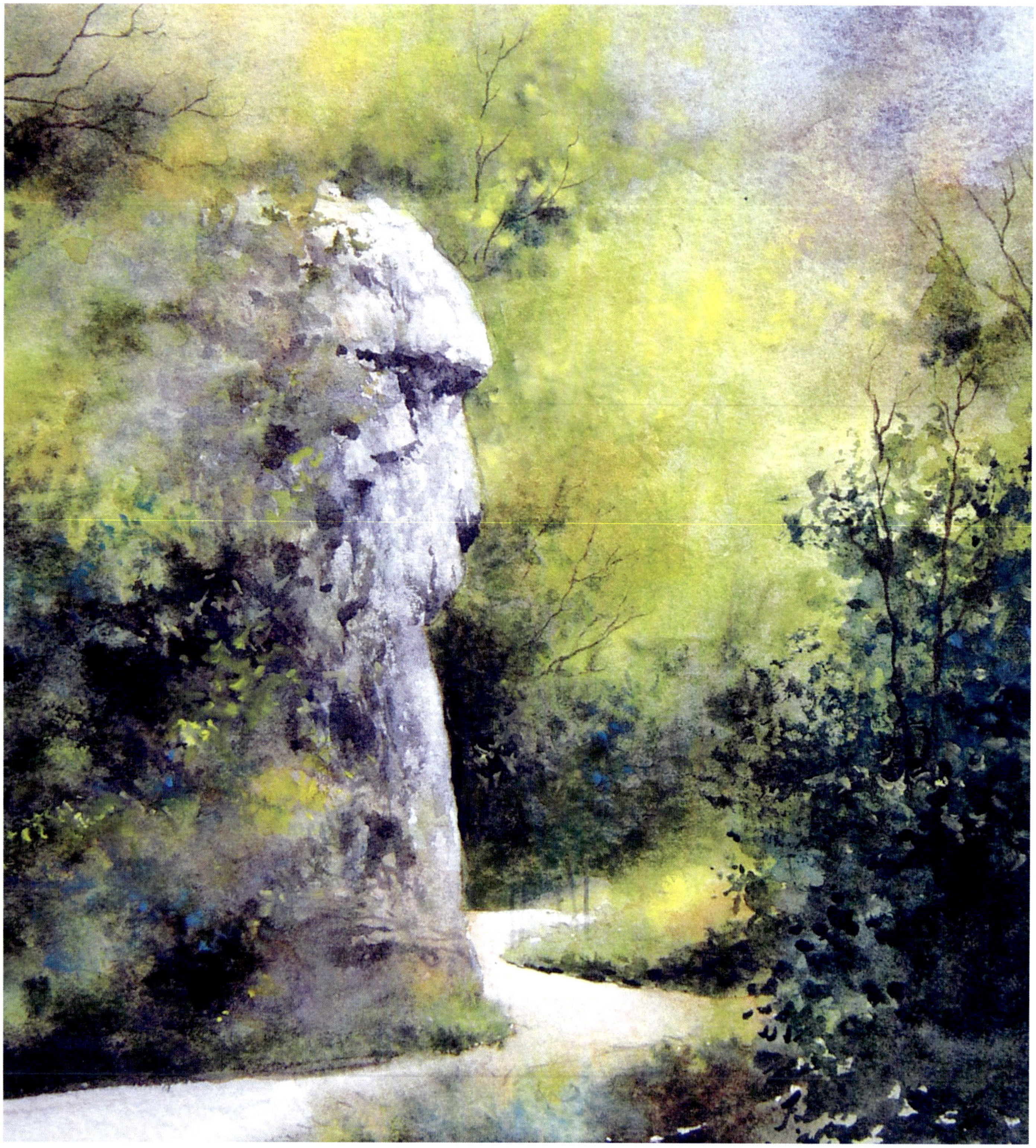

Lion's Head Rock, Dovedale

This natural curiosity is called Lion's Head Rock, for obvious reasons. This is just a quick watercolour sketch, done with a view to creating a larger painting from it.

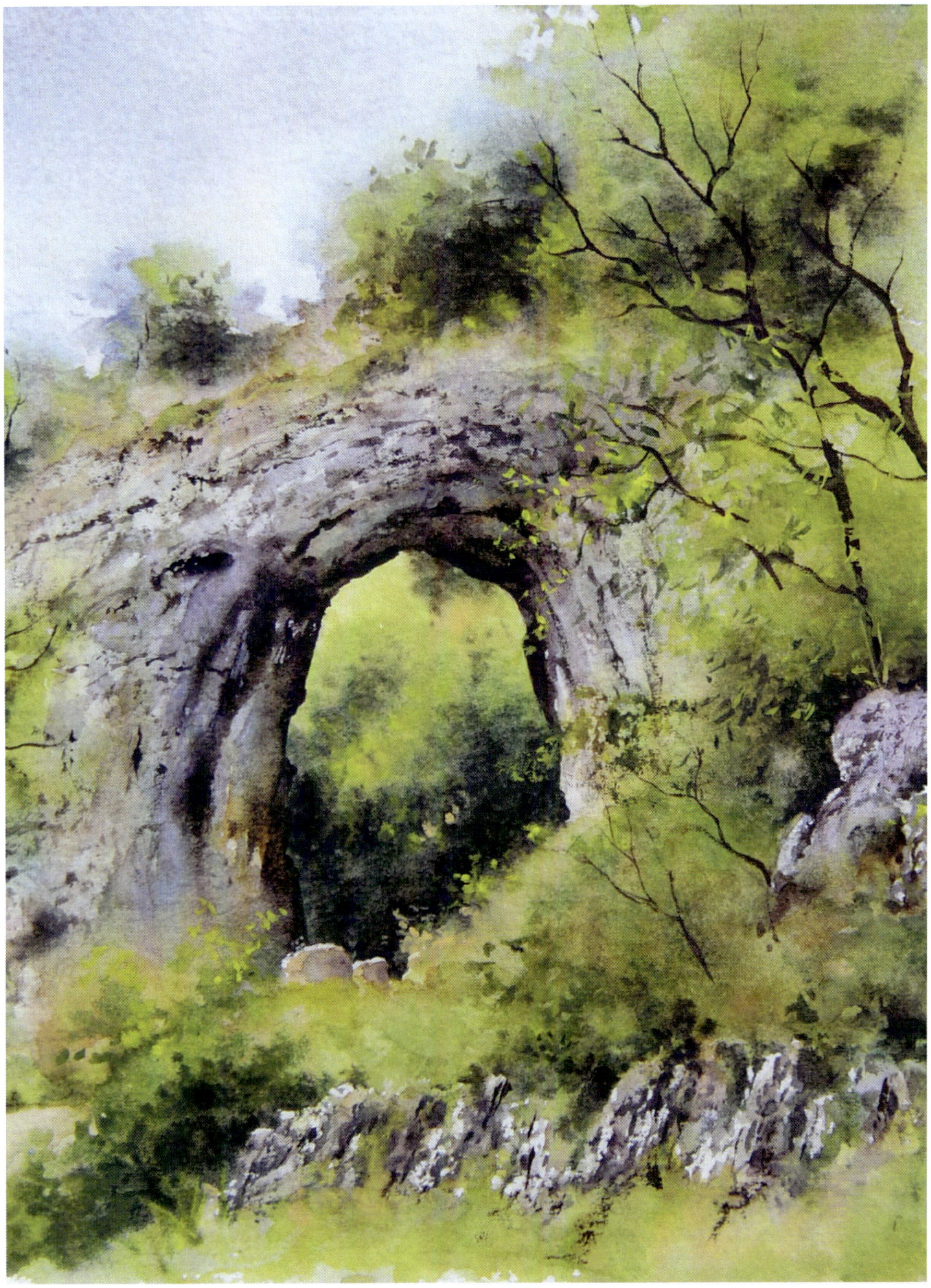

Reynard's Cave, Dovedale

This is a small watercolour of one of a few natural caves found in Dovedale that were used at one time by shepherds for shelter. The cave opening frames the abundance of foliage, and the deep, dark shadow area on the underside of the cave contrasts with the bright summer colours.

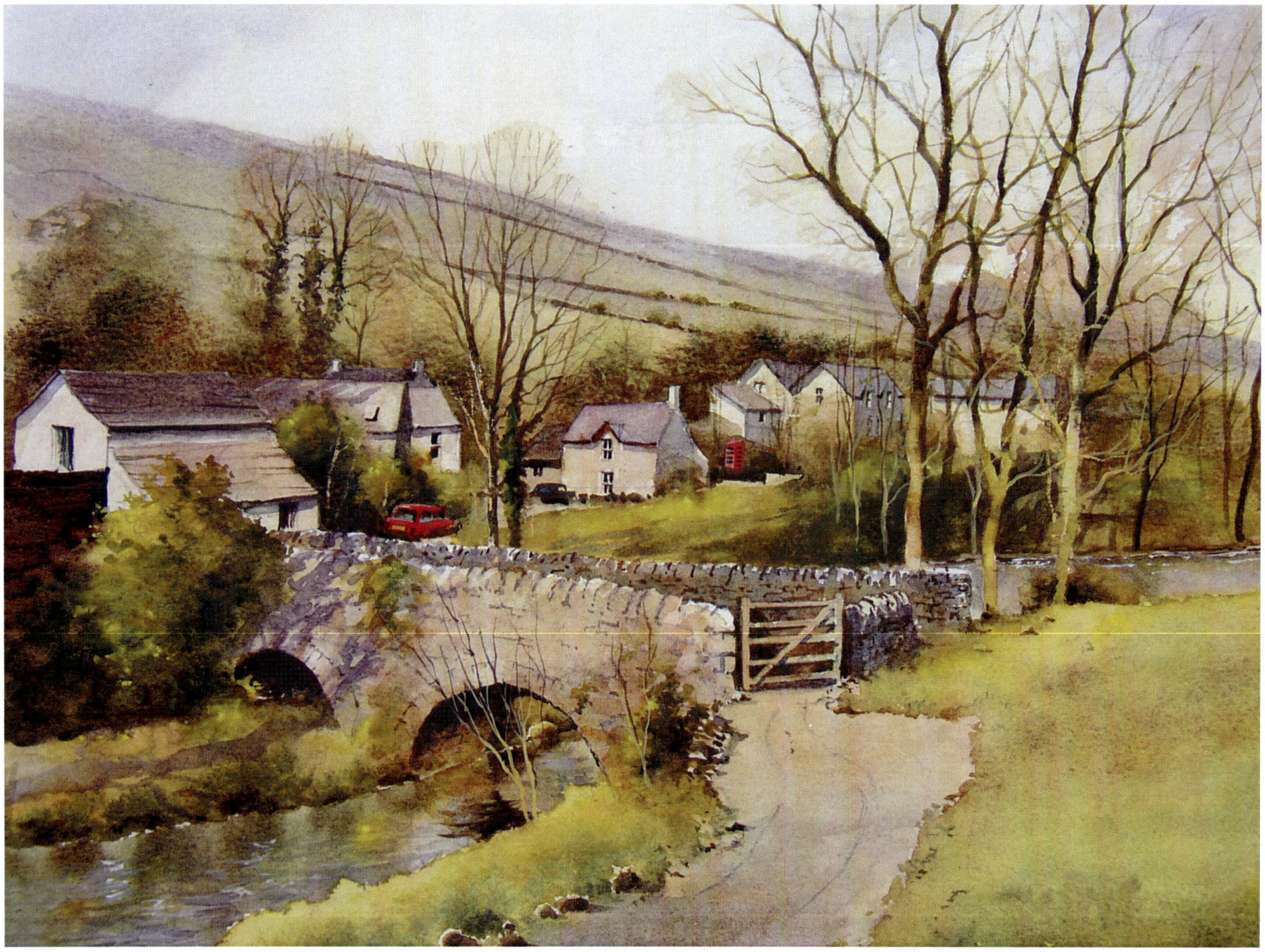

Viator's Bridge, Milldale

At the northern end of Dovedale, the path crosses an ancient and narrow packhorse bridge known as Viator's Bridge, the name being based on the Latin word for 'traveller'. The path leads into the tiny village of Milldale, a scene featured on many Peak District calendars, and included in numerous books of Peak District photographs. There's a good reason for its popularity among artists, photographers and walkers alike, as it is a ready-made composition, with the eye being lead over the little rustic bridge into the assortment of houses and cottages glimpsed amongst the trees. The tall trees on the right provide an excellent 'L' shaped composition, with the scene completed by the slope of distant meadows.

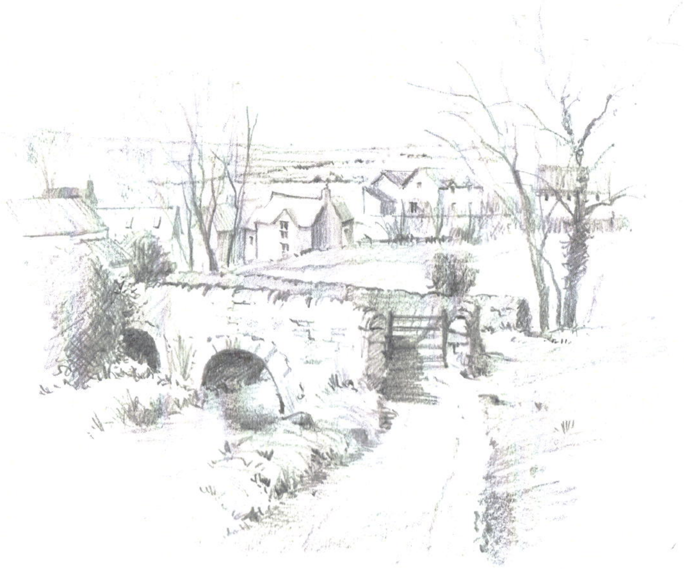

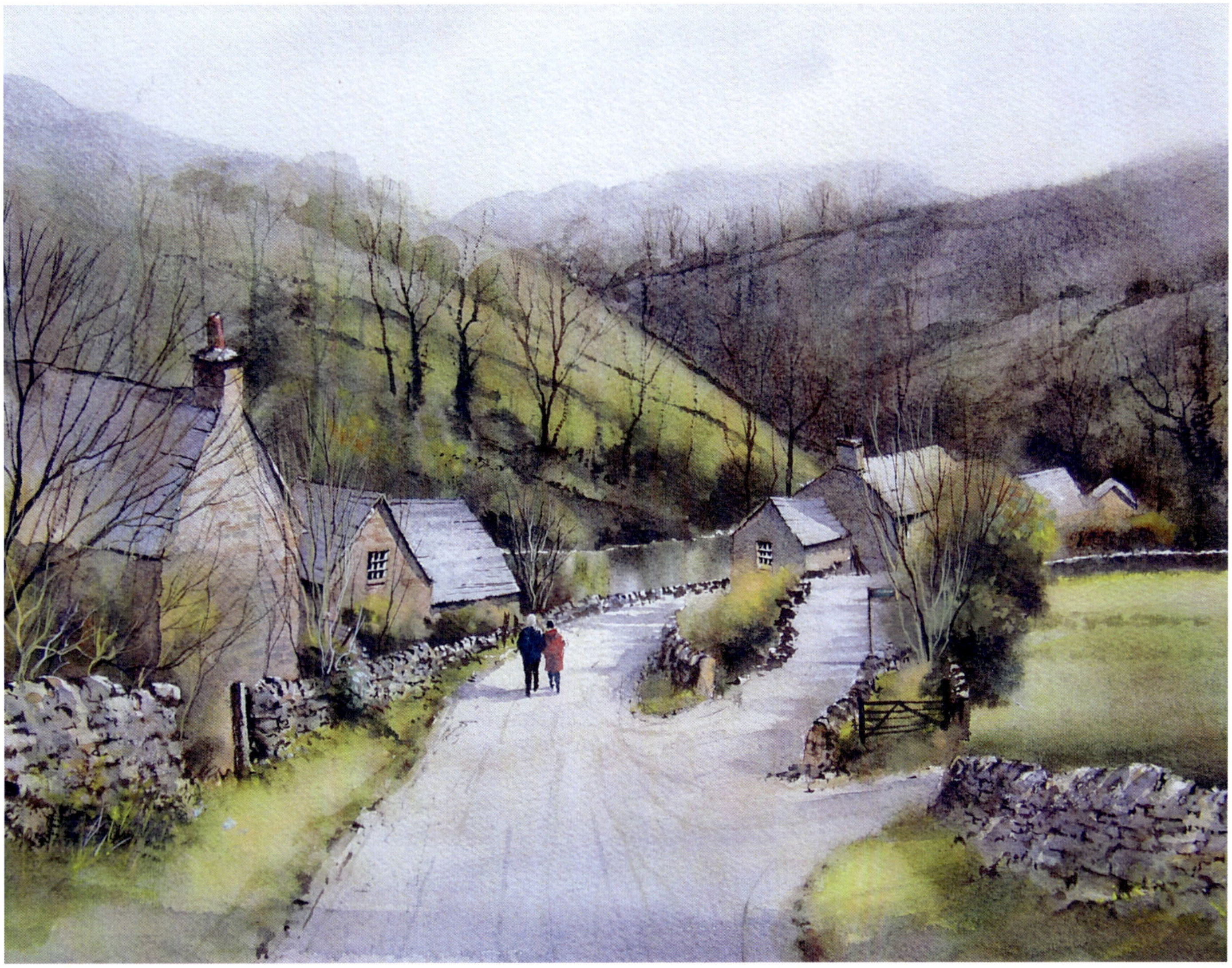

Looking down to Milldale

I have ended this section on Dovedale by taking another high viewpoint; this time looking back down over Milldale. The hill on the left and the jumble of rooftops catch the sunlight, in contrast with the cool grey of the distant hills.

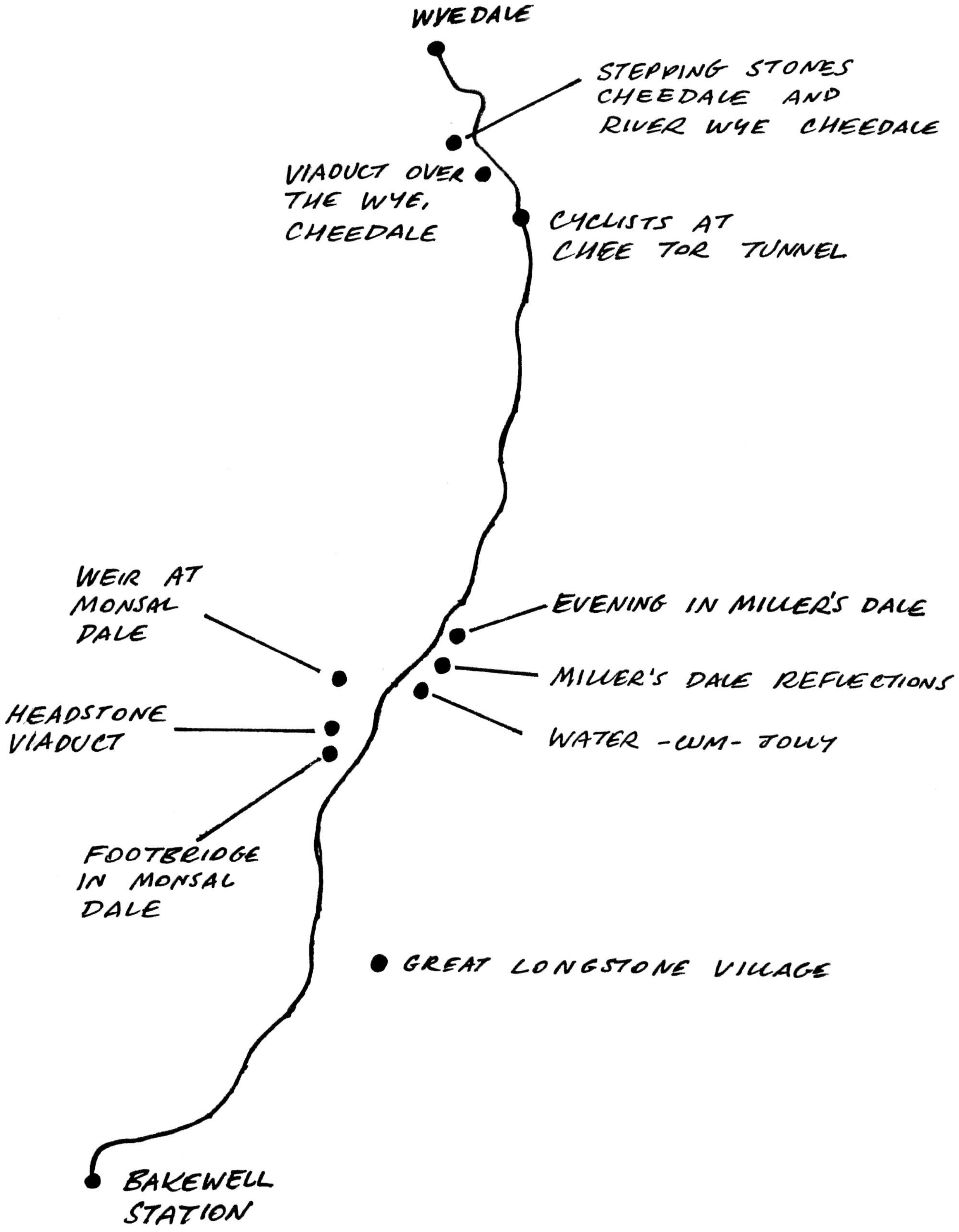
WYEDALE
STEPPING STONES CHEEDALE AND RIVER WYE CHEEDALE
VIADUCT OVER THE WYE, CHEEDALE
CYCLISTS AT CHEE TOR TUNNEL
WEIR AT MONSAL DALE
EVENING IN MILLER'S DALE
MILLER'S DALE REFLECTIONS
HEADSTONE VIADUCT
WATER -CUM- JOLLY
FOOTBRIDGE IN MONSAL DALE
GREAT LONGSTONE VILLAGE
BAKEWELL STATION

2 *The Monsal Trail*

Another favoured area of the Peak District, rich in painting subjects, is this 8.5 mile (13.7 km) trail that follows a section of the former Manchester, Buxton, Matlock and Midlands Junction Railway, built by the Midland Railway in 1863 to link Manchester with London. The line was closed in 1968 and remained unused for twelve years before being taken over by the Peak District National Park. It runs from Coombs Viaduct just one mile east of Bakewell, to the Topley Pike junction in Wye Dale, which is just three miles south east of Buxton. It follows the River Wye valley, running parallel to the A6.

Until May 2011 parts of the trail were inaccessible due to three of the tunnels being closed for safety reasons; but many of the paths diverted around these closed tunnels, afforded beautiful scenery ideal for painting. It is this loose connection that links all the paintings in this section.

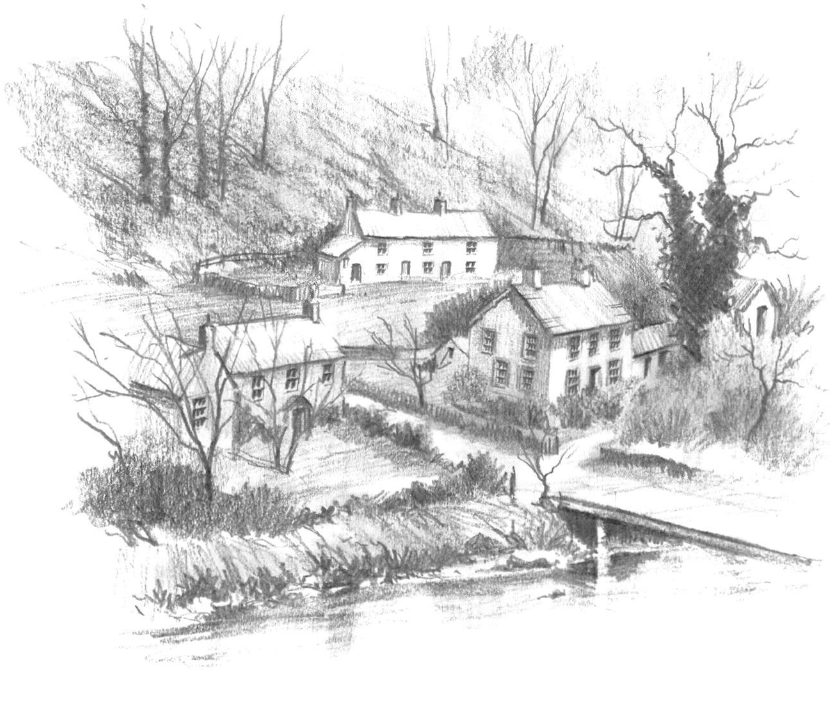

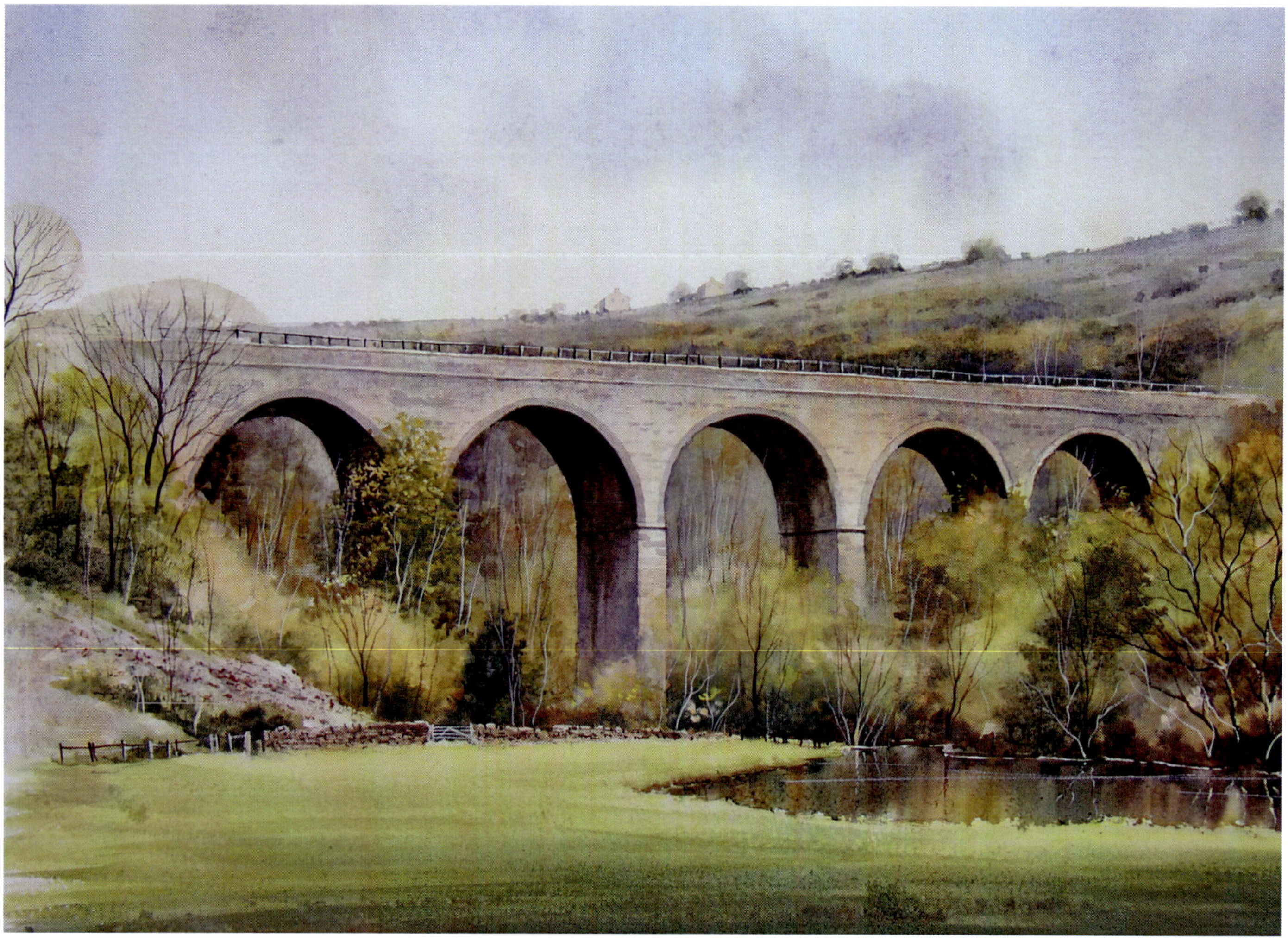

Headstone Viaduct, Monsal Head

This is arguably one of the Peak District's most impressive structures, although there were concerns at the time of construction that it would destroy the beauty of the dale. John Ruskin, a poet and conservationist at the time, criticised the building of the railway. The following quote from him is actually displayed on the Viaduct:

'The Valley is gone – and now every fool in Buxton can be in Bakewell in half an hour and every fool in Bakewell at Buxton'.

When the railway was closed there was talk of demolishing the Viaduct, but due to considerable opposition a preservation order was placed on the structure in 1970.

It is interesting to see the same view in winter on the opposite page.

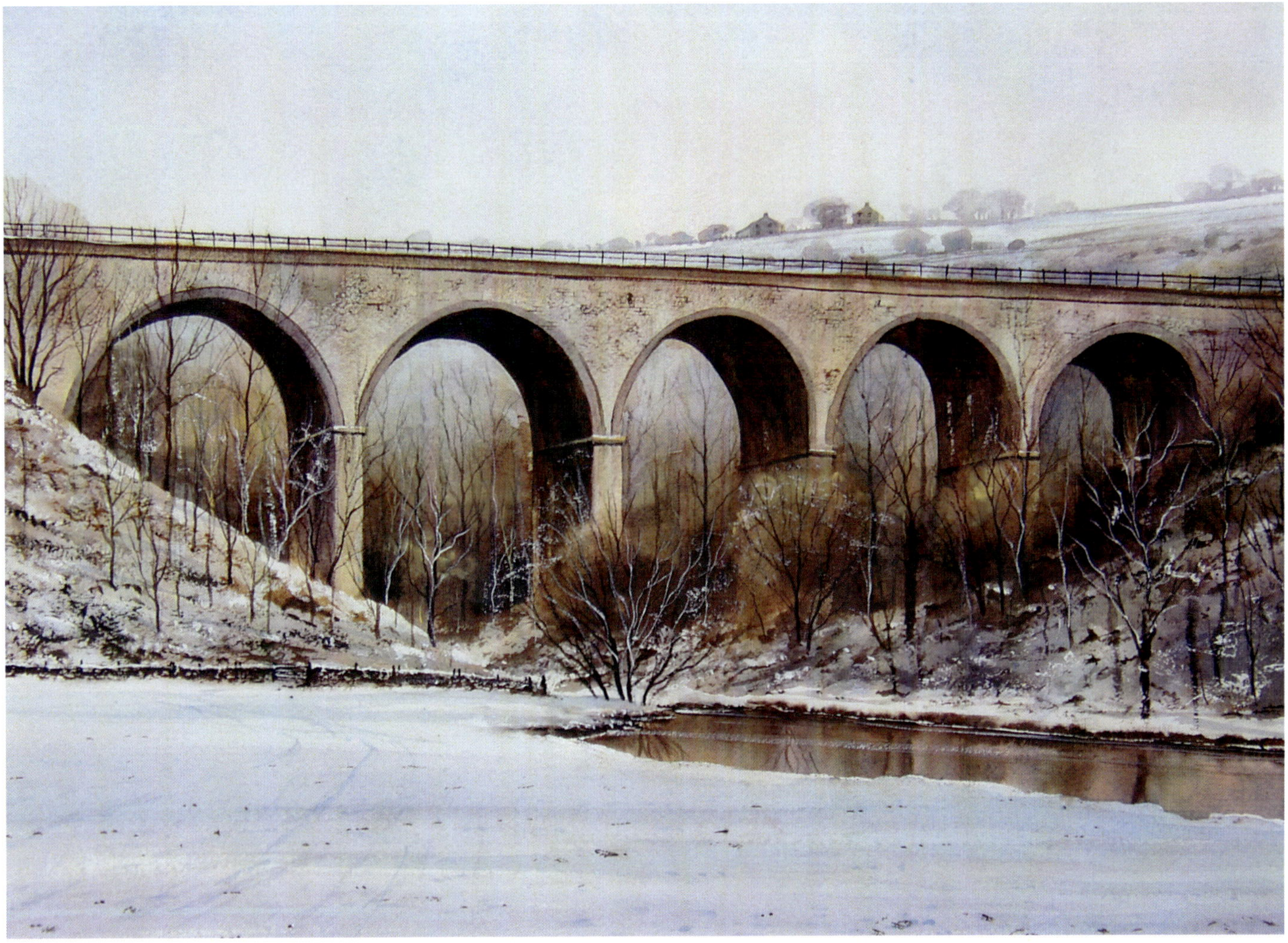

The challenge of achieving the correct shape and persective of the Viaduct is appealing, along with the way the base of the structure dissolves into the soft shapes of all the trees and foliage, with just a glimpse of reflections in the River Wye. I spent quite a lot of time drawing the Viaduct prior to applying any paint; it was important to observe that the width of each arch became narrower as they receded.

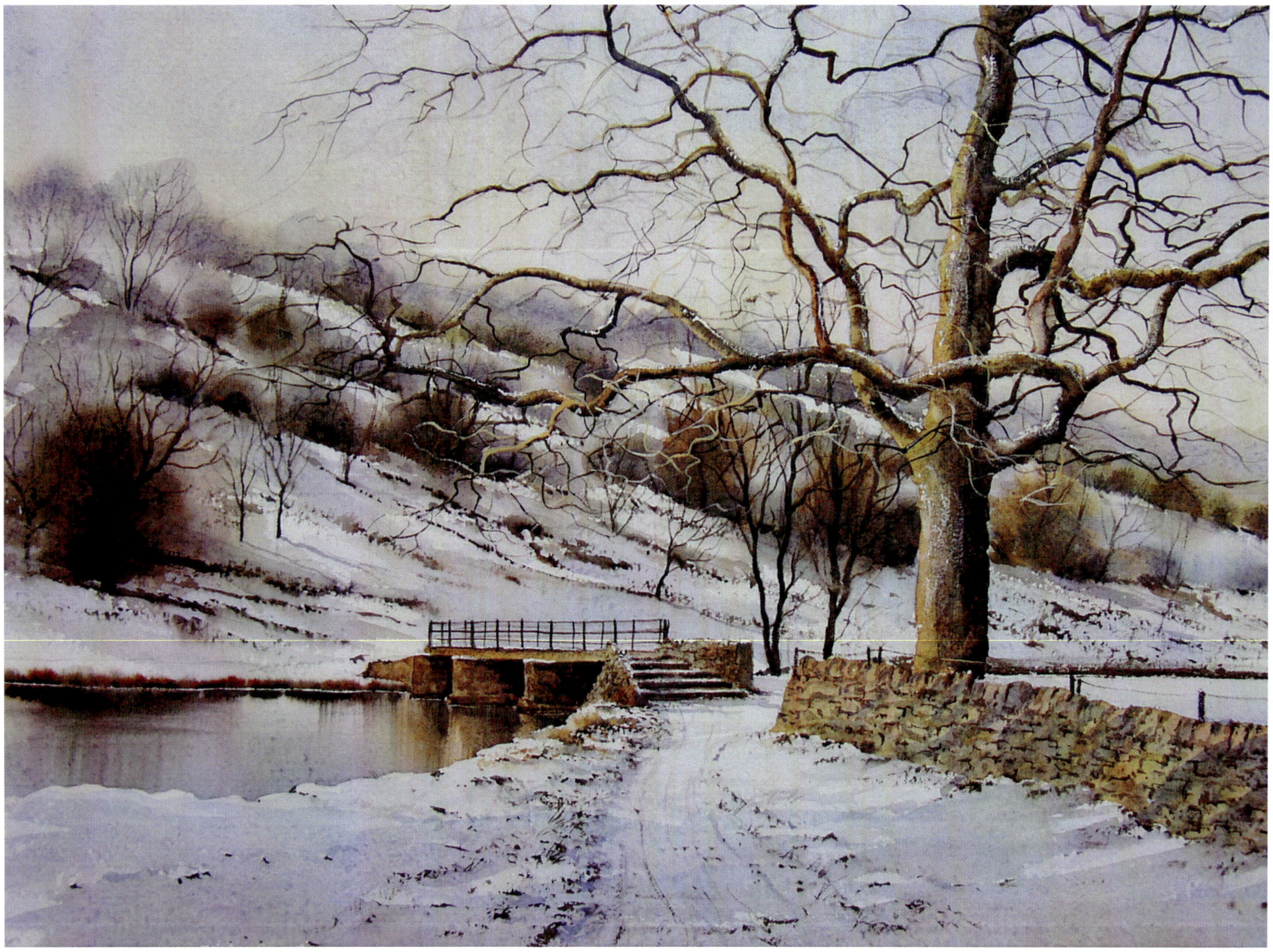

Footbridge in Monsal Dale

In order to get the view of the Headstone Viaduct on the previous page, I crossed this small bridge. On the approach the bridge stood out as an ideal painting subject due to the strong 'L' shaped composition and the way the slope of the hill leads the eye to the large tree.

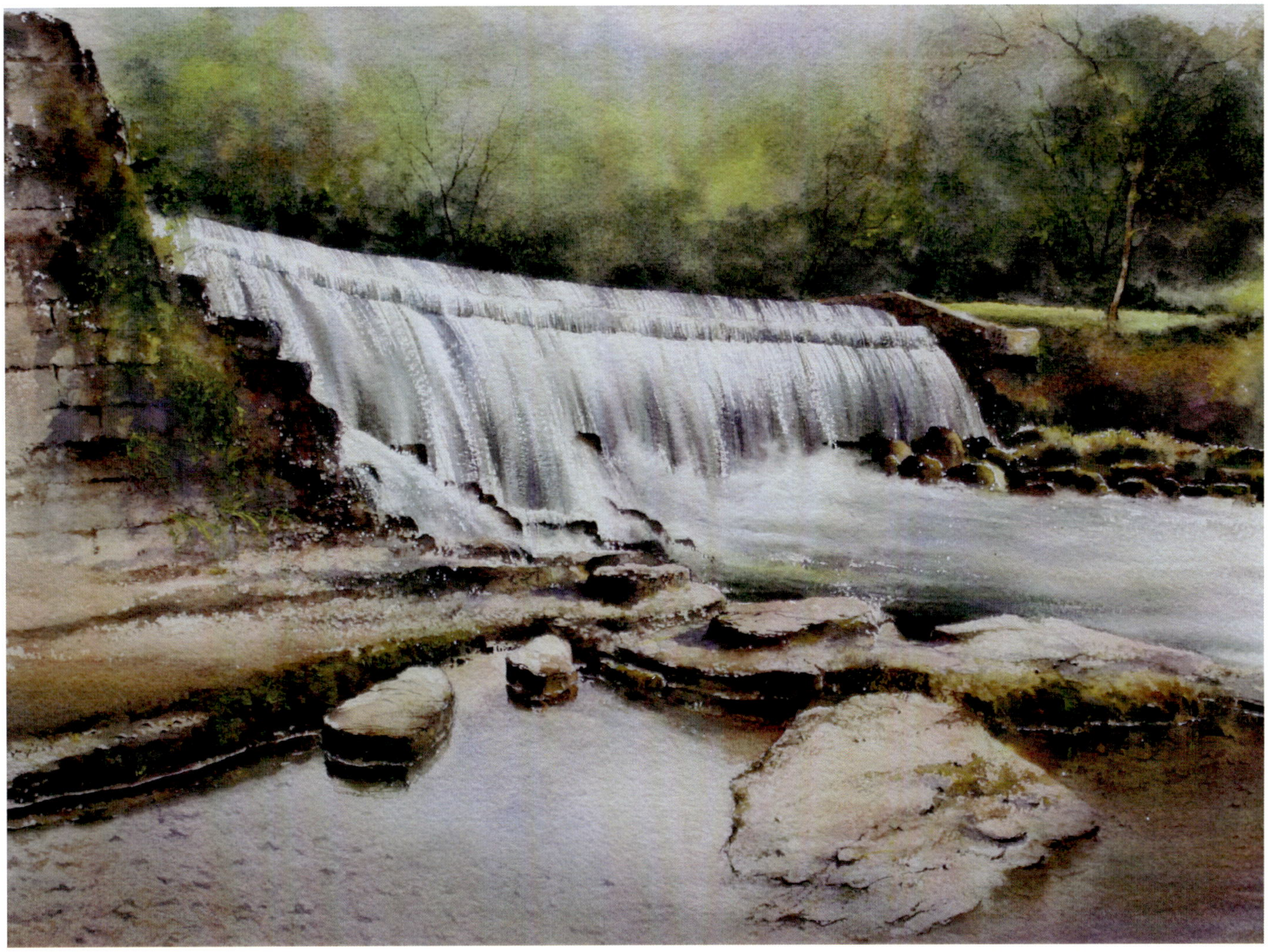

Weir in Monsal Dale

A little farther down the river from the viaduct the water rushes over the drop of the weir. Again quite a challenge to paint; the key is to use a rake type brush which has gaps between the hairs at the end (almost comb-like), and leave plenty of white paper.

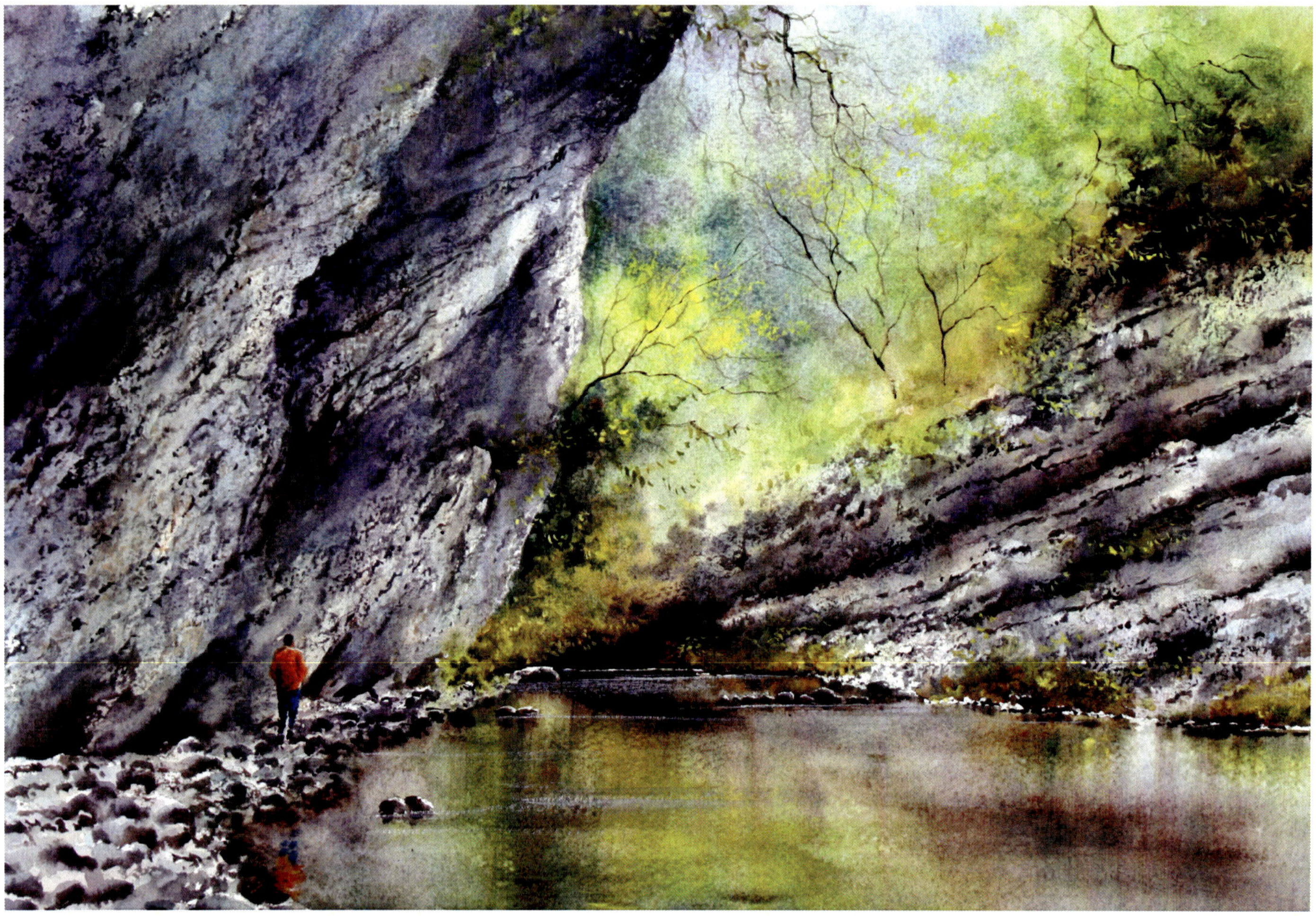

Stepping Stones, Cheedale

Just a short detour from the Monsal Trail is the beautiful winding gorge of Cheedale which is flanked by limestone cliffs. These impressive natural structures sometimes tower 300 feet above the path, in some places overhanging it. At times this overhang means leaving the path and using stepping stones to continue the walk; this can be a problem if the River Wye is in flood as it can be impassable.

I chose a very rough surface paper for this painting to suggest the rough texture of the limestone. The figure plays a surprisingly important role in the scene as it gives it scale, emphasising the sheer height of the rocks and the extent of the overhang; it also gives me an opportunity to introduce a hint of colour that doesn't exist anywhere else in the painting.

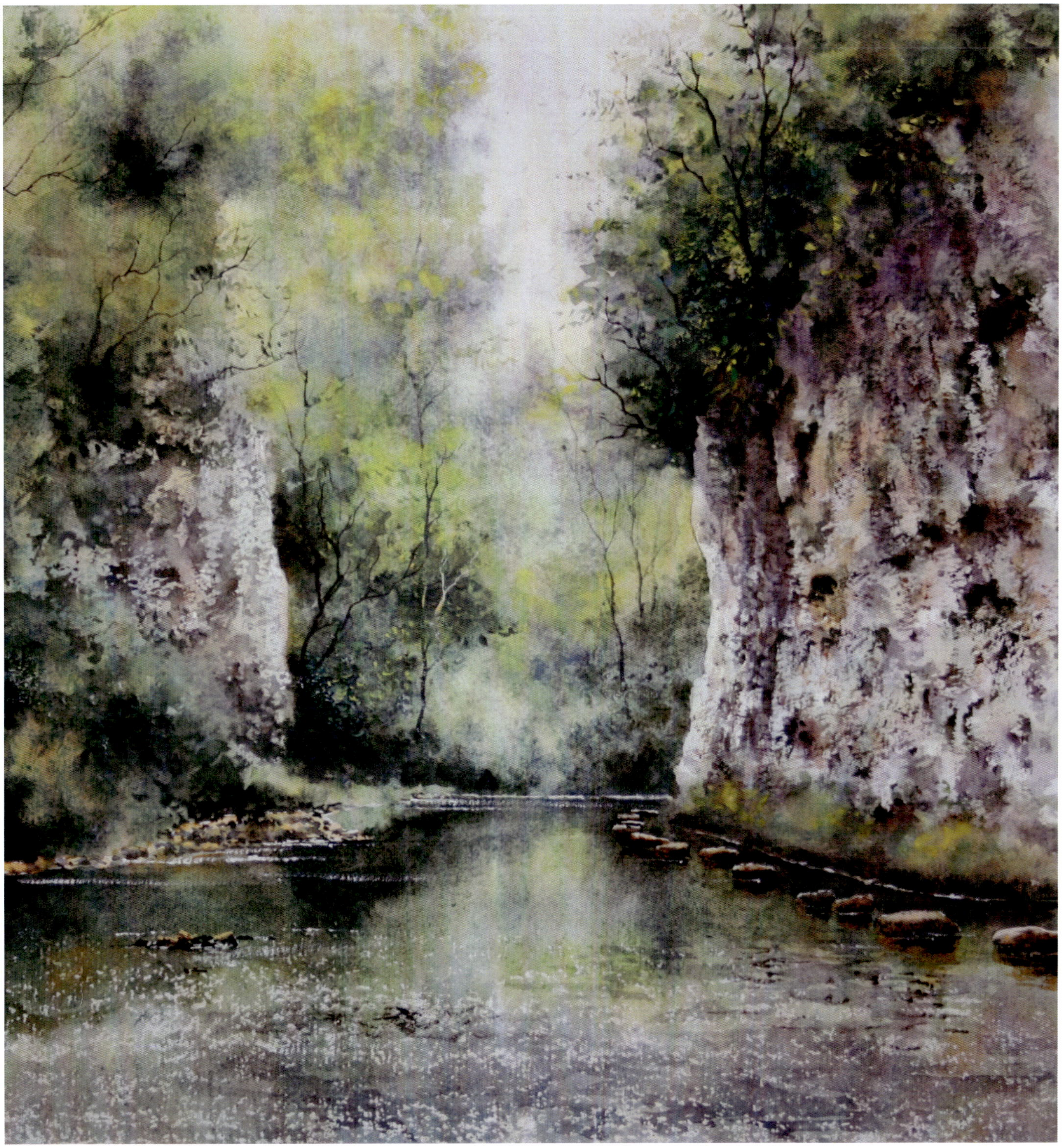

The same stepping stones as the scene overleaf, but in a more unusual, almost square format. To achieve the effect of ripples and reflected light on the surface of the river, wax resist was applied to the paper prior to applying the paint.

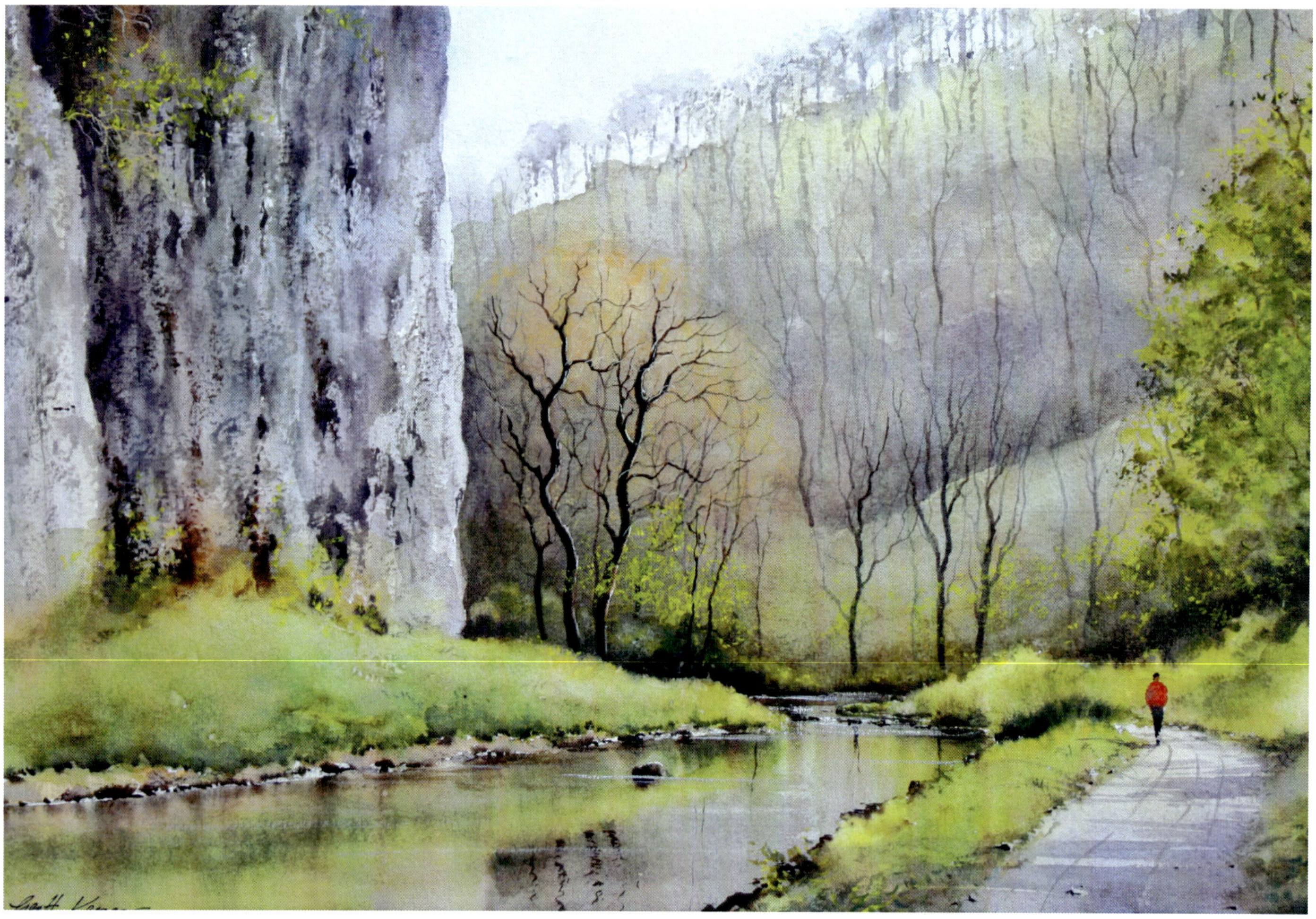

River Wye, Cheedale

The converging lines of the path and river, dominated by the limestone cliffs on the left, provides a pleasant composition. To create the light orange halo shape around the trees in the centre, I used the slightly opaque colour of Naples yellow; this opaque quality works when painting a lighter colour over an already painted background.

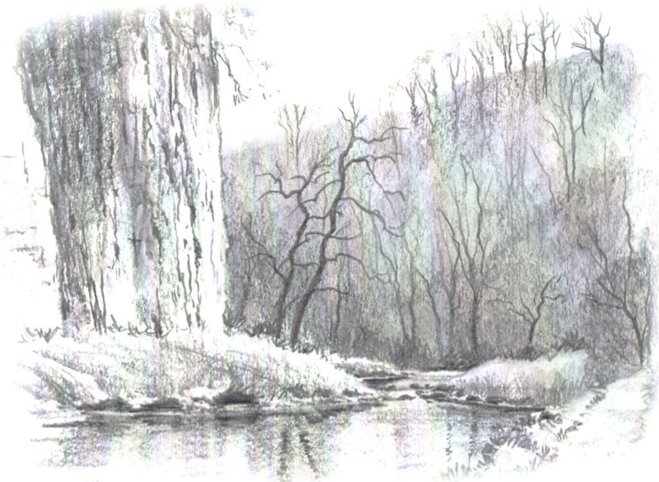

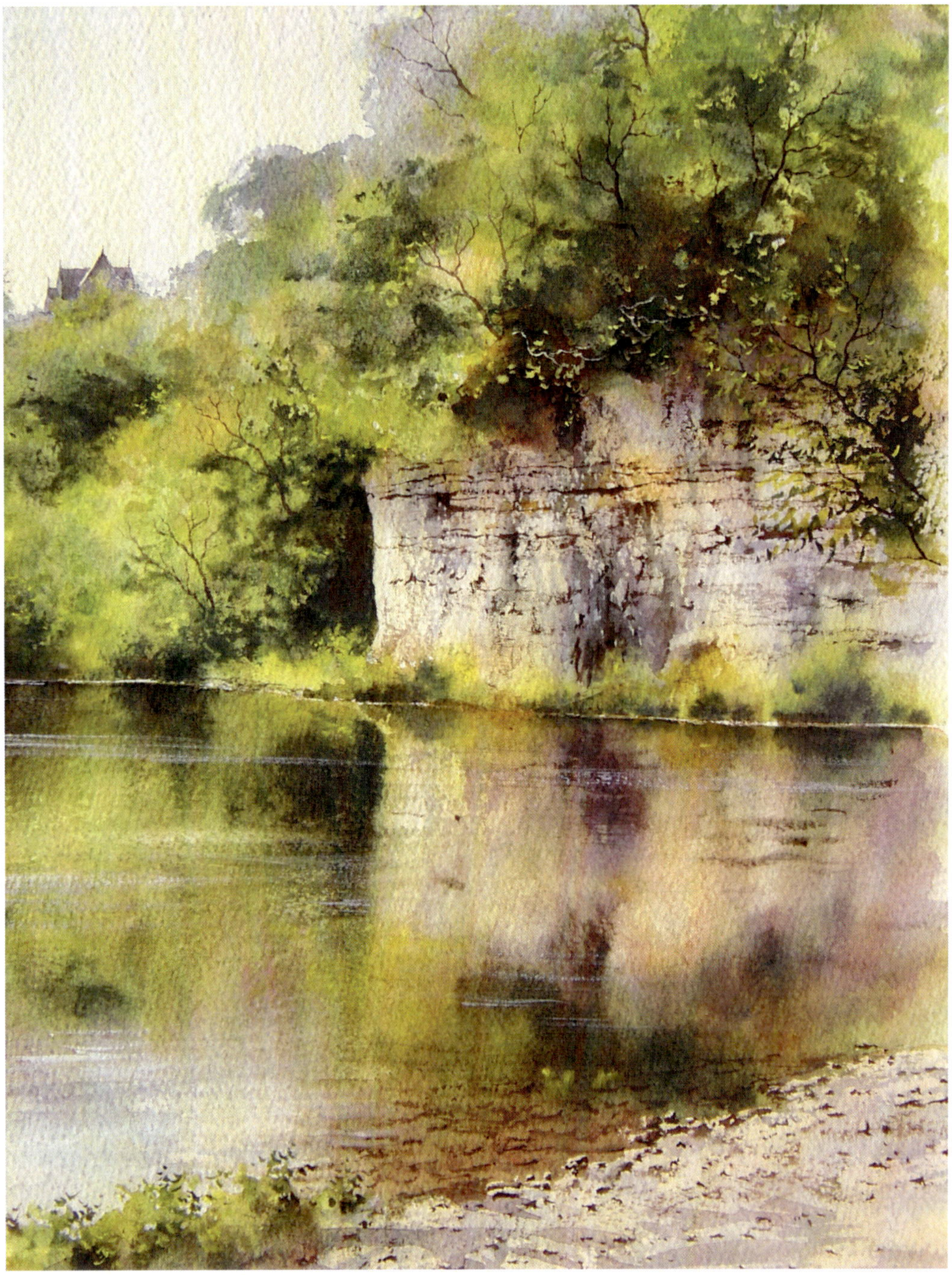

Water Cum Jolly, Miller's Dale

A short walk down a steep path from the Monsal Trail leads to this particularly scenic little dale, next to Cressbrook Mill.

The challenge with this painting was to make the reflections to look convincing. Rather than painting a mirror image, an impression of reflection was achieved by brushing the colours into a wet background, before blurring them with vertical strokes of a flat brush. I deliberately introduced some warm, orange/brown colours into the greenery and into the rock face to give a sense of warm sunlight.

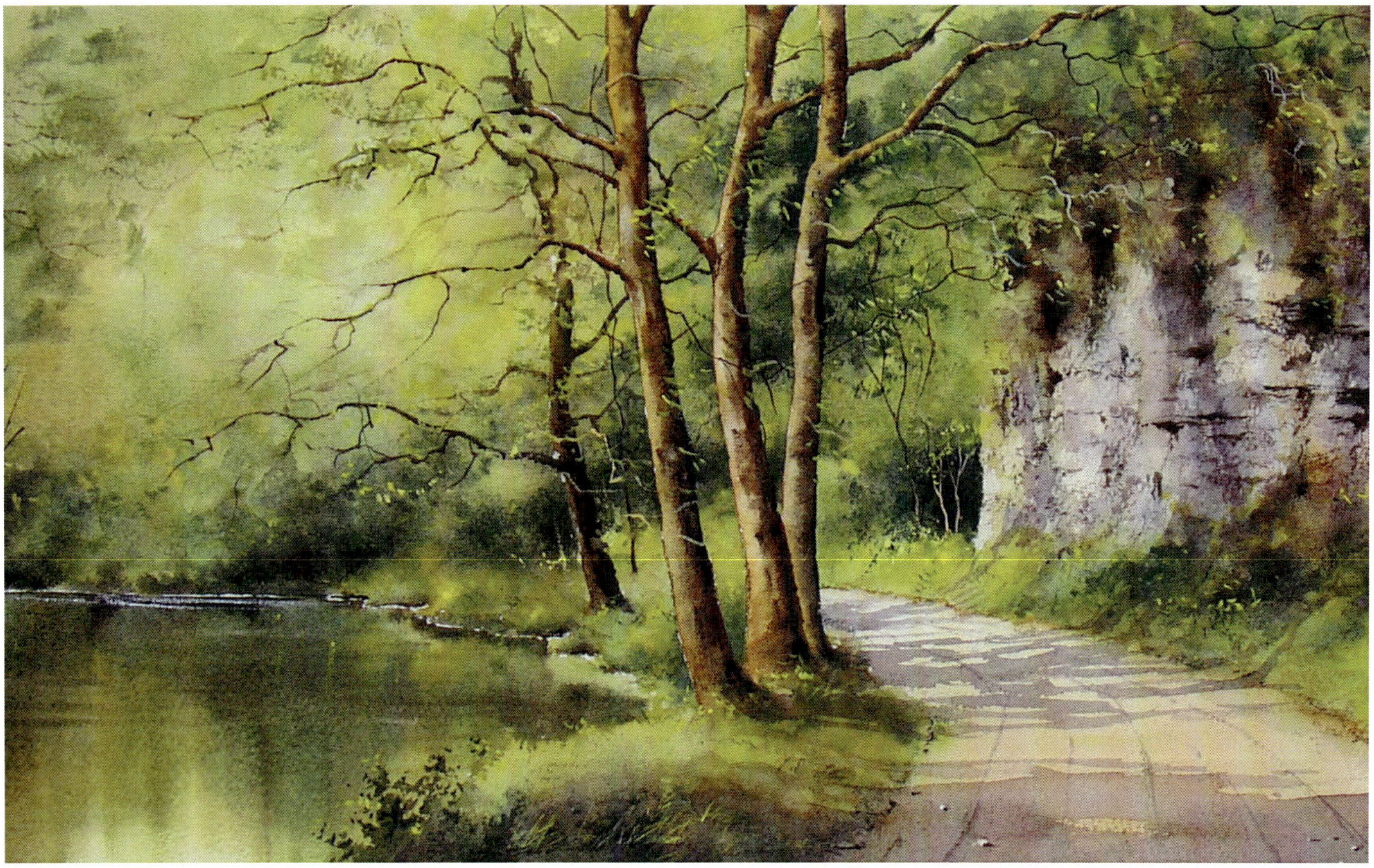

Miller's Dale Reflections

Just further along from Water Cum Jolly on the path towards Litton Mill are many inspiring subjects for a landscape artist.

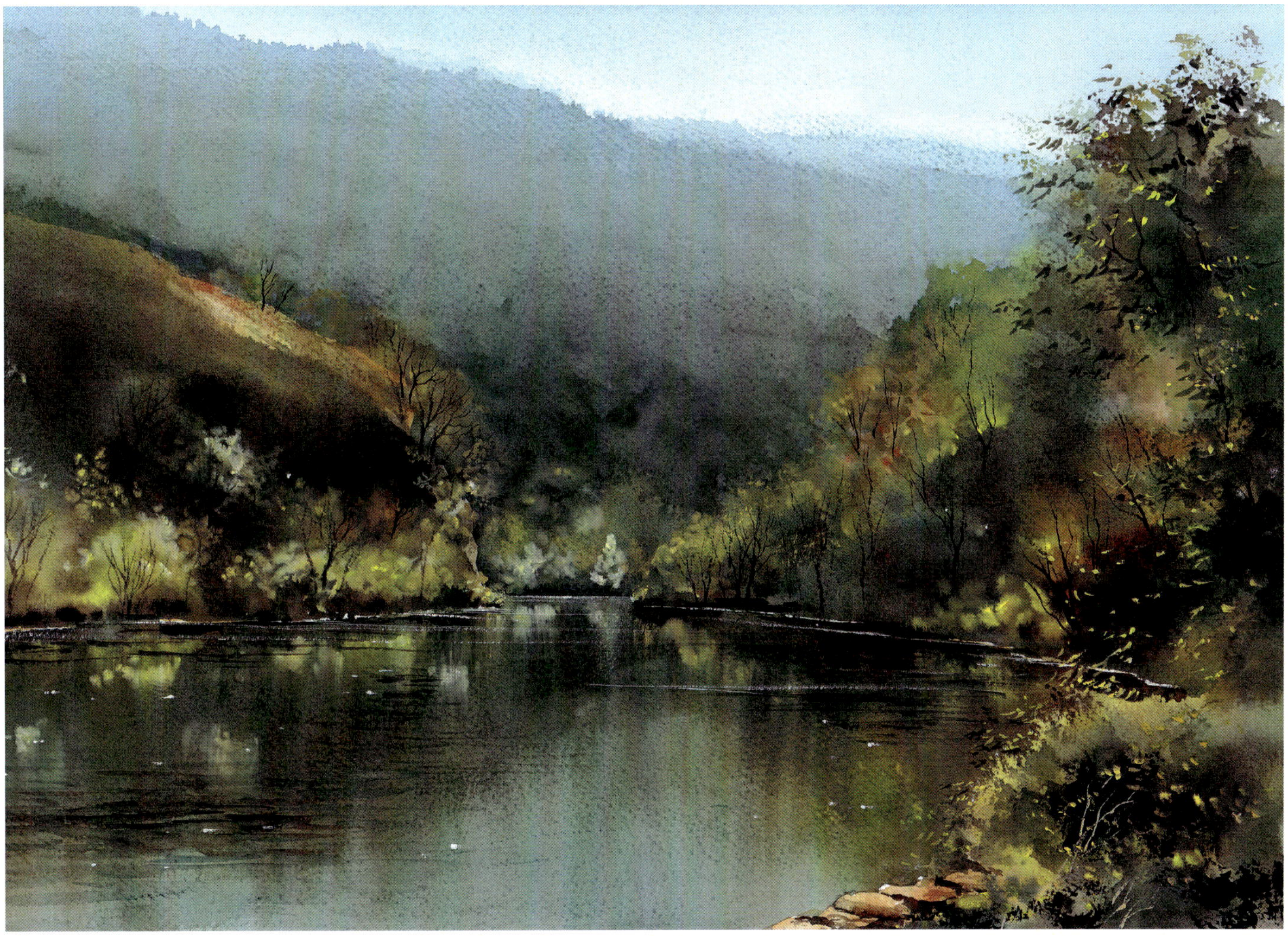

Evening in Water Cum Jolly

Revisiting a favourite location at a different time of day can feel like painting a different subject, with a different set of challenges.

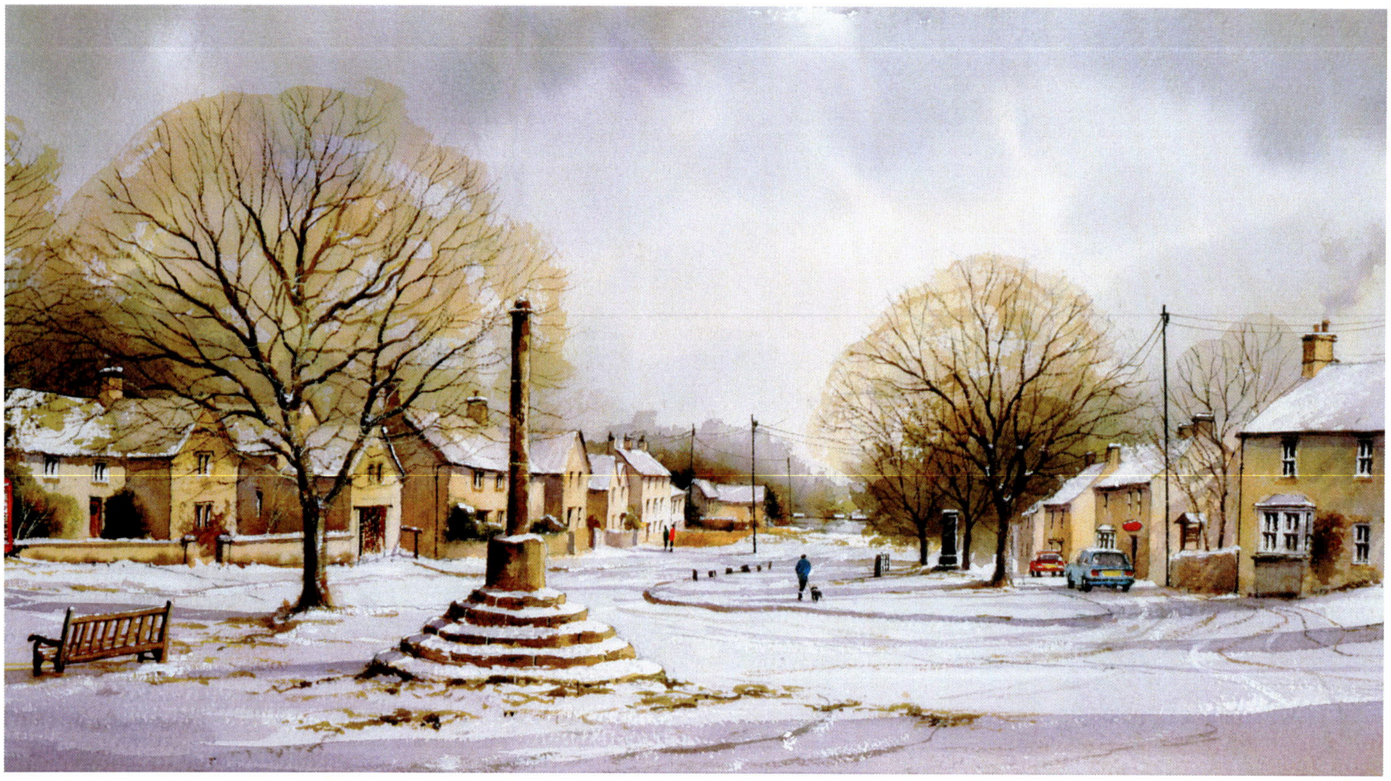

Great Longstone Village

Just a short walk from the Monsal Trail is the village of Great Longstone, which stands on high ground under a range of hills called Longstone Edge. I was careful to compose the picture with the monument to the left of centre which grouped successfully with the large tree, bench-seat and phone box gives plenty of foreground interest.

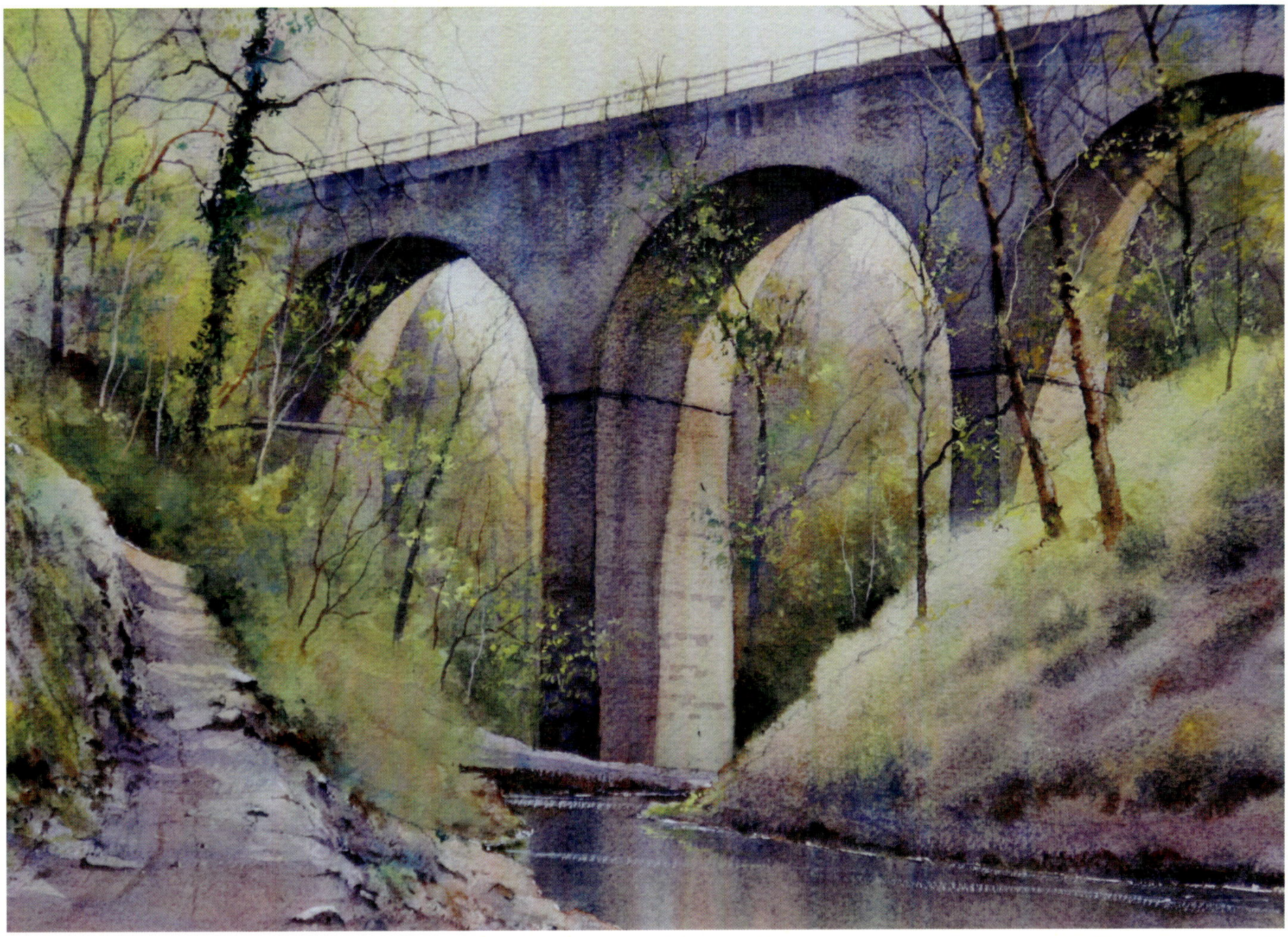

Viaduct over the River Wye in Cheedale

The viaduct is a spectacular structure which dominates the scene. I love the shadow on the underside of the middle arch and how nature seems to frame the angular shapes. A subject like this demands careful drawing, because if the basic structure doesn't look convincing, no amount of painting technique will rescue it.

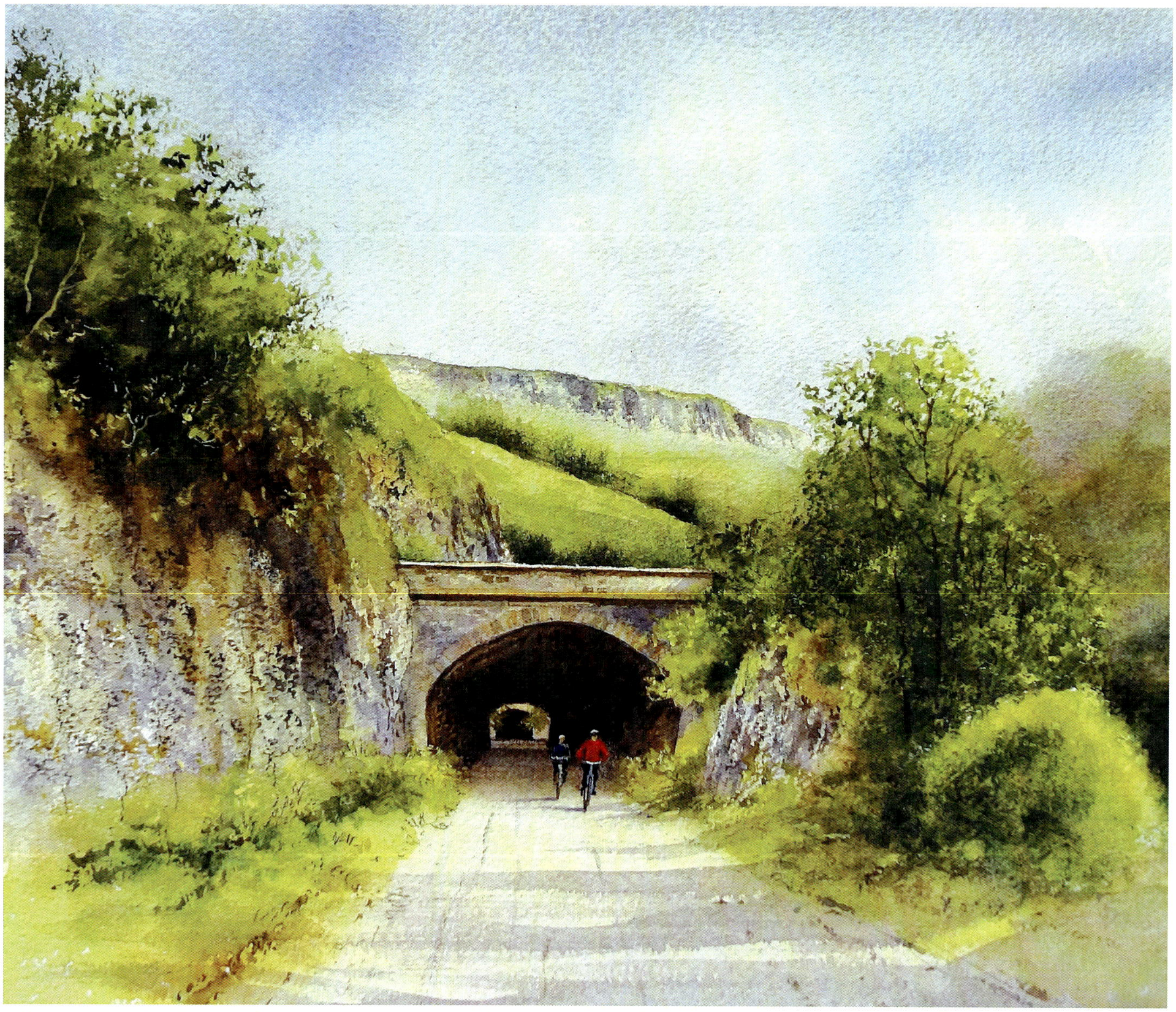

Cyclists at Chee Tor Tunnel

In this scene I tried to achieve impact by contrasting the rich dark tone under the tunnel with the bright light catching the foliage and rocks that frame it on either side. The glimpse of the entry to the next tunnel beyond the cyclists draws the eye into the scene.

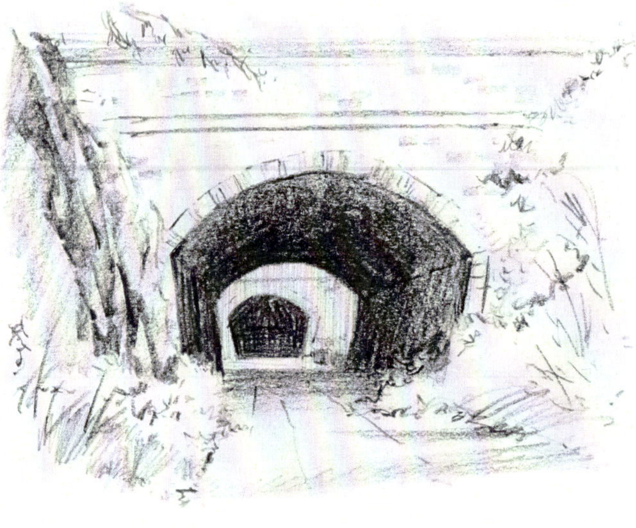

3 *On and Around The Edges*

The 'Edges' are a gritstone escarpment that runs along the eastern side of the Peak District. They are the last remains of the gritstone which originally covered all of the Peak District, most of which was scraped off by glaciers in the last ice age. They are notable for their unusually shaped gritstone tors – created by the ravages of the strong winds – and the marvellous views of the Peak District landscape.

Many of these hills have been quarried to produce millstones that have been transported across the country; indeed you can still see examples of these millstones, abandoned, both on and below the edges. The random groupings of these elliptical shapes make excellent subjects in themselves, and are very popular with both artists and photographers.

Walking from Stanage High Neb in the north to Baslow in the south is an excellent linear walk (downhill in this direction), which affords unrivalled views and much inspiration for the artist. It is along this path, with a few diversions into woods and along riverside paths to create circular walks, that I discovered the scenes to paint featured in this section.

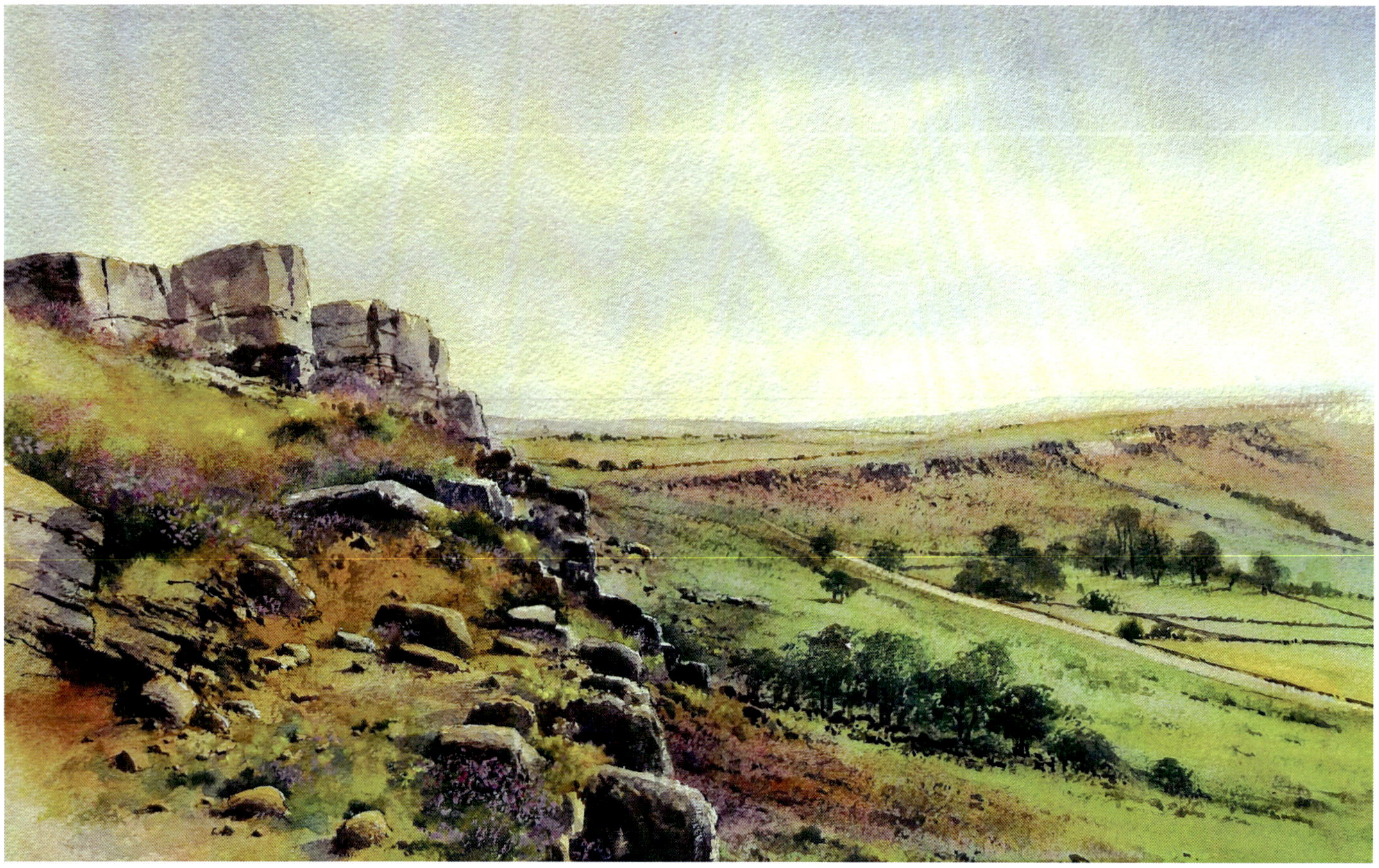

Heather on Baslow Edge

Although not usually my favourite time of year to paint landscape subjects, the abundance of heather on Baslow Edge in August provides an excellent contrast with the greens. The contrast of the heather against the dark shadowy areas is accentuated by adding a touch of opaque white to the crimson colour, before using just a few dashes of it with a fine brush, to suggest the tiny flowers of the heather. The bright light on the top edge of the stones, is achieved by leaving it as almost white paper, to contrast with the dark colour of the shaded areas, this helps to separate the foreground edge from the distant edge that runs along the horizon.

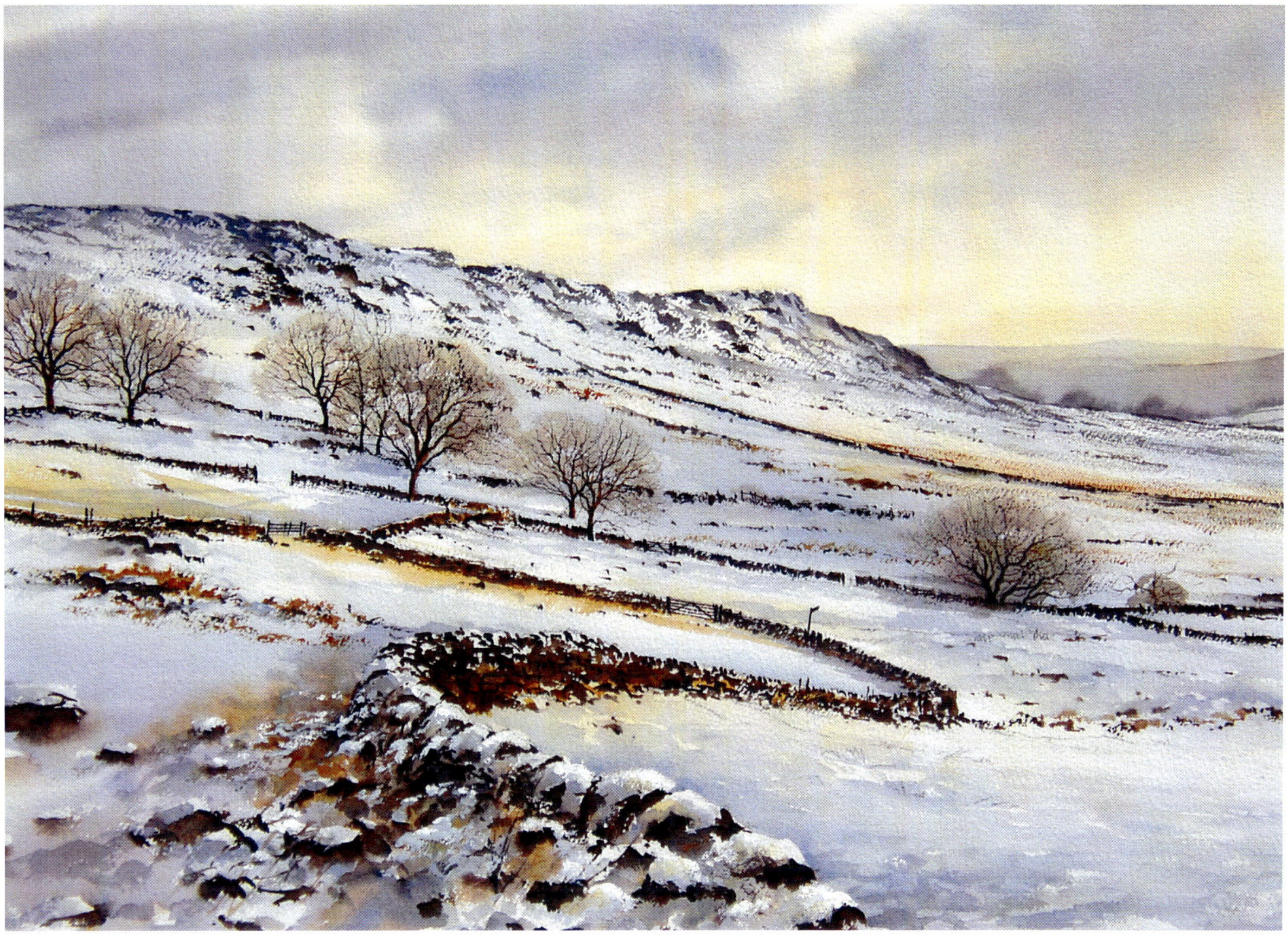

Baslow Edge from Curbar Gap

Between Baslow Edge and Curbar Edge is an old coaching road which comes up to Curbar Gap. It is from this road that I have painted the above scene; looking up towards Baslow Edge. The snaking shape of the old dry-stone wall leads the eye into the middle distance.

Curbar Gap can be a cold, bleak place on a winter's afternoon; a feeling captured by painting cold blue/grey shadows across the snow-clad hill, reinforced by the glimpse of orange in the sky.

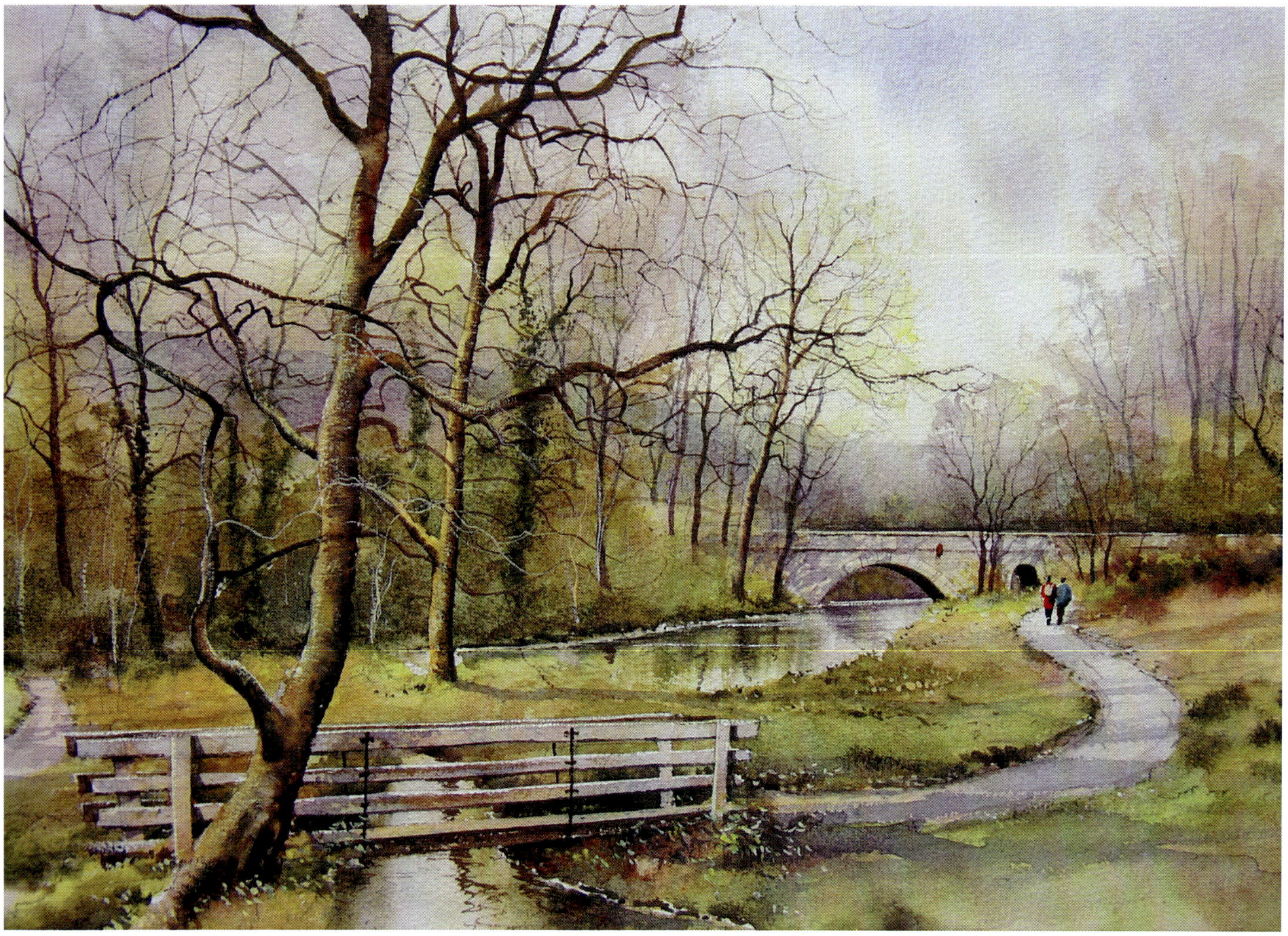

The Path to Calver Bridge

Calver Bridge has been the subject of many of my paintings over the years. The approach to the bridge is from the small footbridge crossing the brook in the foreground. On the left a large tree forms an 'L' shaped composition, with branches pointing to the focal point.

In *Calver Bridge in Winter,* at the top of the adjacent page, the bridge was painted from a closer viewpoint, again with an 'L' shaped composition, but this time with the tree on the right. This was a more speedily executed painting than on the previous page, giving it a feel of spontaneity. Wax resist was used to suggest the light glinting on the slightly rippled surface of the water.

On the adjacent page, bottom, (*Calver Bridge in Summer*), features a much calmer, more tranquil version of the same scene; here the river is almost still, with the undisturbed surface of the water rendering the reflections almost mirror-like. Opaque lemon yellow used for the trees in front of the bridge, and cooler blue/grey greens for the trees behind the bridge; help to separate middle distance from the far distance.

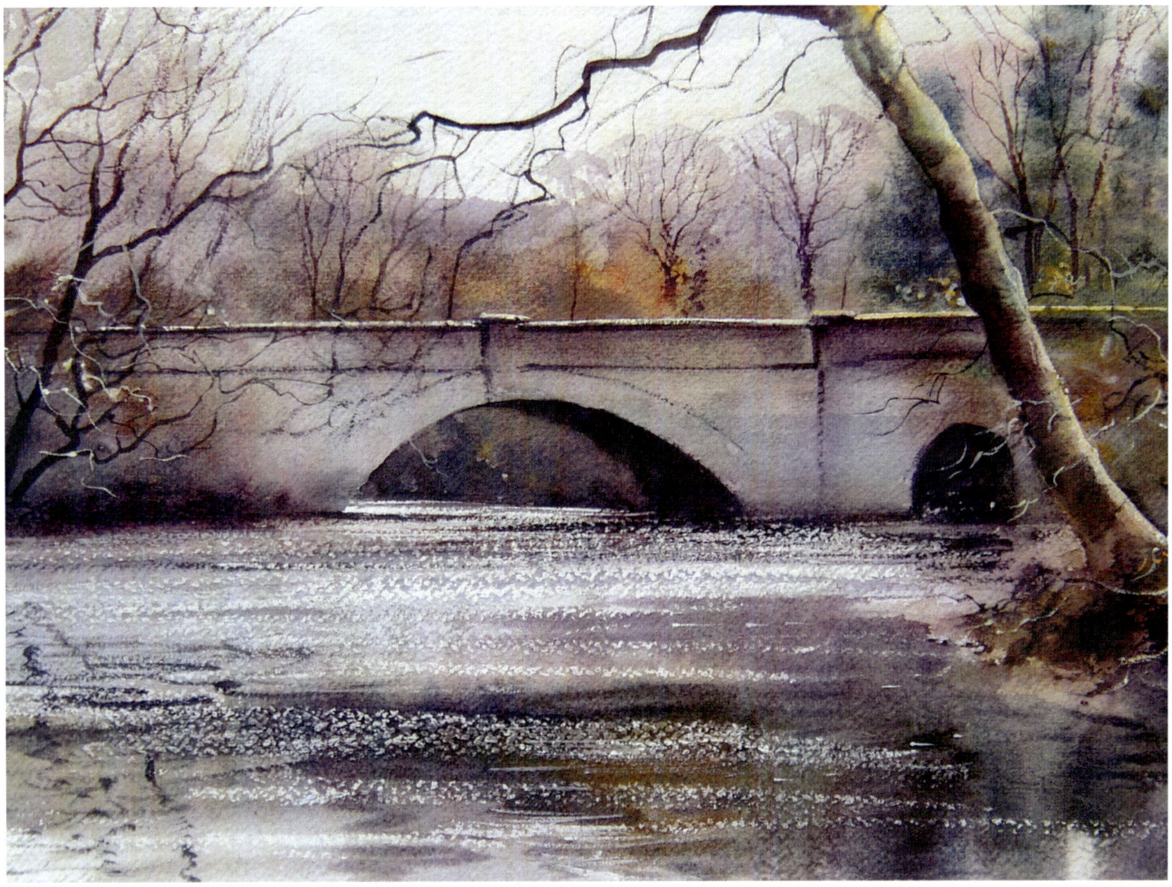

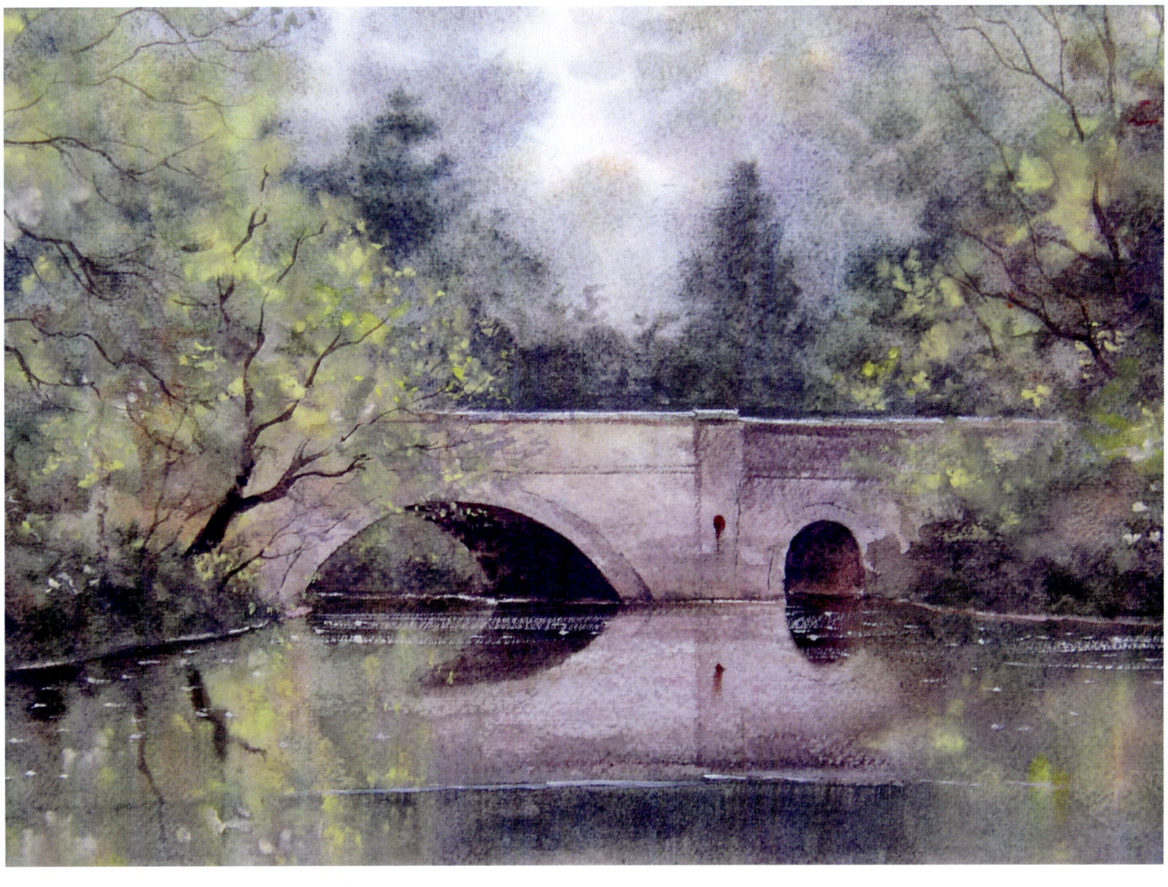

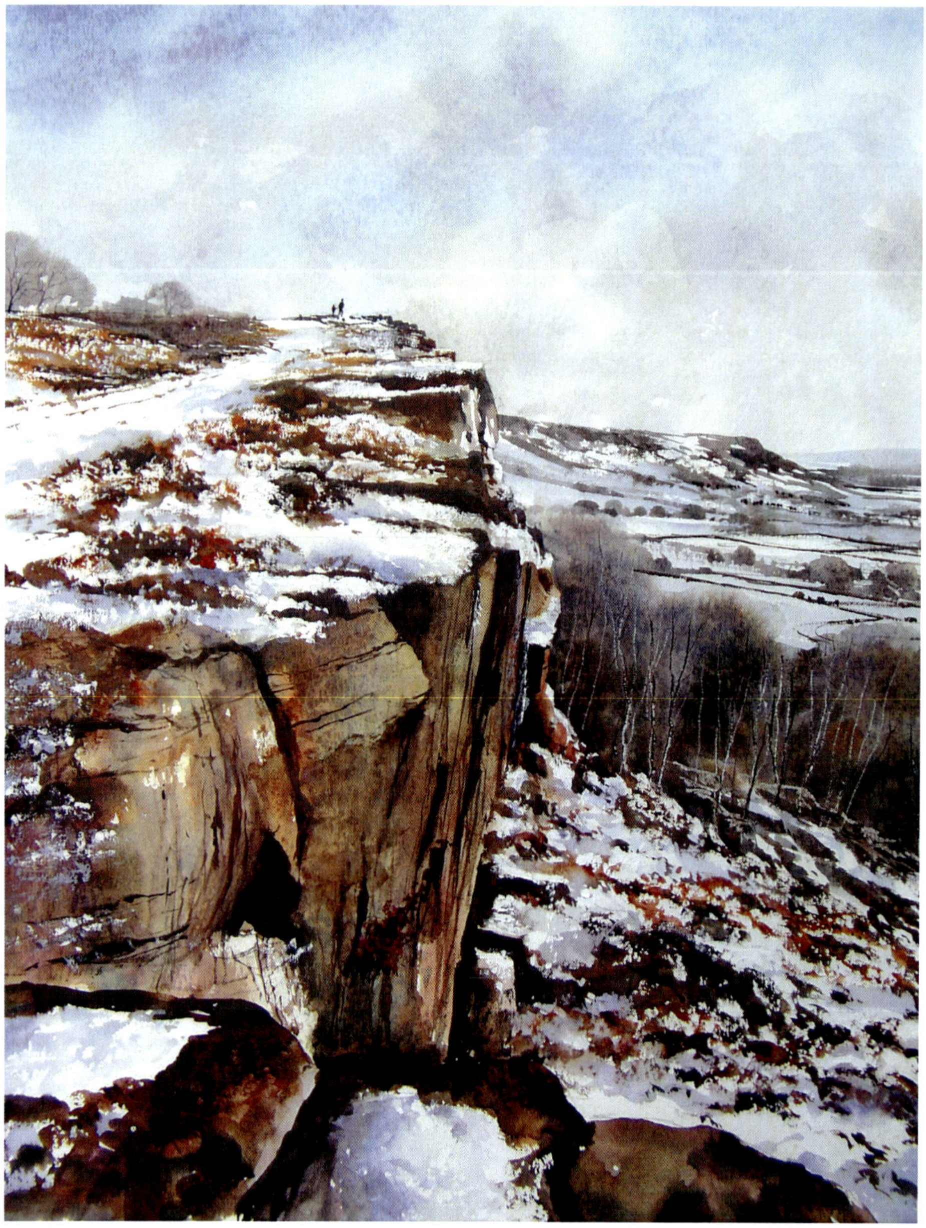

Froggatt Edge in Winter

This was painted from a photograph taken on a cold blustery day. In the studio I made a start while the experience of being on the exposed, windy edge was still fresh in my mind.

A 'portrait' format aided in capturing the feeling of height, and I really enjoyed trying to capture the texture and rugged surface of the rocks, leaving white paper, with just a few hints of blue shadow to suggest the thin coating of snow. The addition of a couple of tiny figures way off in the distance gives the composition a sense of scale.

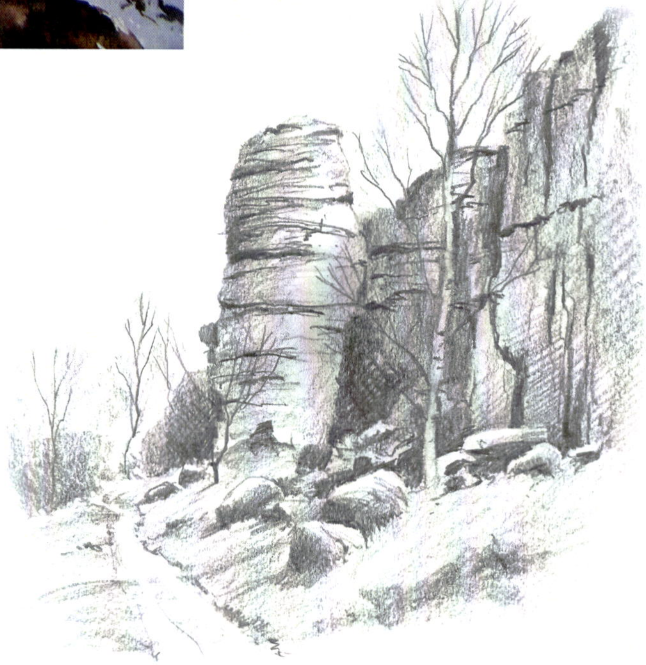

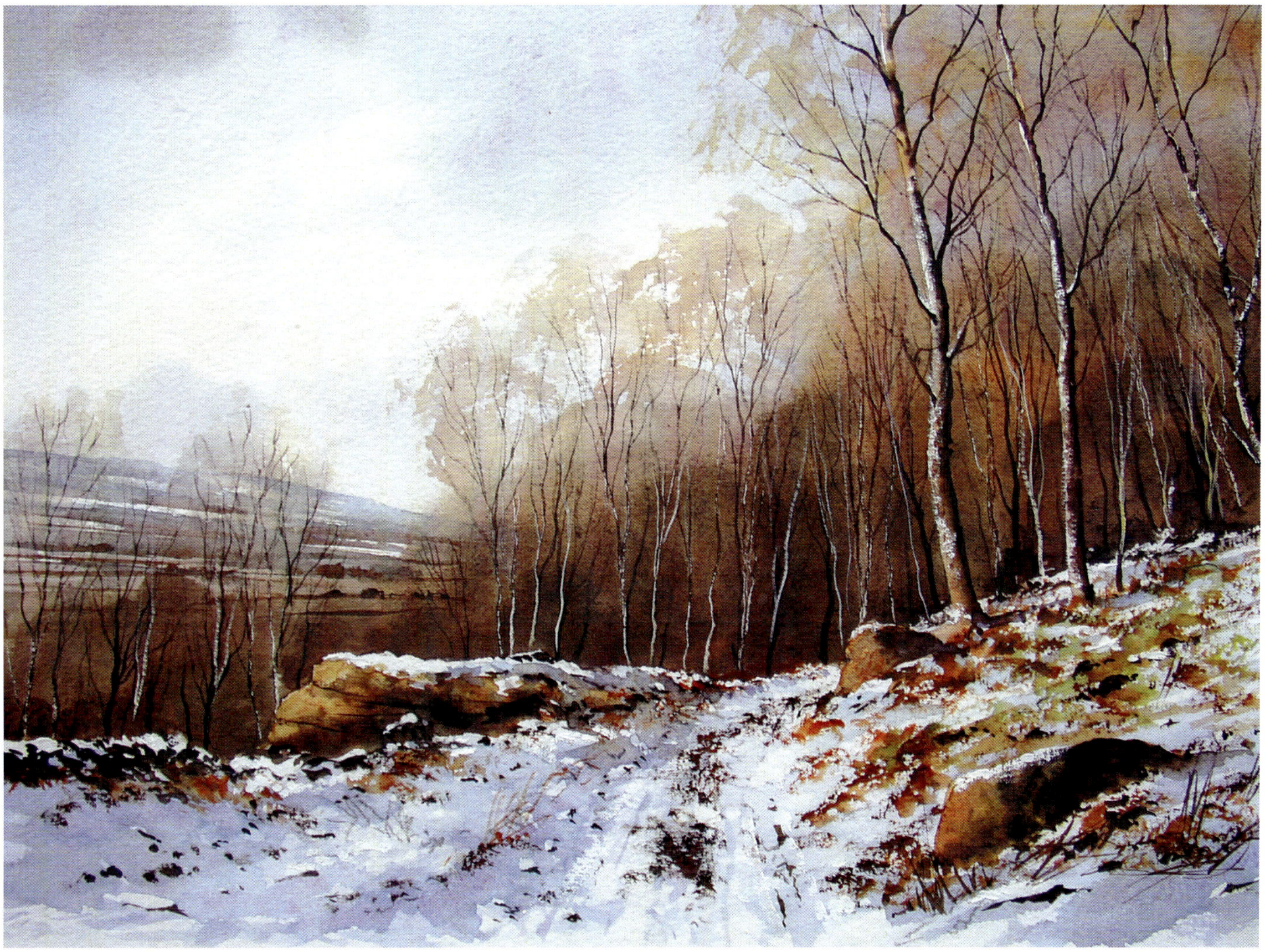

Froggatt Woods

Still in mid-winter and just below Frogatt Edge, this snow covered woodland provides an excellent subject; the misty shapes of the tree tops and distant clouds mean it is ideally suited to watercolour. Contrast this with the painting overleaf, which features the same path in summer; and this could be a different place, a reason I love the varying seasons.

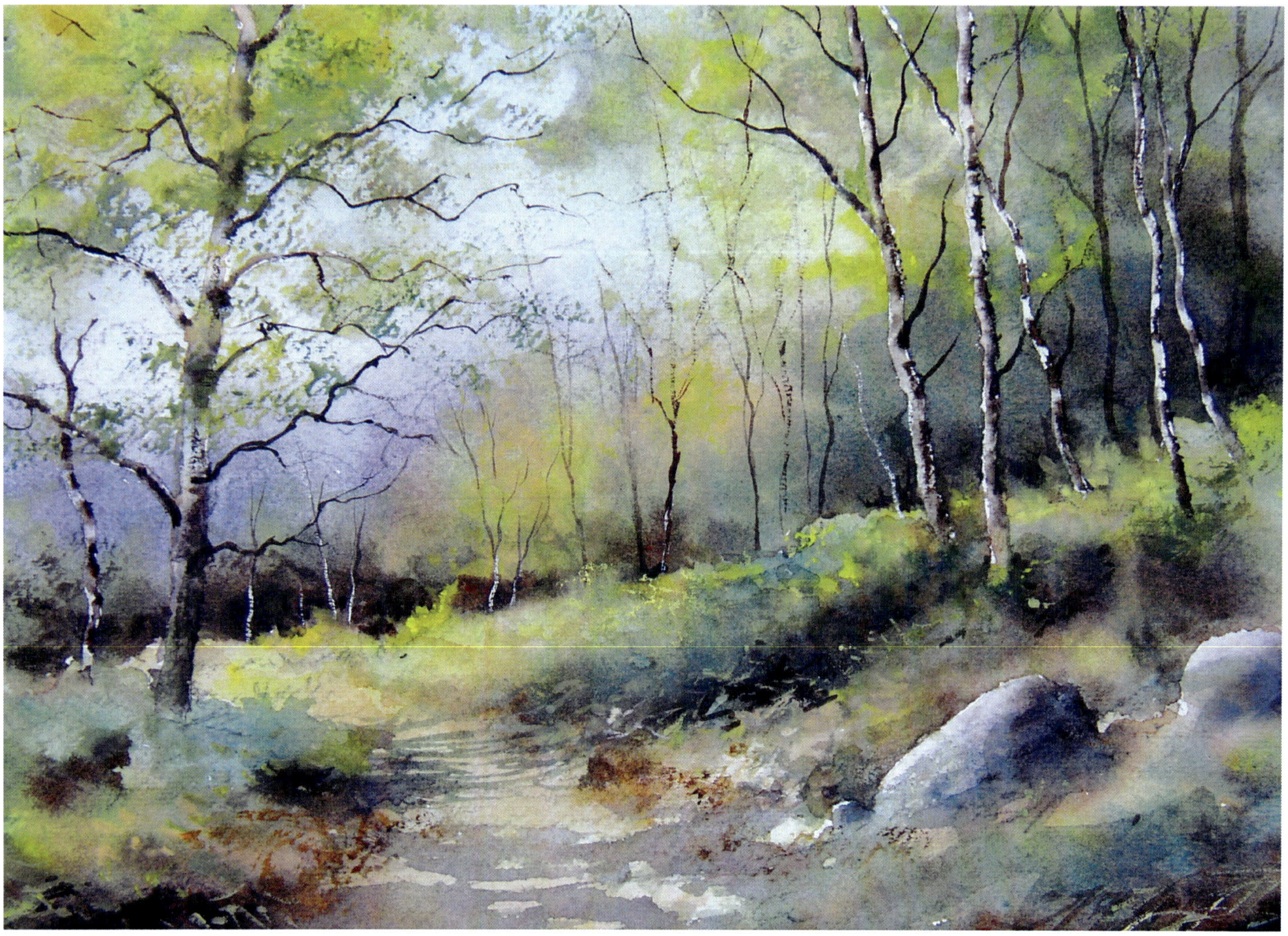

Froggatt Woods

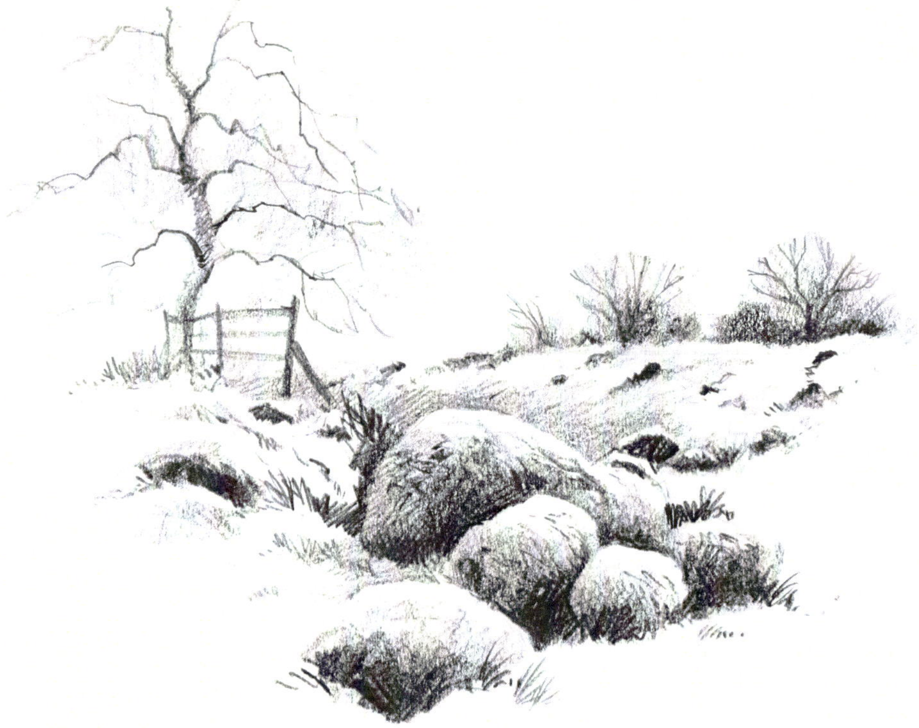

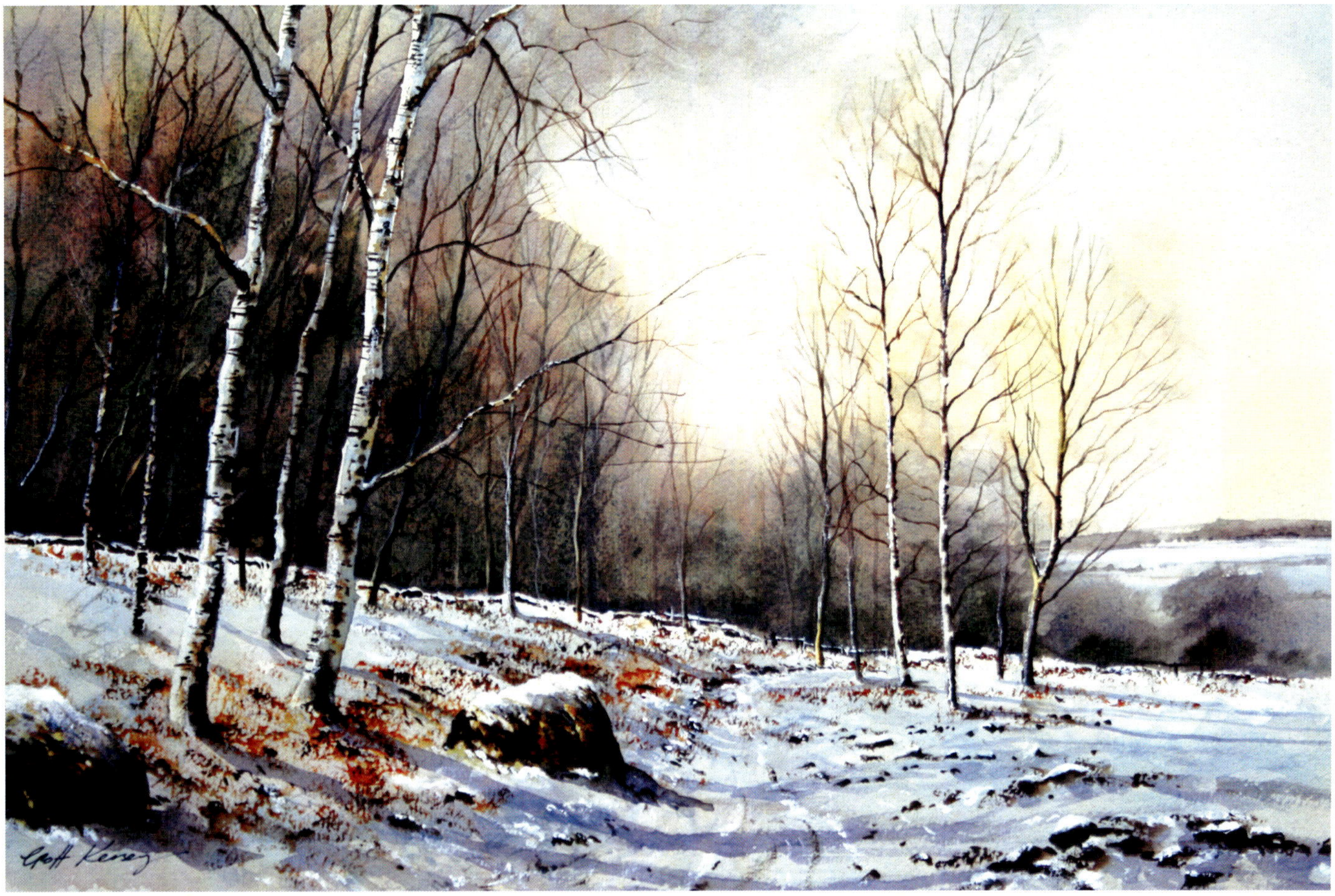

A Wintery Afternoon in Froggatt Woods

Later in the day, further along the same path as on the previous page, I found this beautiful scene looking back towards the woods I had just emerged from. To give the impression of the last remnants of the weak winter sunlight glimpsed beyond the trees, a sheet of buff tinted paper was used, employing white gouache, brushed onto the still wet background. White gouache was also used for highlights in the snow and the lit side of the silver birches, which contrast well with the brooding darks of the distant woods and the yellowing sky.

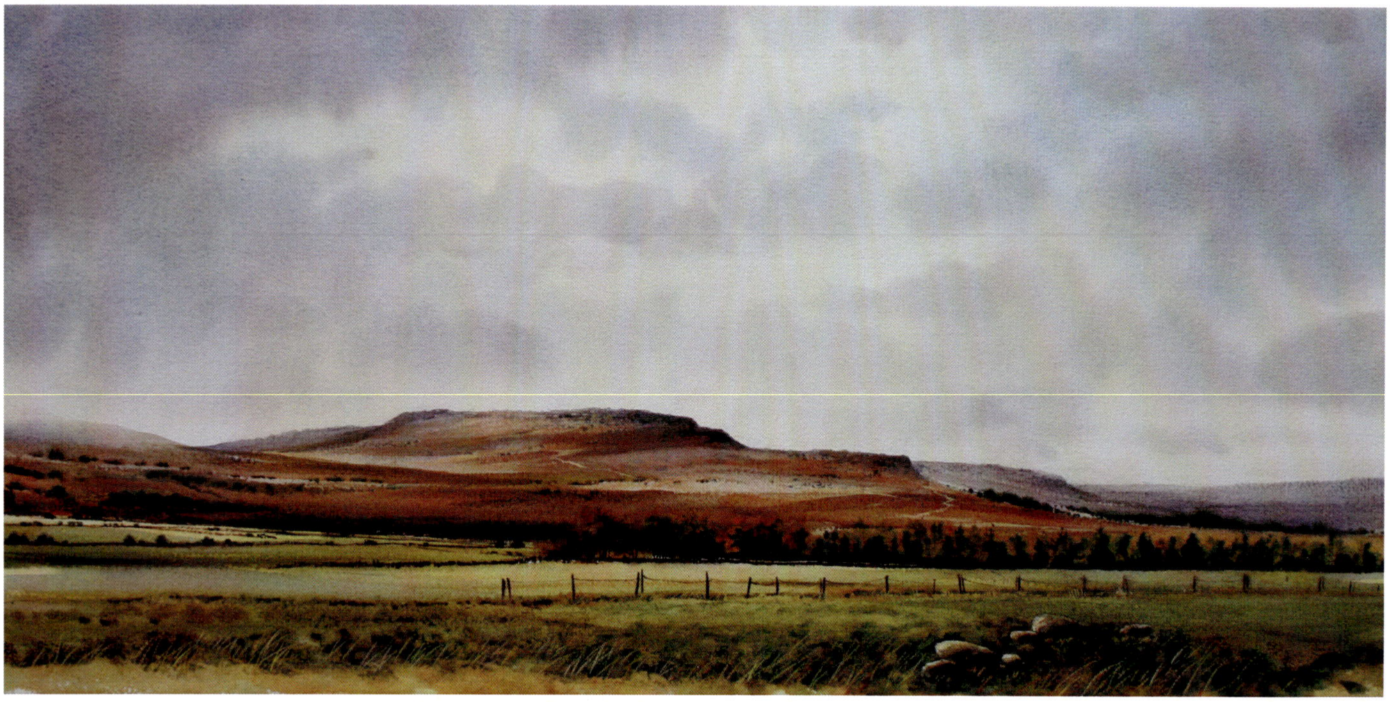

Carl Wark and Higgar Tor from Longshaw

The hill known as Carl Wark lies close to Higgar Tor, between Stanage and Burbage Edges. It rises high above Burbage Brook forming a natural defensive position, and long ago it was used as a fort. The remains of the large gritstone blocks that formed the walls of the fort can still be seen on the sides of the hill. To capture the panoramic view the length of the painting is more than twice the height, whereas a more traditional format has a length approximately 1.5 times the height.

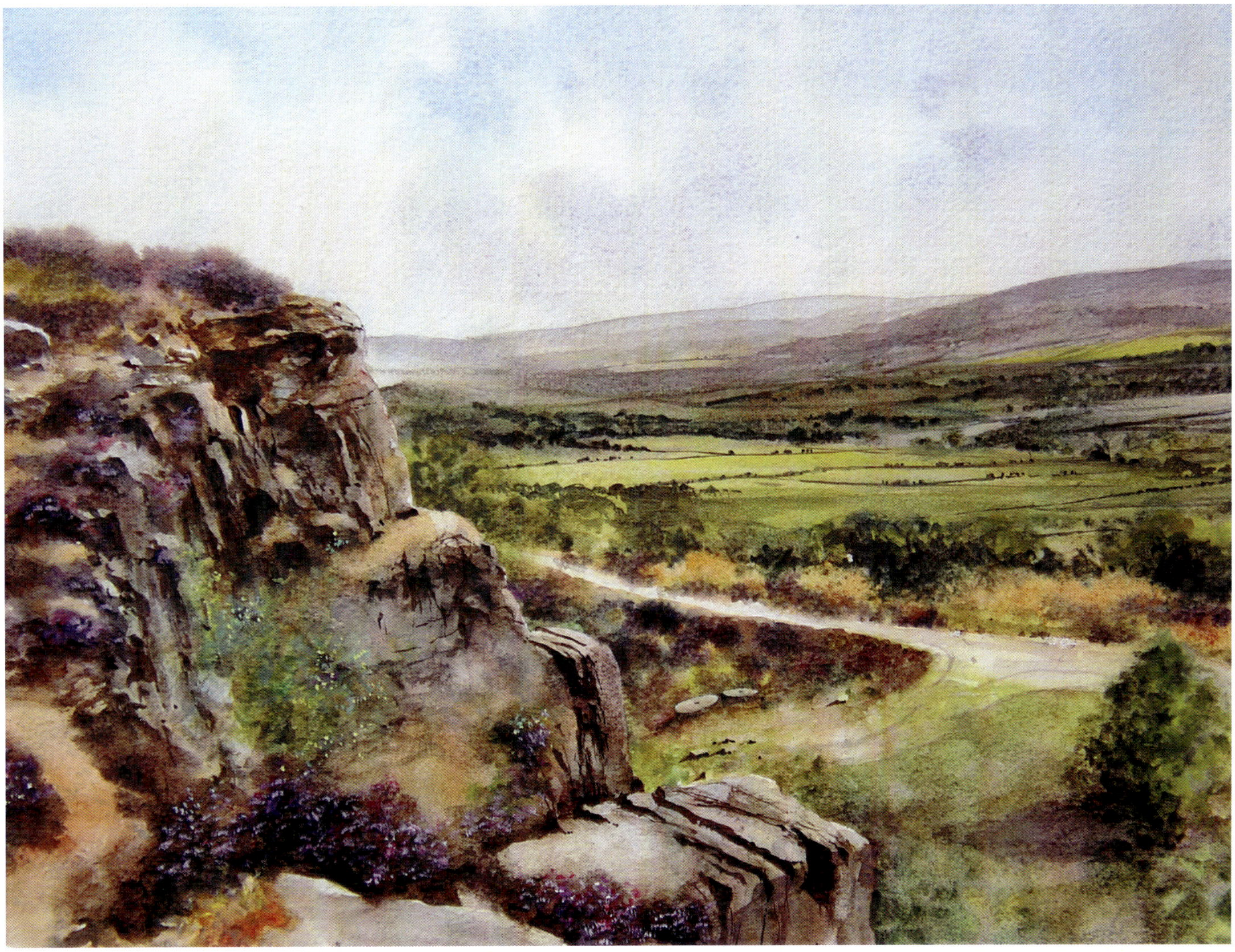

Millstone Edge

This scene appealed to me as much for the view beyond the edge as the edge itself, so I endeavoured to capture the best of both. In the foreground the soft shapes of the heather are contrasted with the craggy, harder forms of the rocks that it nestles between. In the backdrop bright sunlight falls on the distant meadows.

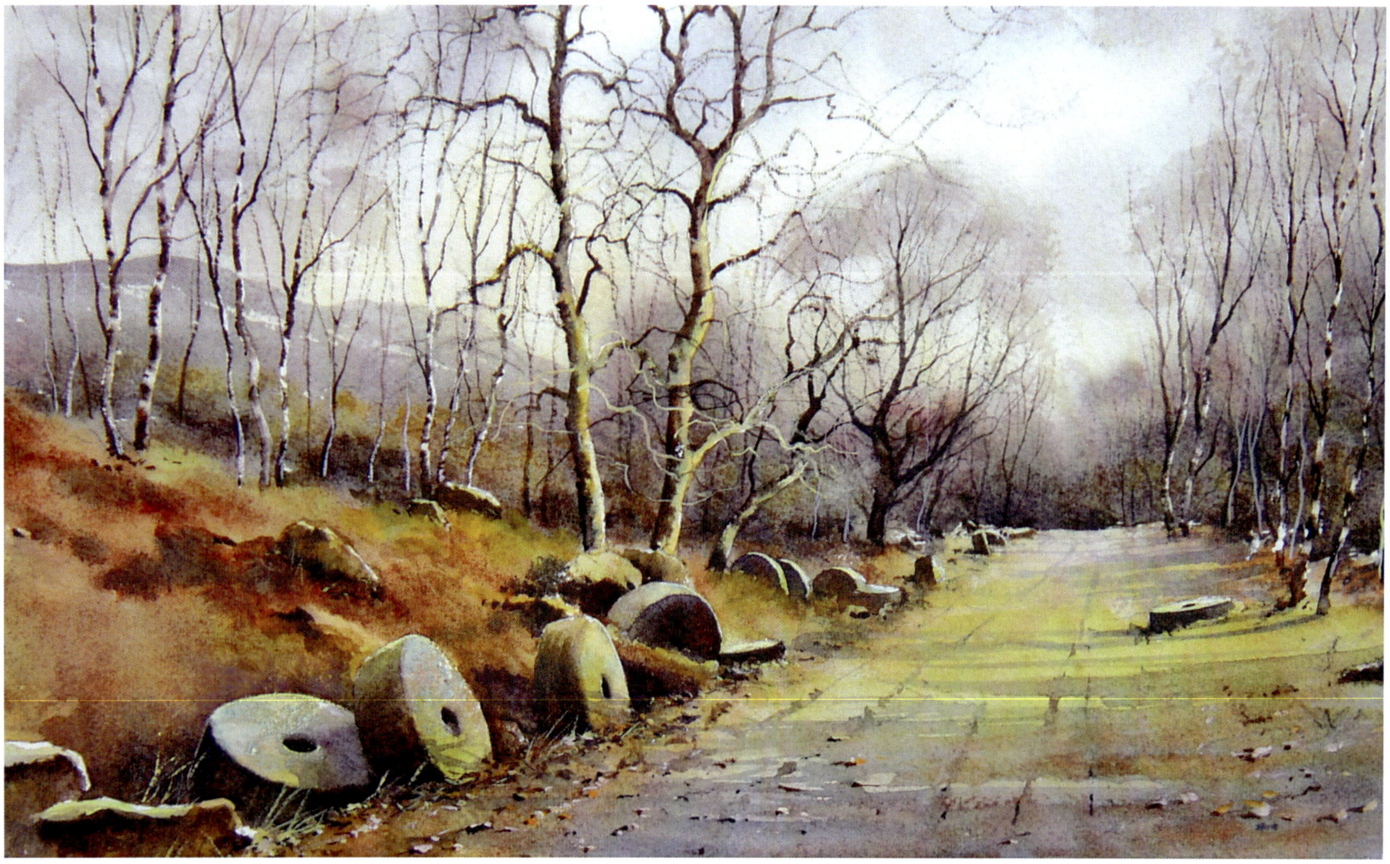

Below Millstone Edge

The haphazard arrangement of Millstones forms the left-hand edge of the path and recede in size to create perspective.

More millstones are featured overleaf, in *Millstones on Stanage Edge.* These rough hewn elliptical shapes can be tricky to get right, so a few preparatory pencil sketches (see opposite) help prior to tackling the painting.

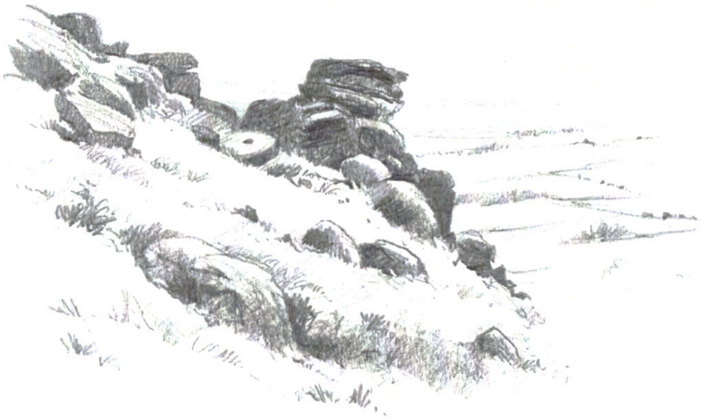

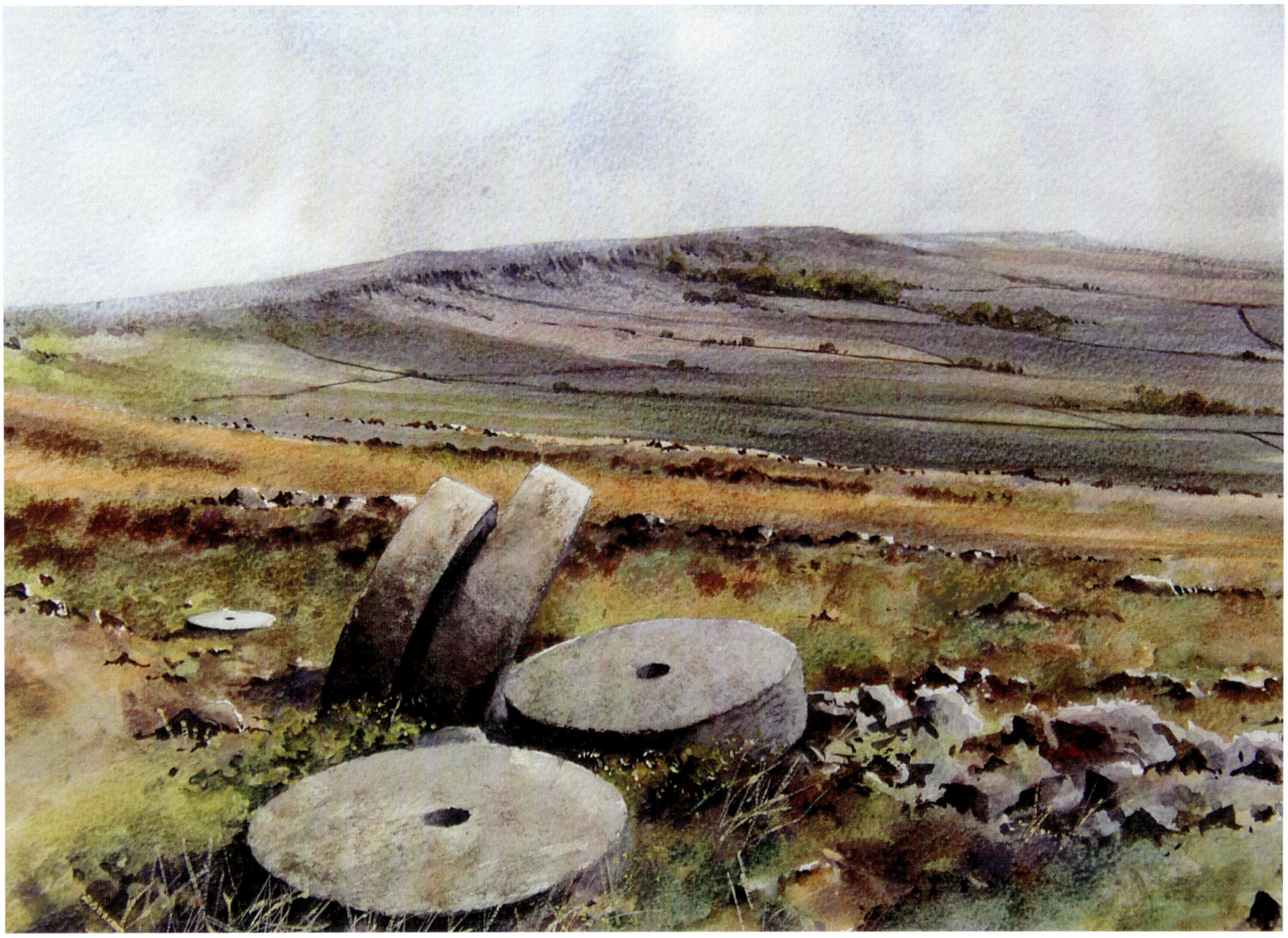

Millstones on Stanage Edge

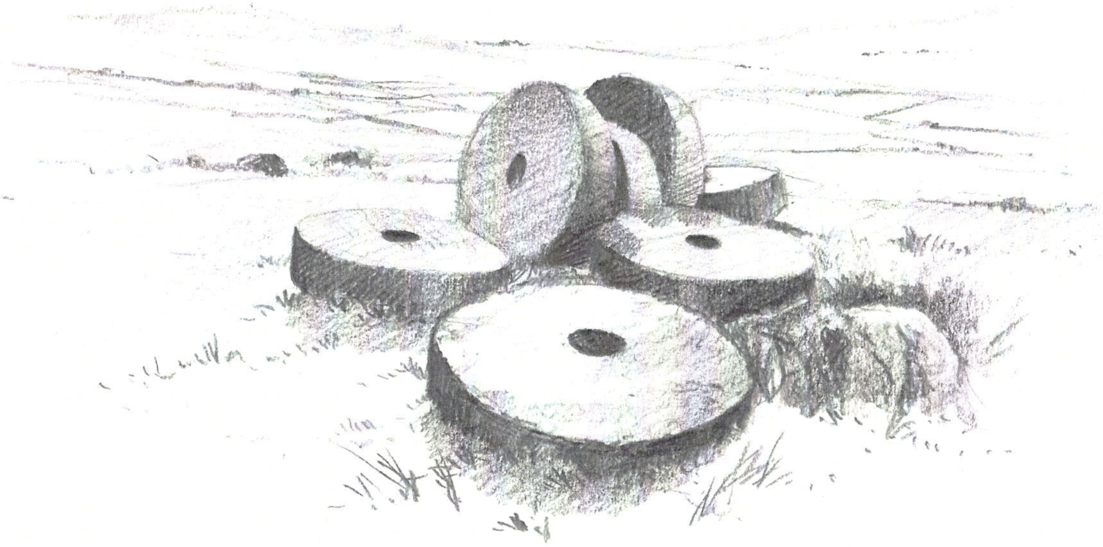

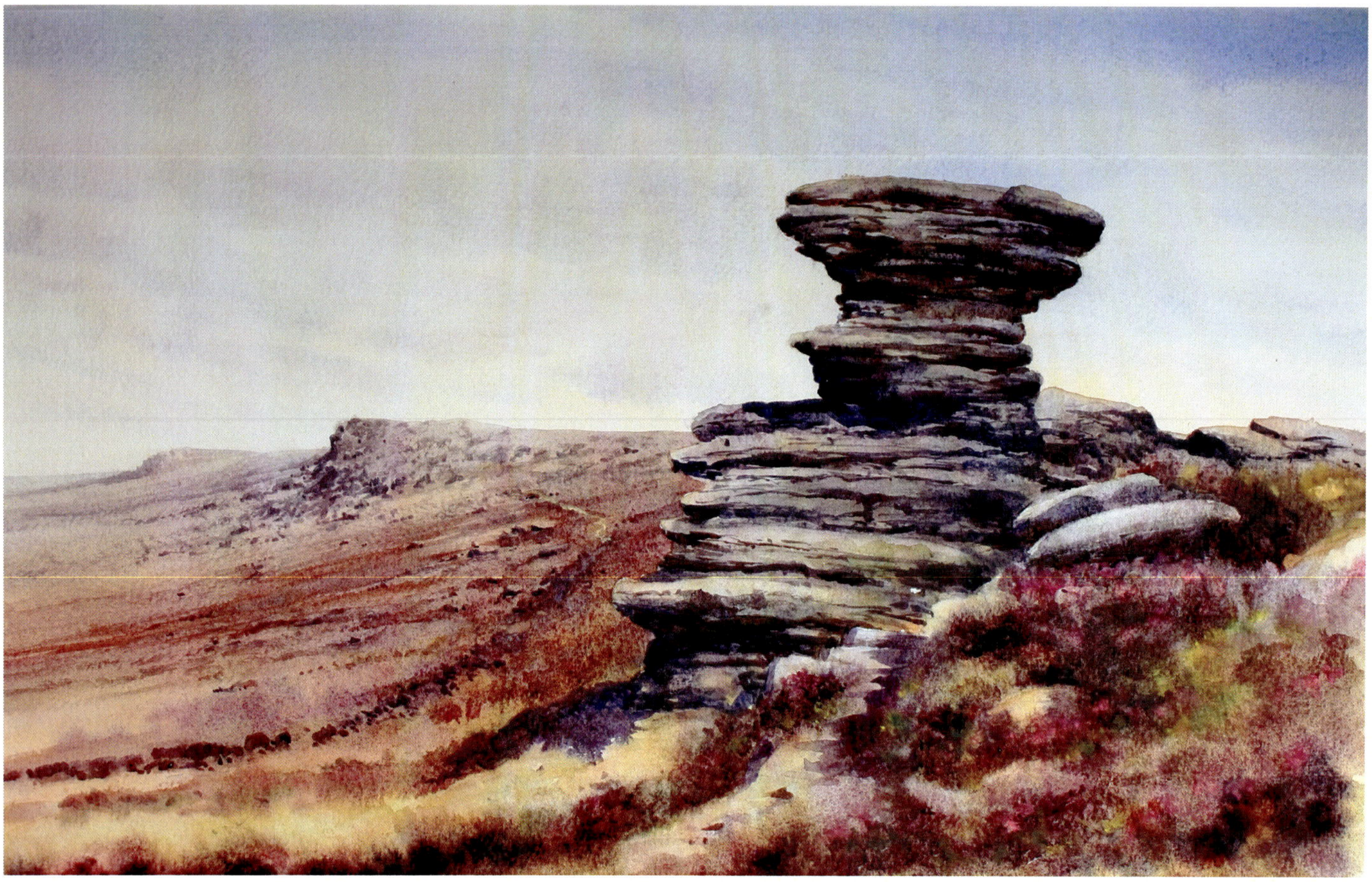

Salt Cellar, Derwent Edge

Many of the unusually shaped gritstone tors to be found along the edges have been named over the years by local residents. These include 'The Coach and Horses', the 'Eagle Stone' and many more. My favourite from a painterly point of view is the one with the funkiest shape, the 'Salt Cellar', shown here with Derwent Edge in the background. The rock formation leans into the hillside, almost bracing itself against the strong winds.

By exploring the variety of colours contained within the rock, purple, green, grey, violet and yellow can be seen. In areas that at a glance may appear just grey or brown, a painting will often benefit from a slight exaggeration of colour. The temptation with a subject like this is to carry on painting that bit too long, and overdo the detail, putting in every little crack and crevice. I always stop every so often and question if any more detail is needed.

4 Woodlands, Forests and Tree-Lined Lanes

I find one of the most difficult aspects of working as a professional artist is keeping a fresh supply of inspiring scenes to paint, and I am constantly on the lookout for new material.

It is a big advantage living in the Derbyshire Dales, just on the edge of the Peak District. A short walk away from our home in Darley Dale, I can find tree-lined lanes and wooded paths that over the years and through the different seasons have provided me with much inspiration and material. This means that some of the scenes in this section are not strictly in the Peak District, but they are not far away and I felt the book was richer for including them.

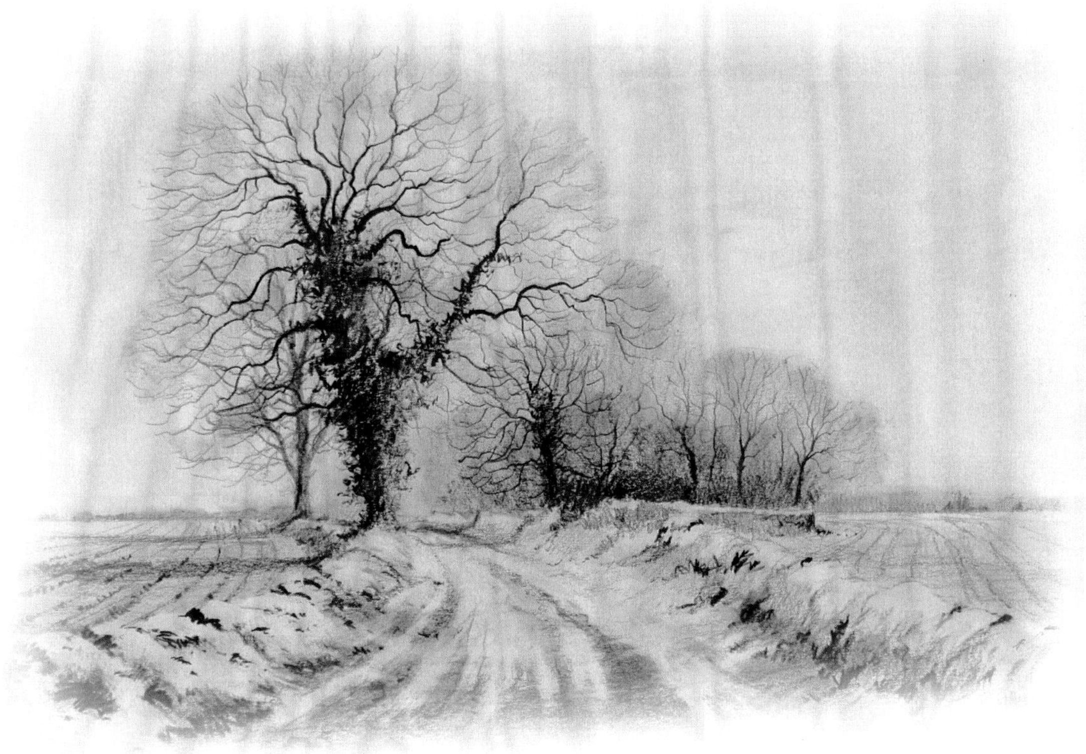

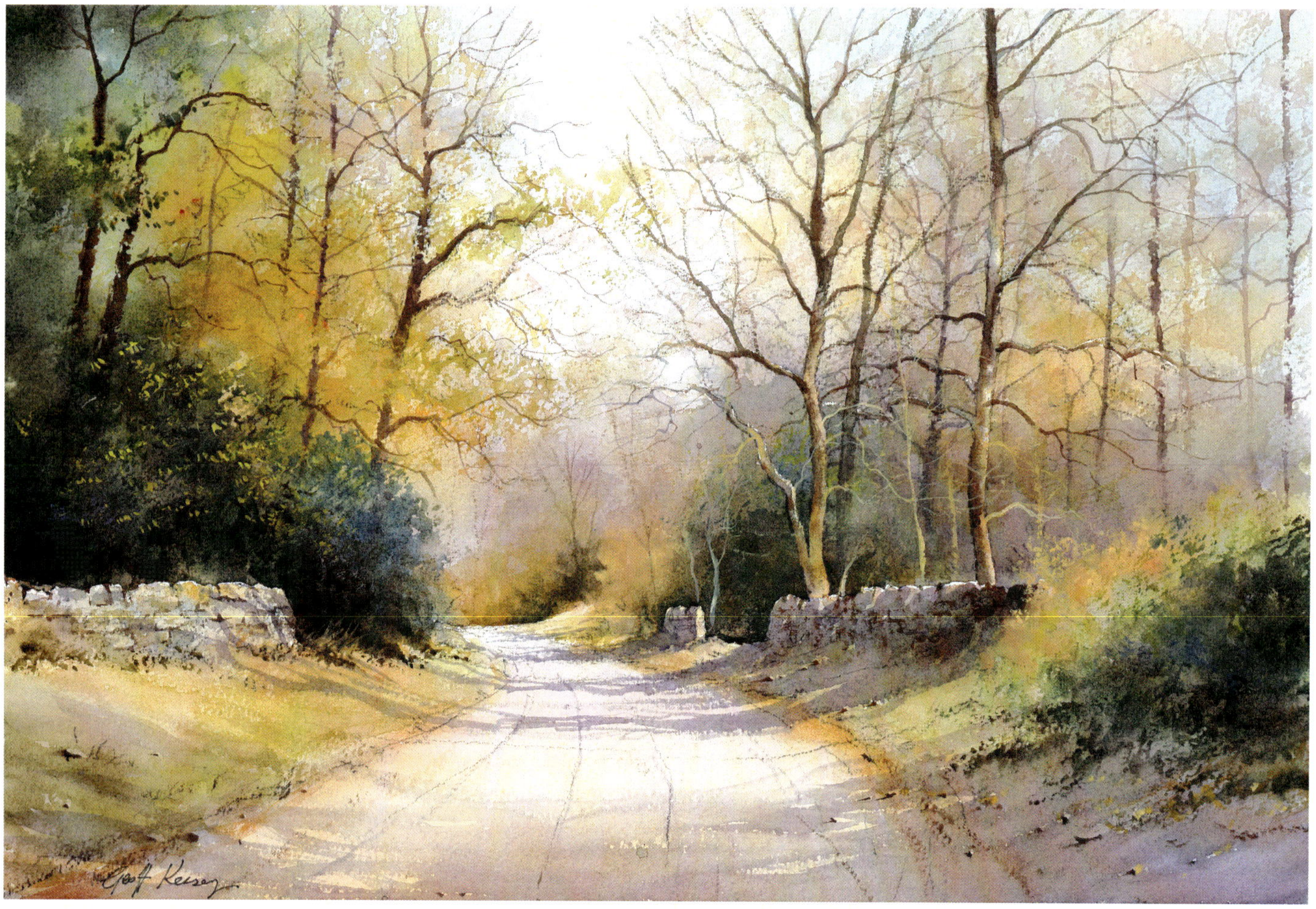

Autumn on Darley Hillside

I am never without my camera, even if it is just a short walk from home to get a bit of exercise. It was on such a walk that I came across this scene, and I knew immediately it would make an ideal painting. It is painted quite late in Autumn and some of the trees have lost their leaves, while others retain some foliage. This gave the opportunity to explore two different tree painting methods in one scene. When approaching this subject I was mindful of the description of autumn as being the season of 'mists and mellow fruitfulness' and have tried to capture this soft, slightly misty look, while employing plenty of warm colour.

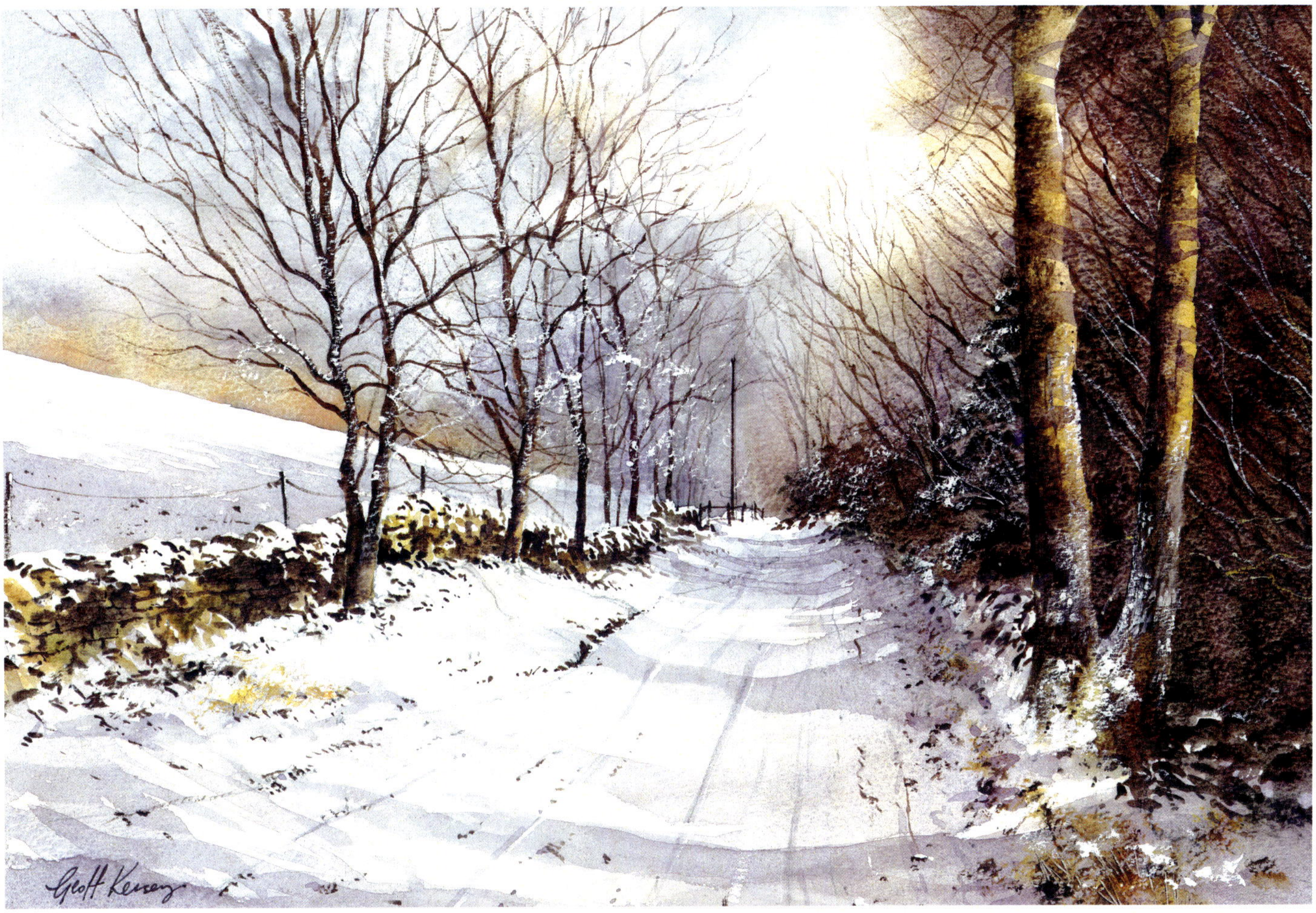

The Path to Halldale Woods

There is a simple perspective that underpins this whole scene. The different aspects of the subject – including the tracks in the path, the dry-stone wall, the diminishing height of the trees on the left, even the suggestions of fence posts – all lead to the focal point, where the path disappears out of view.

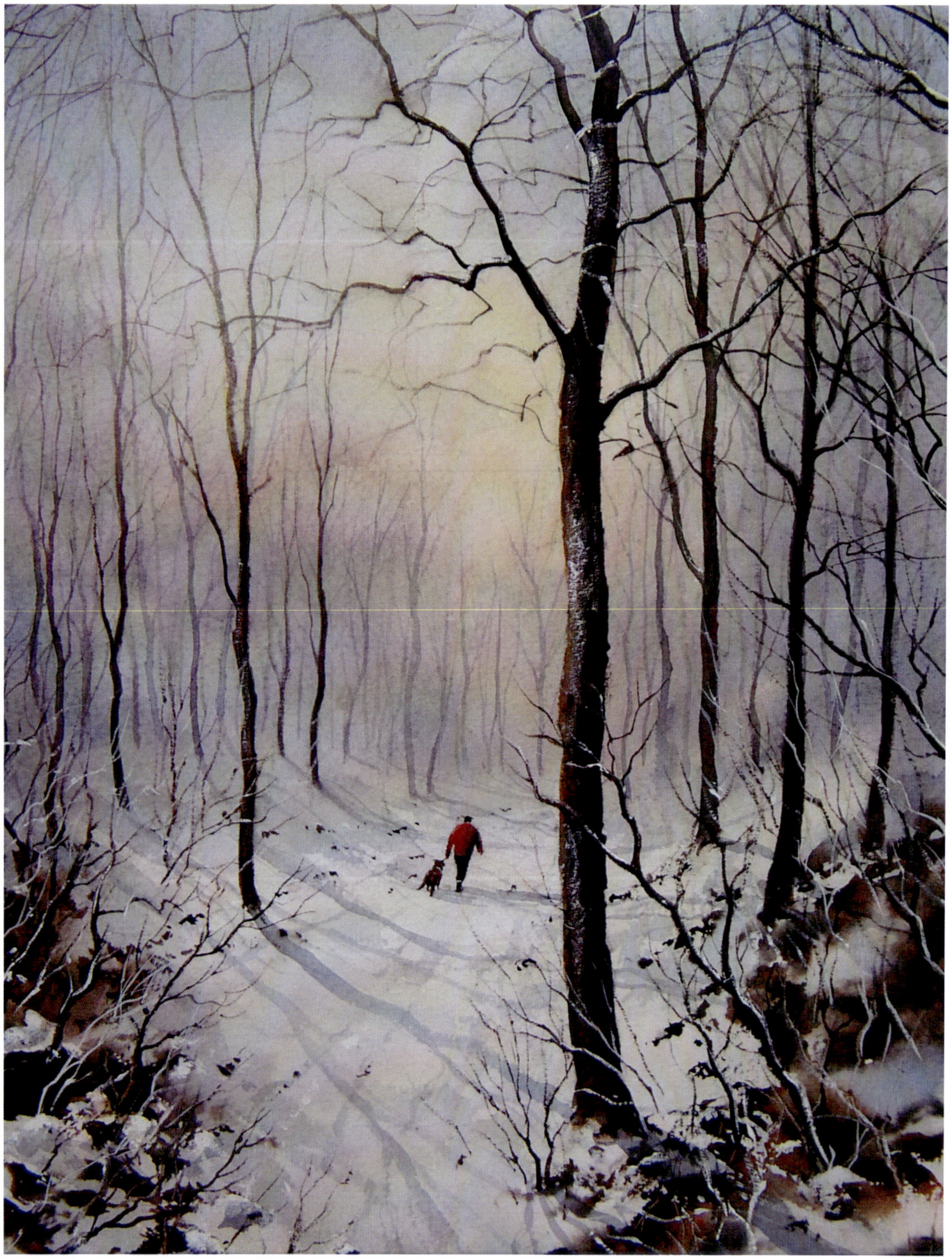

Winter in Halldale Woods

A few years ago I was approached by a charity for a painting suitable to produce as a Christmas card. The above scene seemed ideal as I imagined the walker with the dog heading briskly home in the fading light of a winter's afternoon, which gives the painting a small element of narrative. I stuck to my belief that all paintings – but in particular winter scenes – benefit from a limited palette, using just six colours.

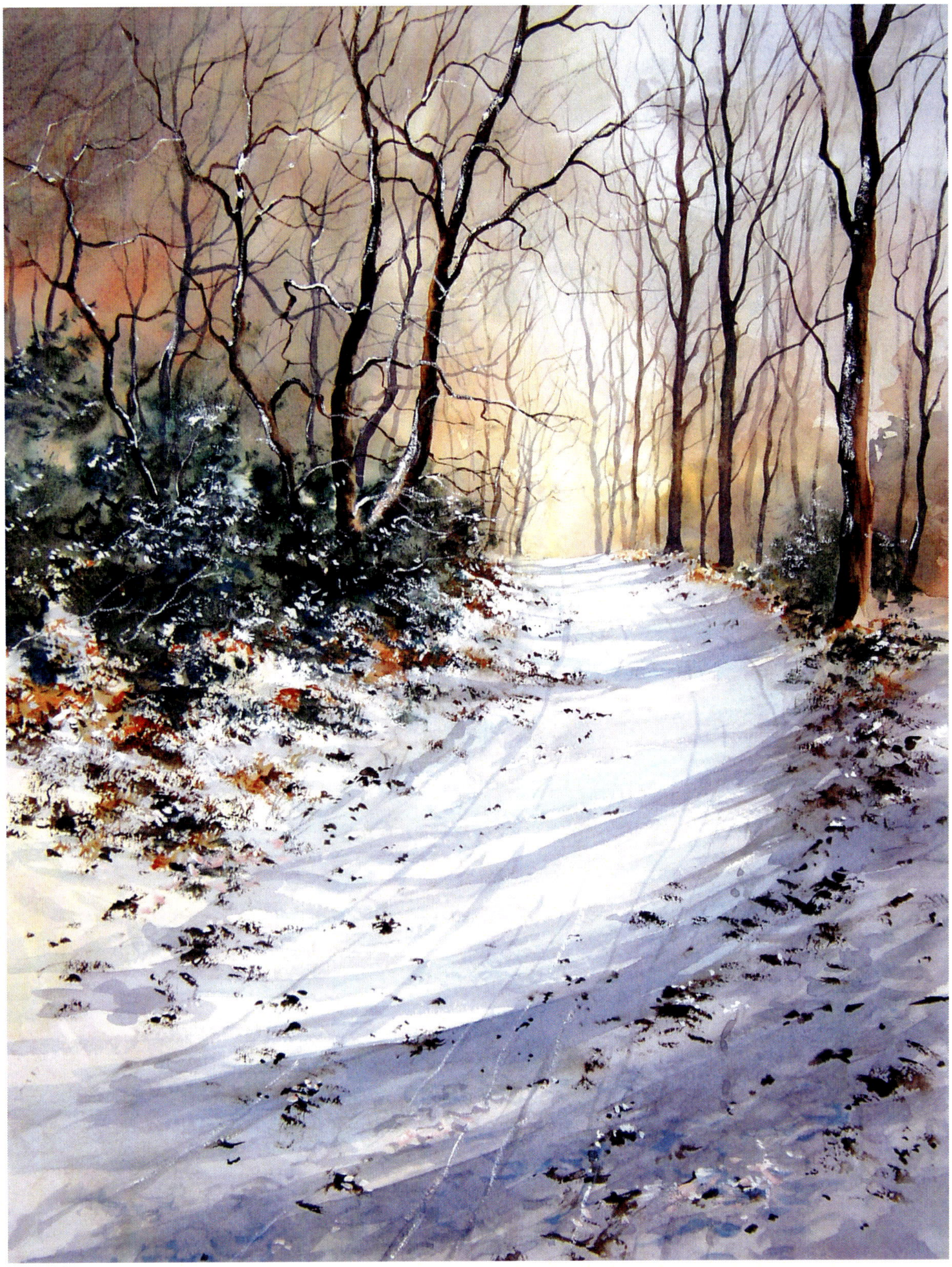

Winter in Halldale Woods 2

Just further along the same path as the painting on the previous page ; but this time with a more orange glow, deliberately contrasted with the rich purple shadows.

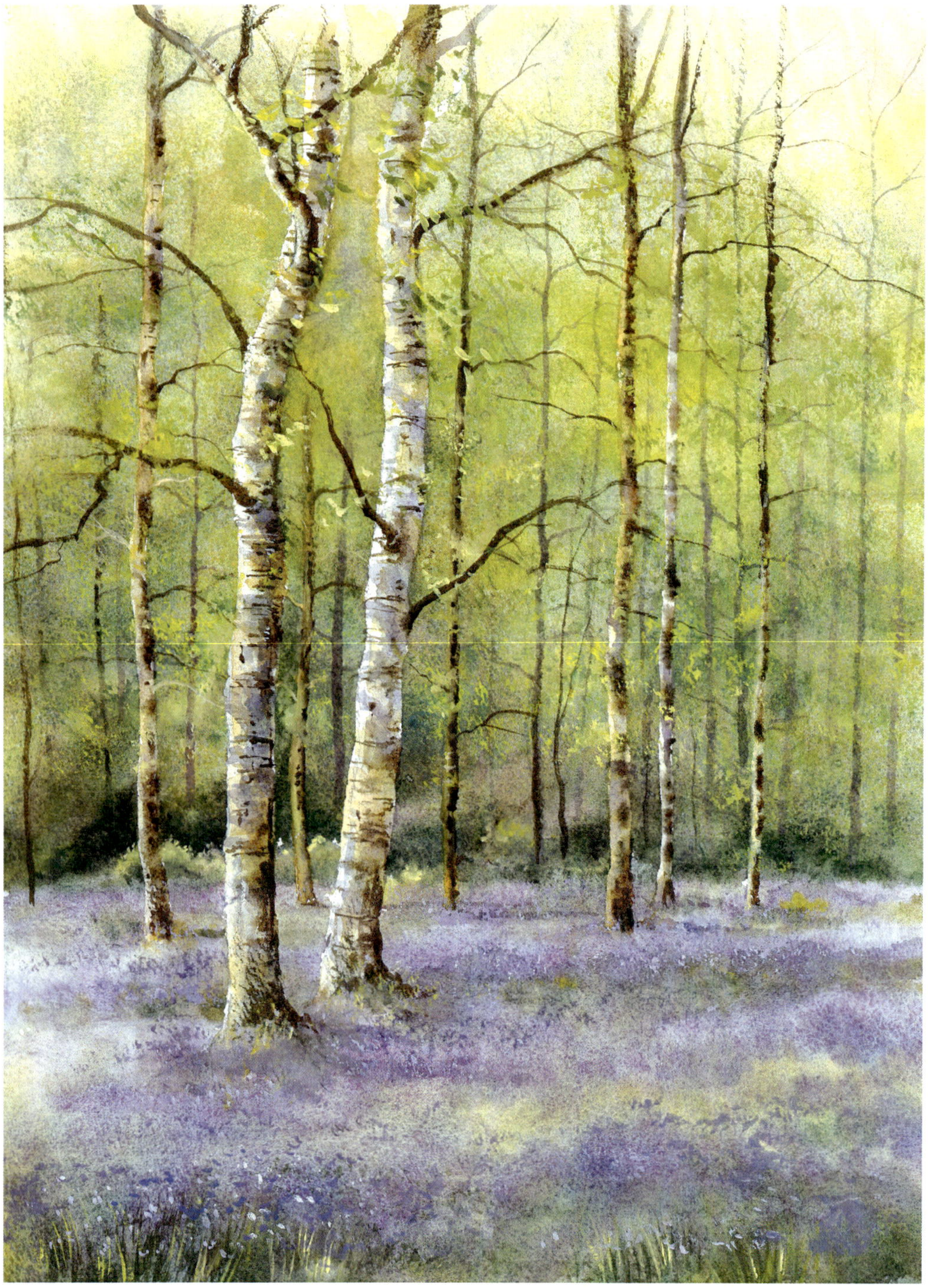

Bluebells at Kedleston Hall

A bluebell woodland scene seems integral to a section on woodlands. The appearance of bluebells is a short but magical time and every year I try to incorporate a few woodland walks in the spring to seek out some fresh subject matter. In the distance individual flowers can't be seen; rather there is a carpet of colour, with individual flowers only becoming more visible in the foreground. Bluebells aren't actually blue; but more of a violet colour, for which I use a mixture of cobalt blue and cobalt violet.

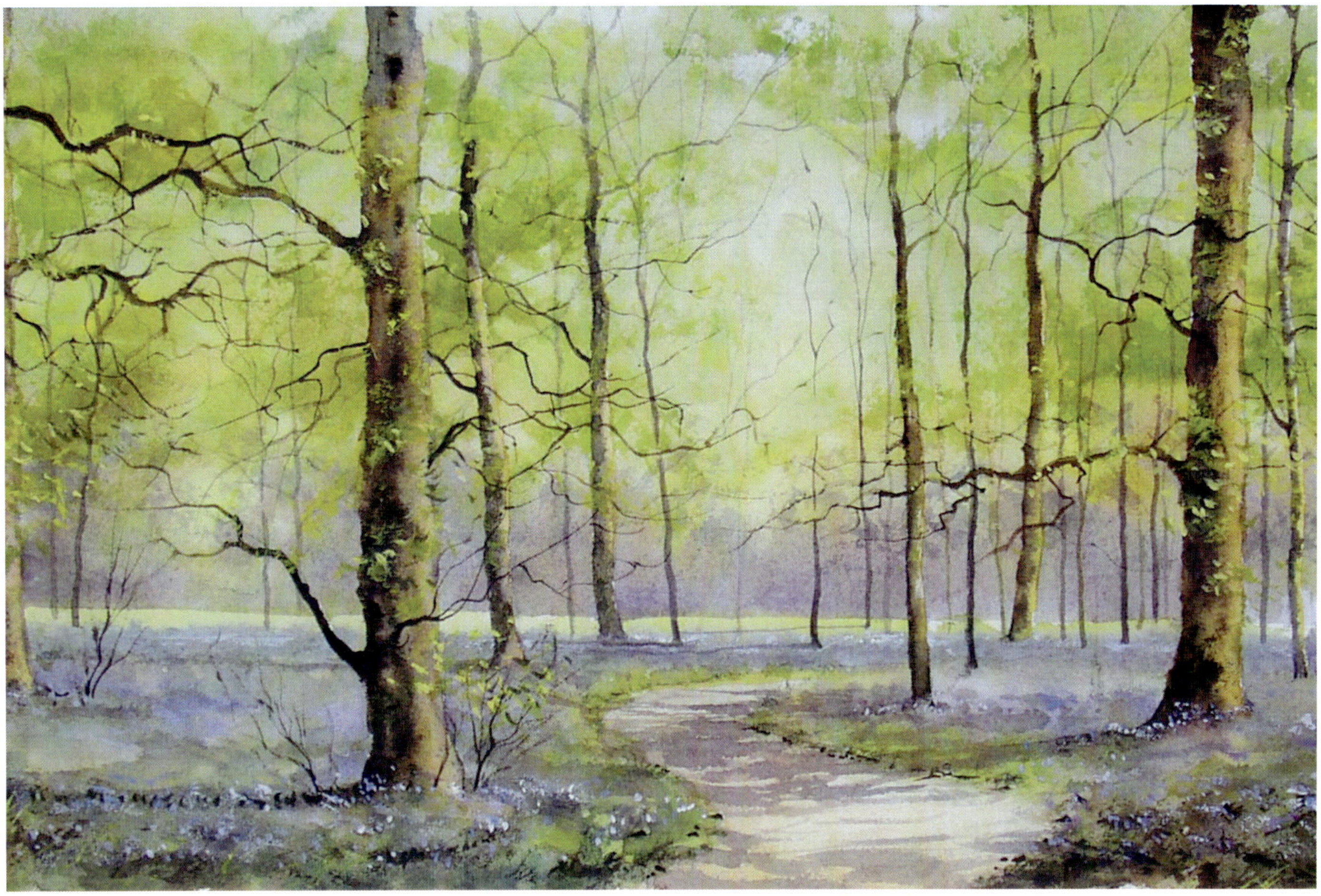

Bluebells at Kedleston Hall 2

Just further along the same path as the painting on the previous page, but a very different format.

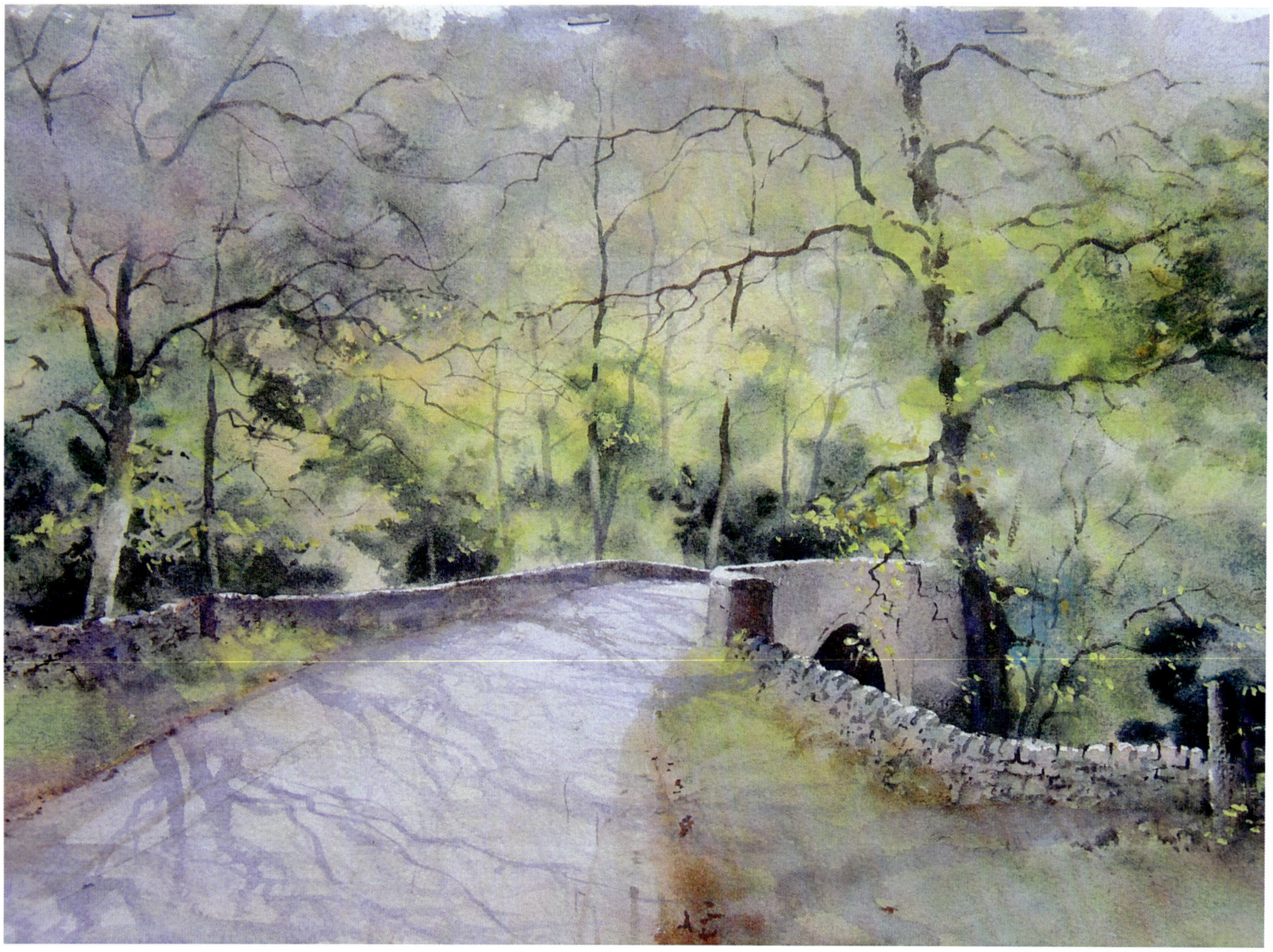

Footbridge in Summer

In this small watercolour sketch, I focused not on detail, but tried to capture the essence of the scene, featuring the warm glow of the colours in the abundant summer foliage. The very fine line of white paper along the top of both walls helps to separate this man-made structure from the mass of trees, while at the same time suggesting that the sunlight is just catching the very top edge of the stone-work.

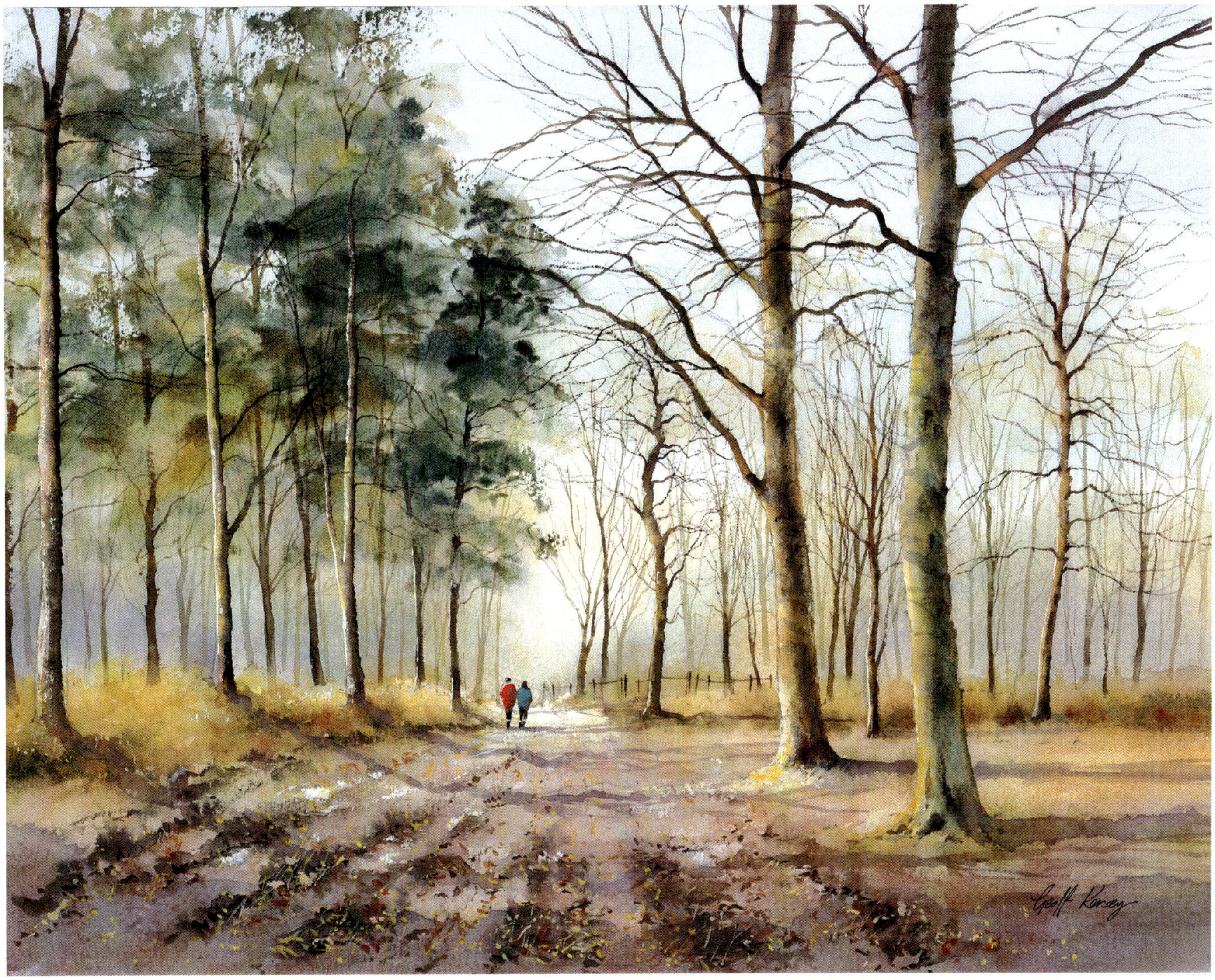

Winter Morning in Manners Woods

There is a footpath from Chatsworth to Bakewell that leads through this scenic woodland. It makes an excellent winter walk, although as can be seen from the painting, it can be a bit muddy. I tried here to capture the crisp freshness of a winter morning, whilst at the same time suggesting that the sun is trying to break through the mist, glimpsed through the trees. The scene is divided into two types of tree: the deciduous ones on the right, contrasted with the firs on the left.

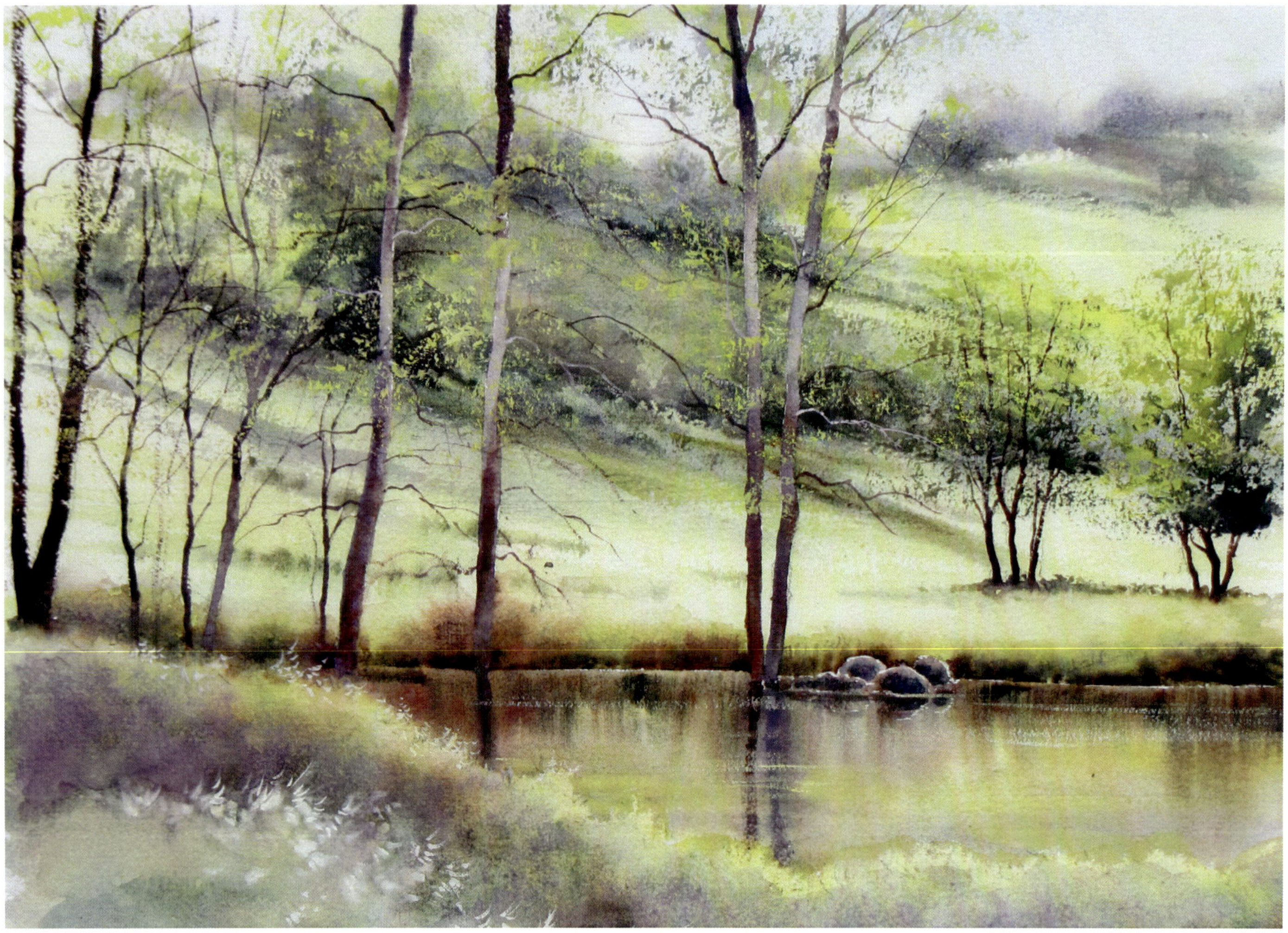

The View from the Studio, Pear Tree Farm

Fringing a small pond, just on the edge of Beamore Wood, is this delightful little view I kept promising myself I would paint. Eventually I completed this little watercolour of the scene as a painting demonstration at an Art Convention.

Due to the limited time and the need to explain what I am doing to onlookers, these demonstration pieces rarely make it to my gallery wall, but I felt in this instance it had a spontaneous quality that was quite pleasing.

5 *Padley Gorge*

Padley Gorge, managed by the National Trust, is a beautiful place full of potential paintings at almost every time of year.

It is a steep sided valley with an excellent stone path that runs from Grindleford station to the Longshaw Estate, and is one of the finest examples of the oak and birch woodland that once covered many Dark Peak valleys. Accessible from the path – if you don't mind a bit of a climb and scramble – runs Burbage Brook, where the water rushes over the boulders when in full flow or meanders between them during the summer.

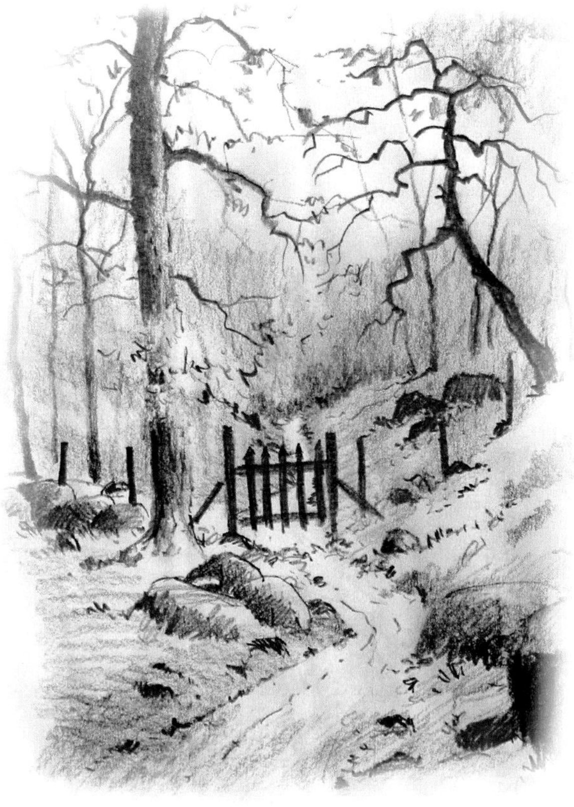

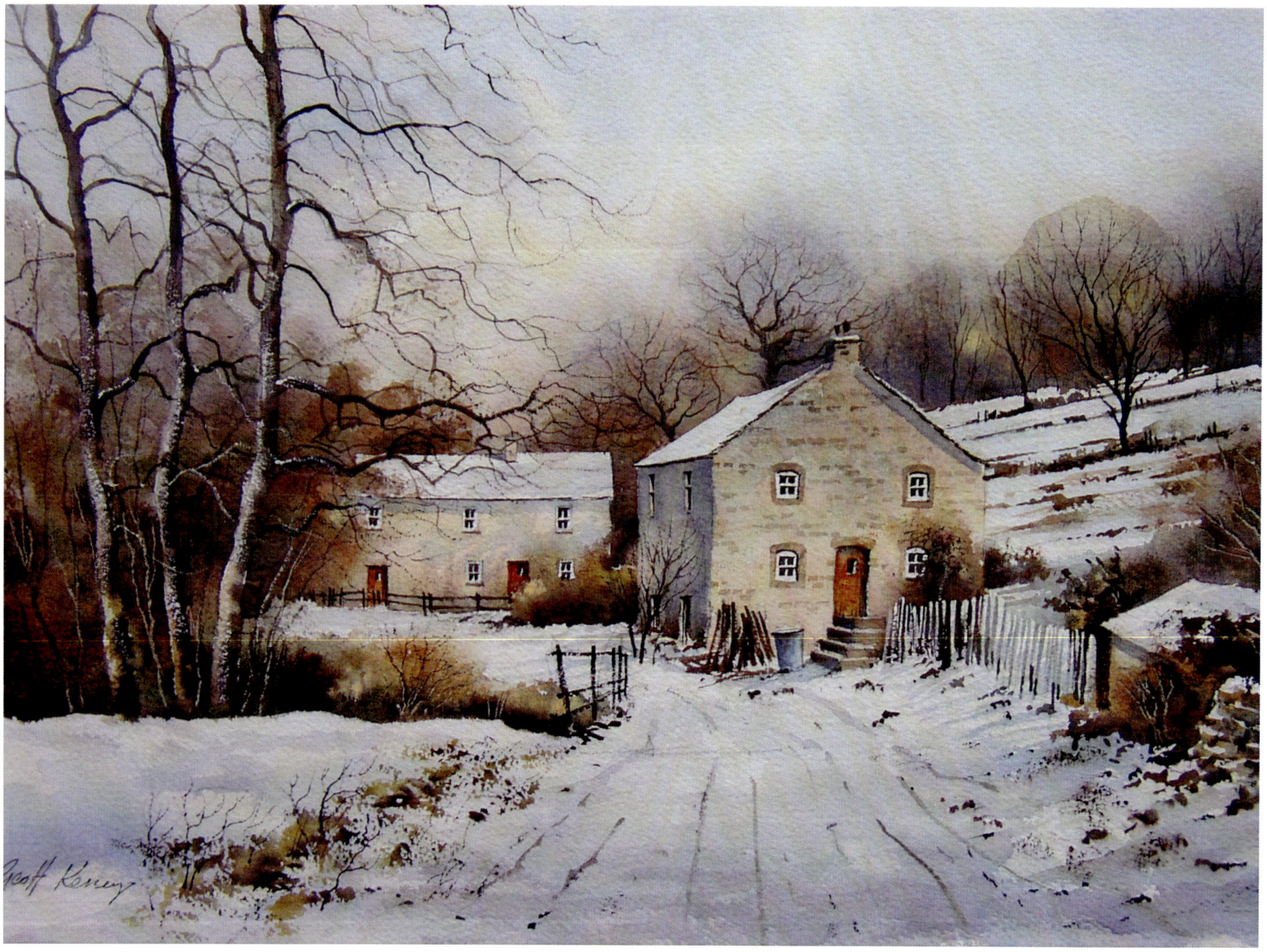

Just before turning right onto the path to start the ascent through the gorge from Grindleford station lies Padley Mill, now a private dwelling. I have always thought this a very attractive building; the lady who bought this painting described it as a 'smiling house', and I can see what she meant. It is a scene that works better in winter, as in summer the foliage on the left partially obscures the cottages.

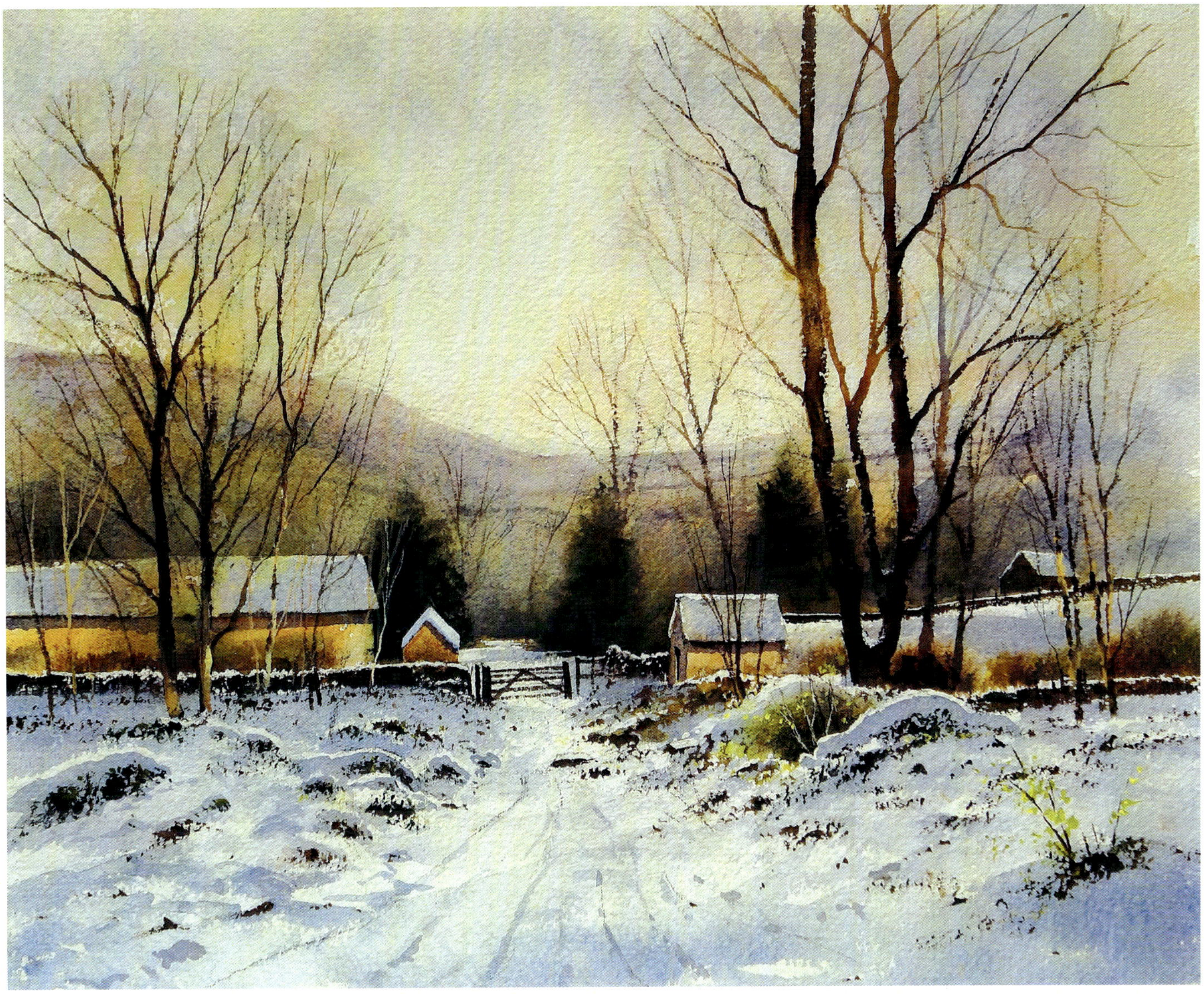

Looking down from Padley Gorge

From an ascending stony path, a look back down the slope provides this excellent composition. Even though this was a cold day I wanted a touch of warmth, so introduced a touch of vermillion into the sky and distant hills. This same hint of warm colour has also been added to the stone-work of the buildings and the tree trunks.

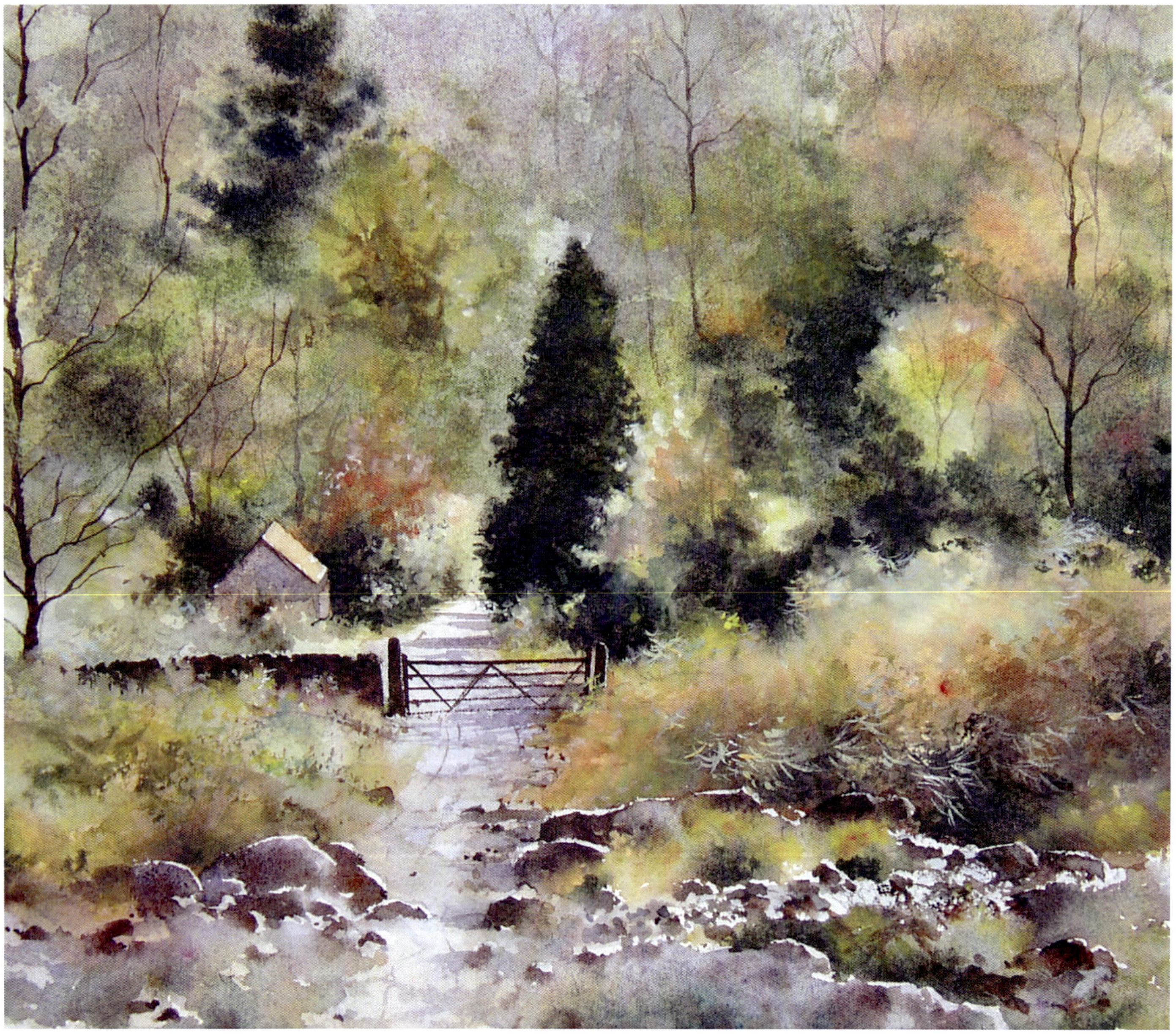

This is the same scene as painted on the previous page, but in autumn, and is a prime example of how the seasons change the look of the landscape. Here I have tried to capture the vivid, bright light reflecting off the partly metalled path and the rich autumn foliage.

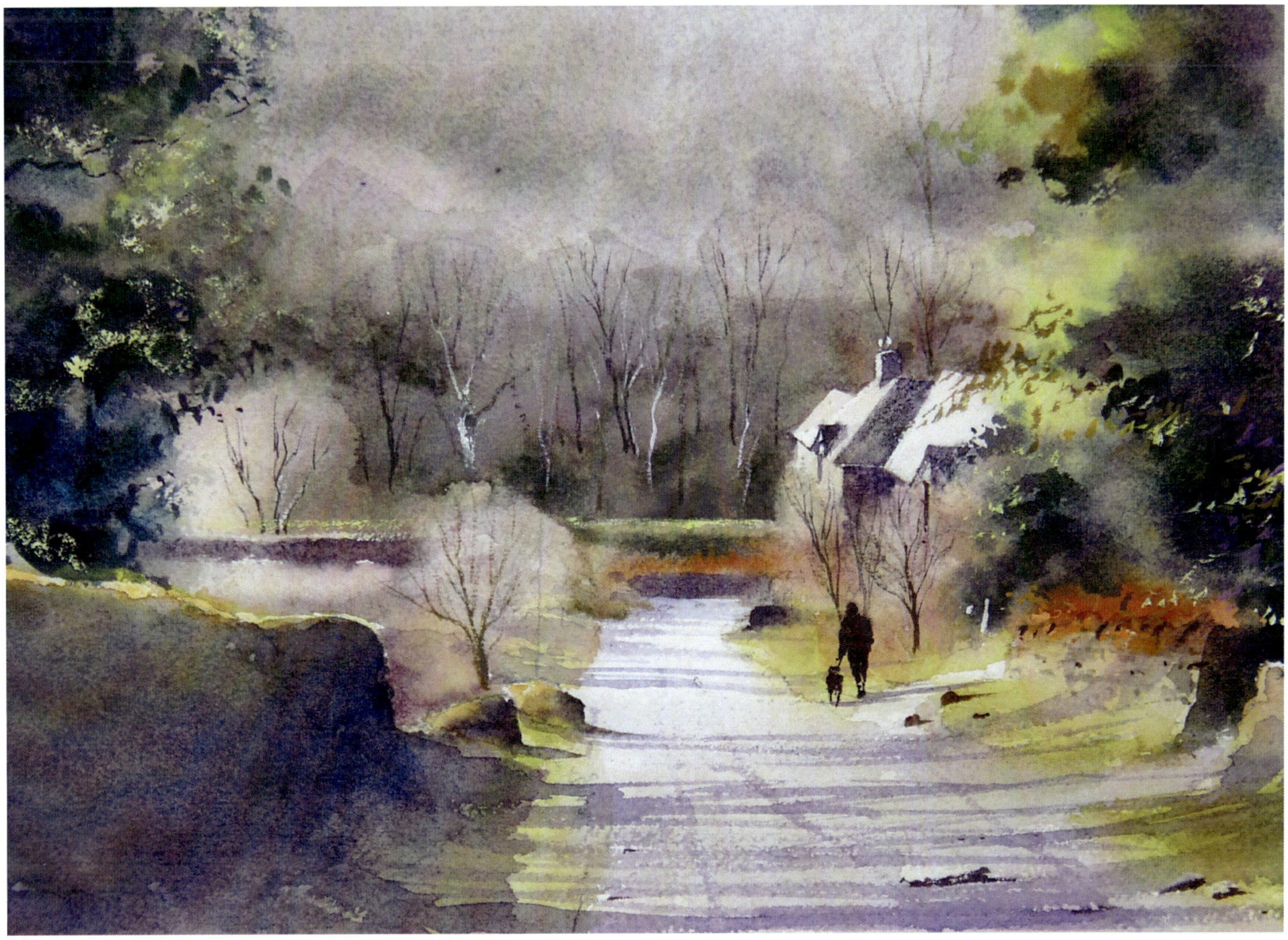

Cottages in Padley

A watercolour sketch of the same path featured on the two previous pages. This represents early spring, with a mixture of winter and spring trees – to my mind a magical time of year for painting. To get a bit of 'oomph' into the scene, I have used deep, fairly dark shadows, contrasted with bright passages: the roofs of the cottages on the right were left as just white paper.

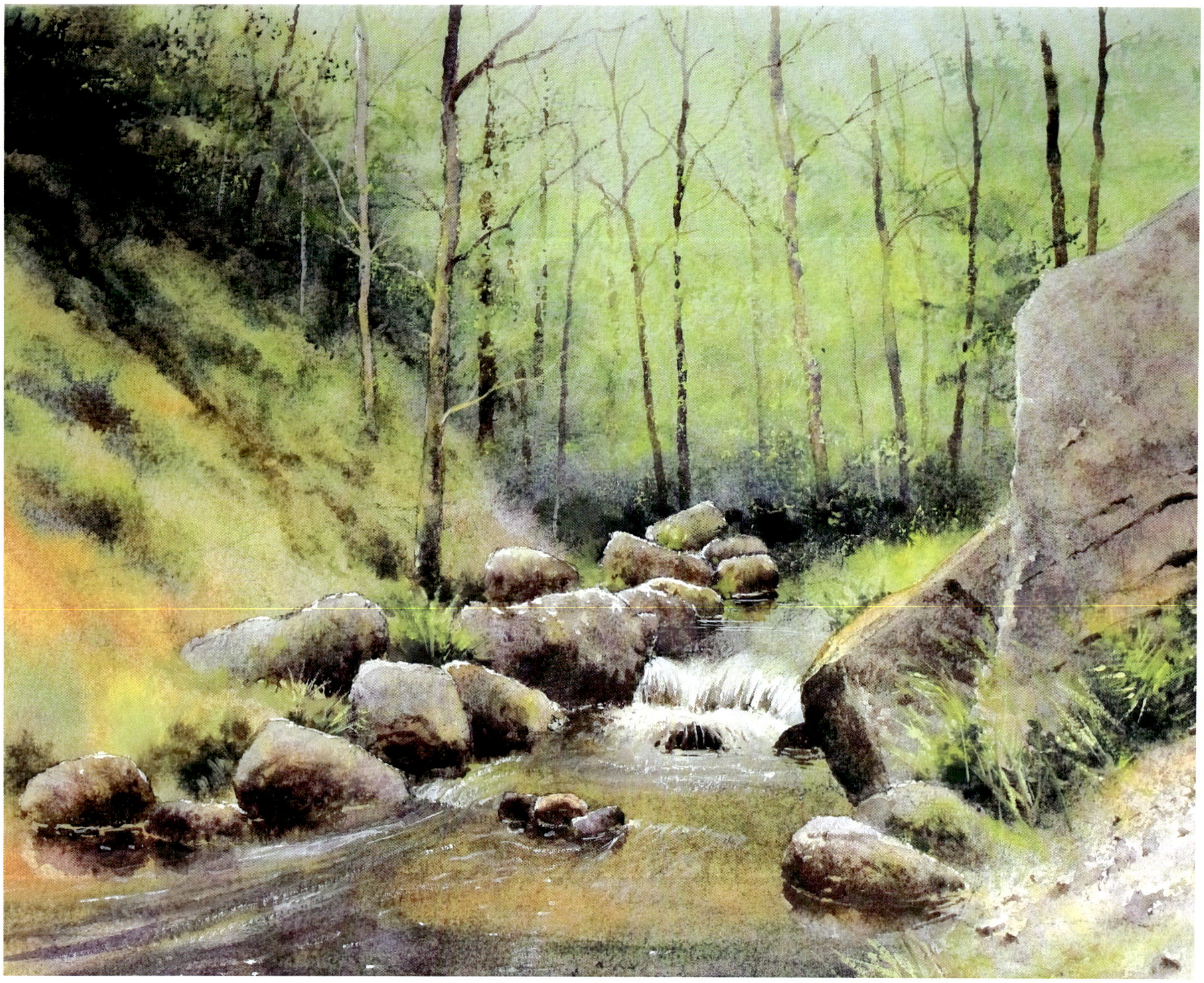

Burbage Brook in Padley Gorge

I always find painting waterfalls challenging, but very rewarding if I can capture the movement of the rushing water. Where the water tumbles over the rocks in the middle distance, masking fluid was used to preserve the white paper, before adding a few strokes of blue and grey paint with a very fine brush to develop the 'rushing' effect. The very last stage of the painting was to add a few streaks of white gouache in the foreground to suggest ripples and movement.

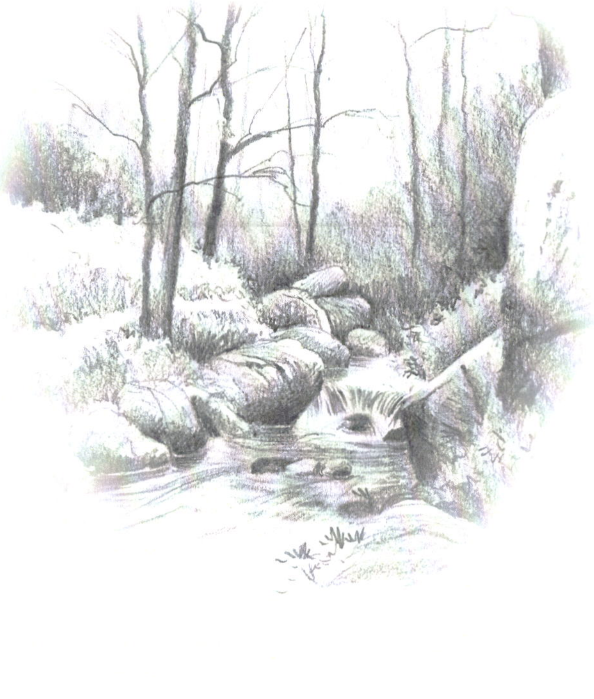

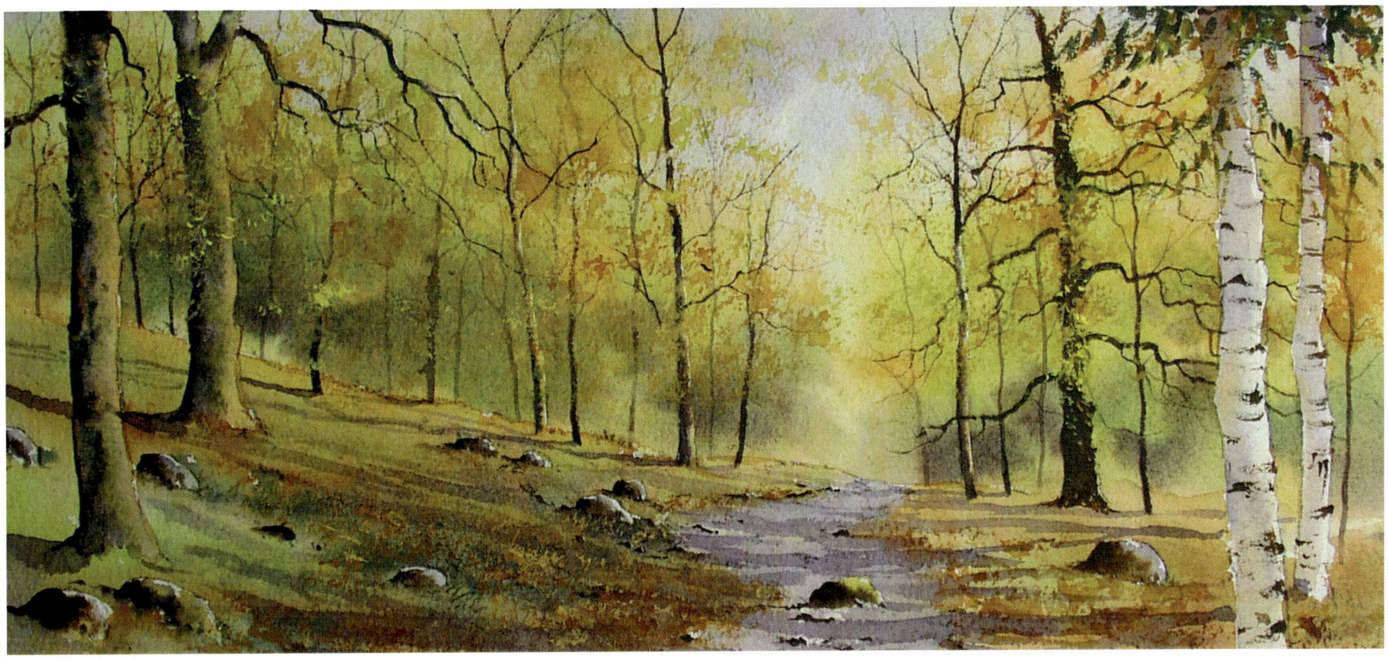

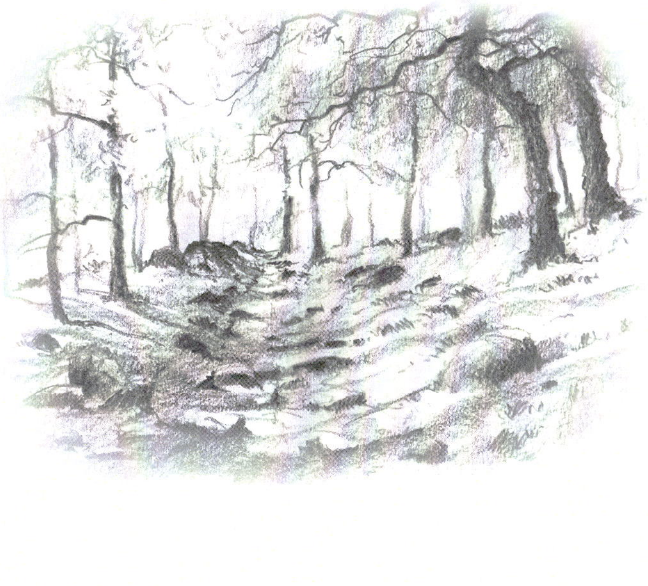

Autumn in Padley Woods

This is at one of the highest points of the path, where it opens out a bit more, providing an inspiring view of the woods in all their autumn glory. I am not sure about the two foreground trees on the left, as they almost match exactly the two silver birches on the right. It makes the composition a little symmetrical, although this is offset to some extent by the fact that the path is not dead centre.

6 *Just Outside The Border: Matlock, Matlock Bath, Cromford Canal and Lumsdale*

Whilst I am aware that strictly speaking none of these locations are actually in the Peak District National Park; they are so rich in painting subjects that I couldn't think of writing this book without including something from each of them.

Living just three miles from Matlock, it has been a convenient source of painting subjects over the years. The two paintings overleaf of Hall Leys Park, right in the centre of the town are an excellent example of how the different seasons can transform the same scene. The first painting (*Autumn in Hall Leys Park*) is from a photo I took on a bright autumn Sunday morning. Having completed the painting, I made a mental note to paint the same view in winter's cloak if snow fell that coming winter (*bottom*, *Winter in Hall Leys Park*). I thought they would look good together, so did not exhibit the autumn painting until I had painted the winter one. I am not sure what I would have done had it not snowed, but in the event they were exhibited and sold as a pair.

A few miles further along the A6 in the Derby direction lies Matlock Bath, built alongside the River Derwent in a steep and beautiful gorge. It was developed as a spa town in the nineteenth century and was very fashionable and prosperous, with the spectacular scenery adding to its appeal. The writer Mary Shelley likened it to 'Switzerland, but on a lower scale'. As a child being taken there almost every year to see the illuminations, it always seemed to me to have the feel of a seaside resort despite being nowhere near the sea.

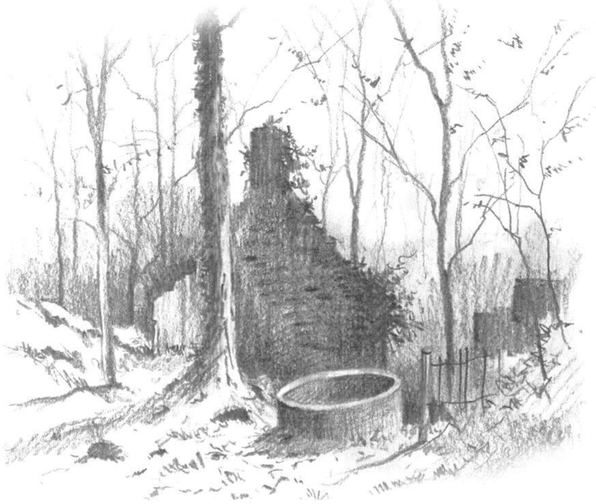

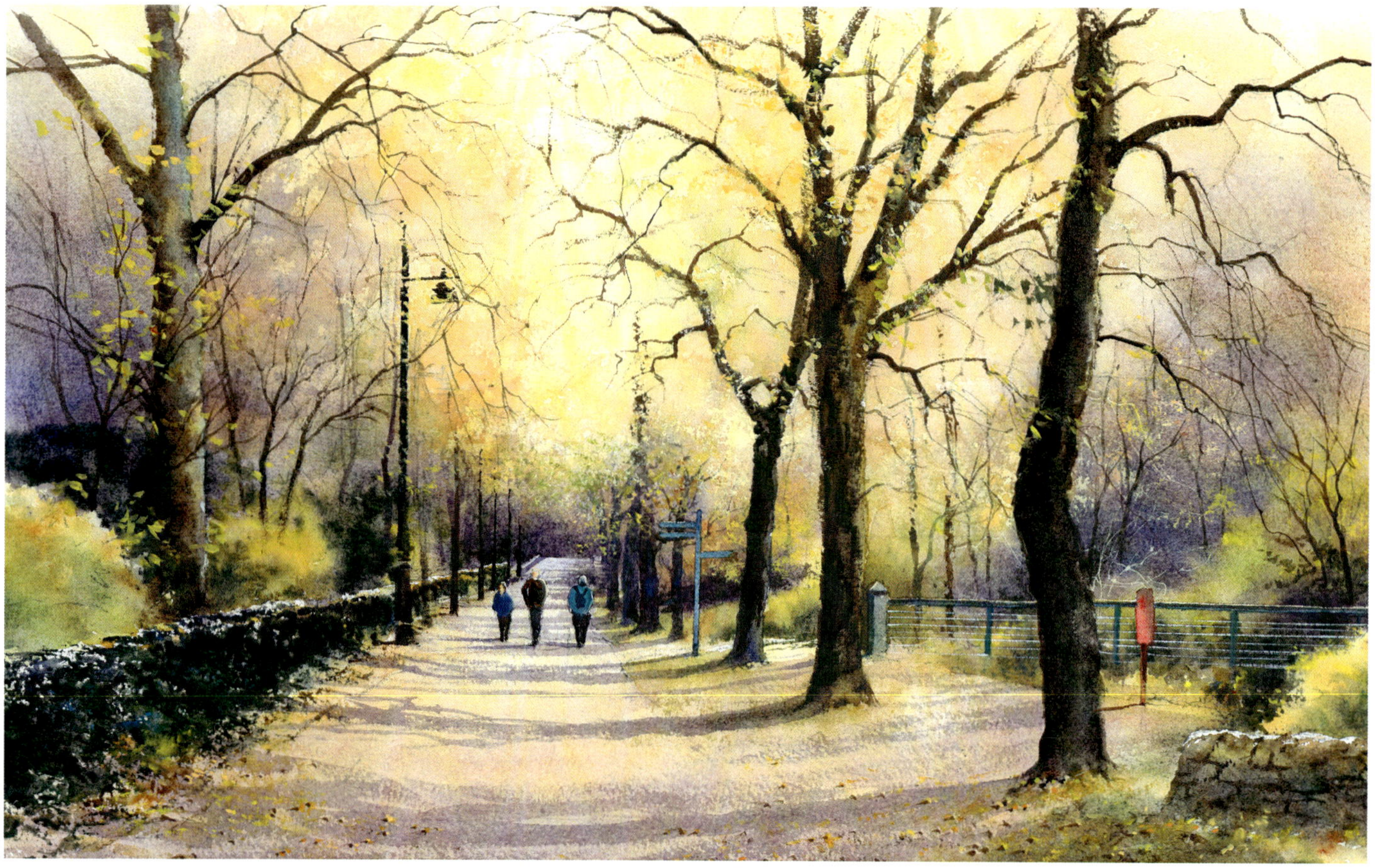

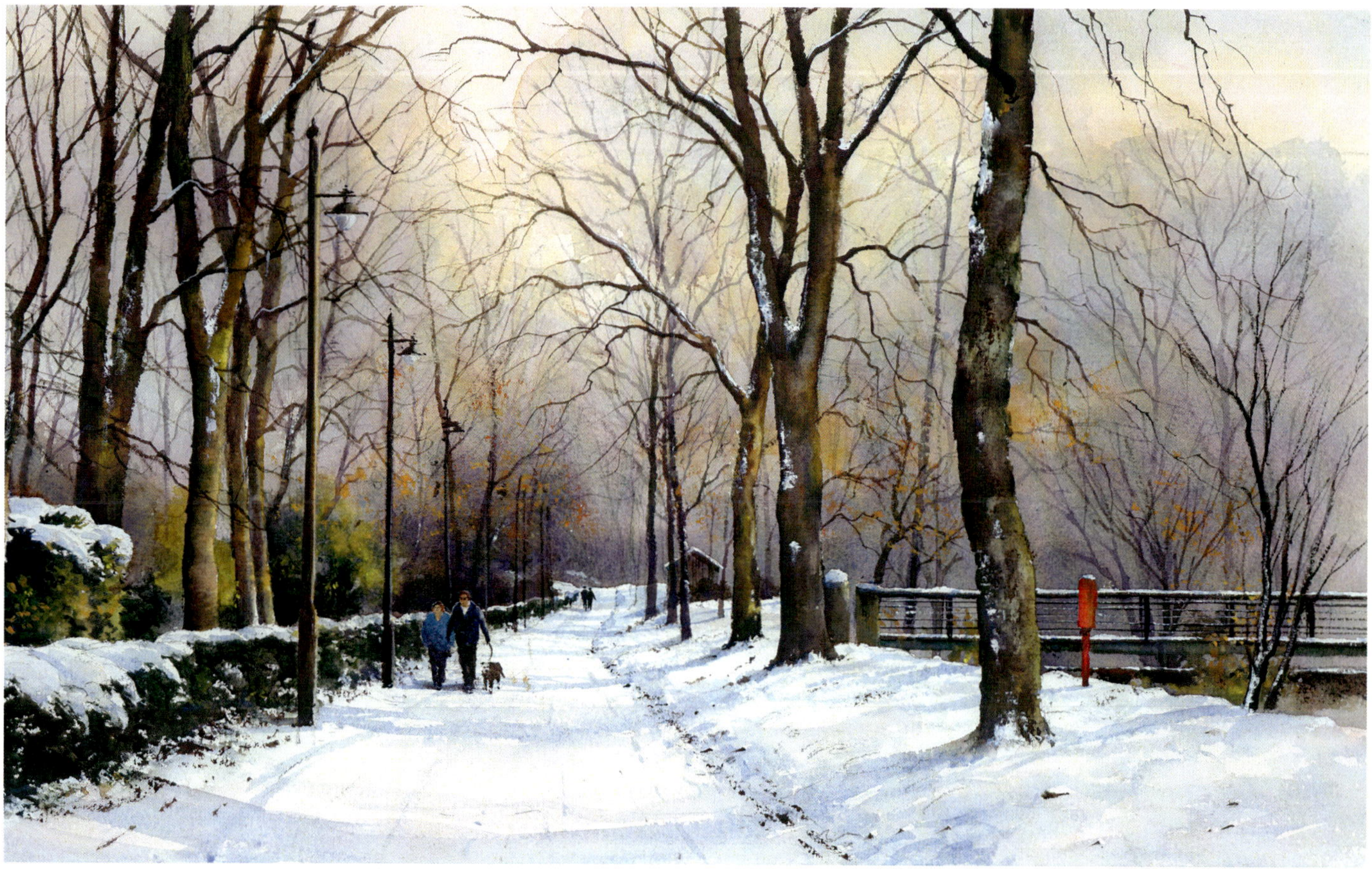

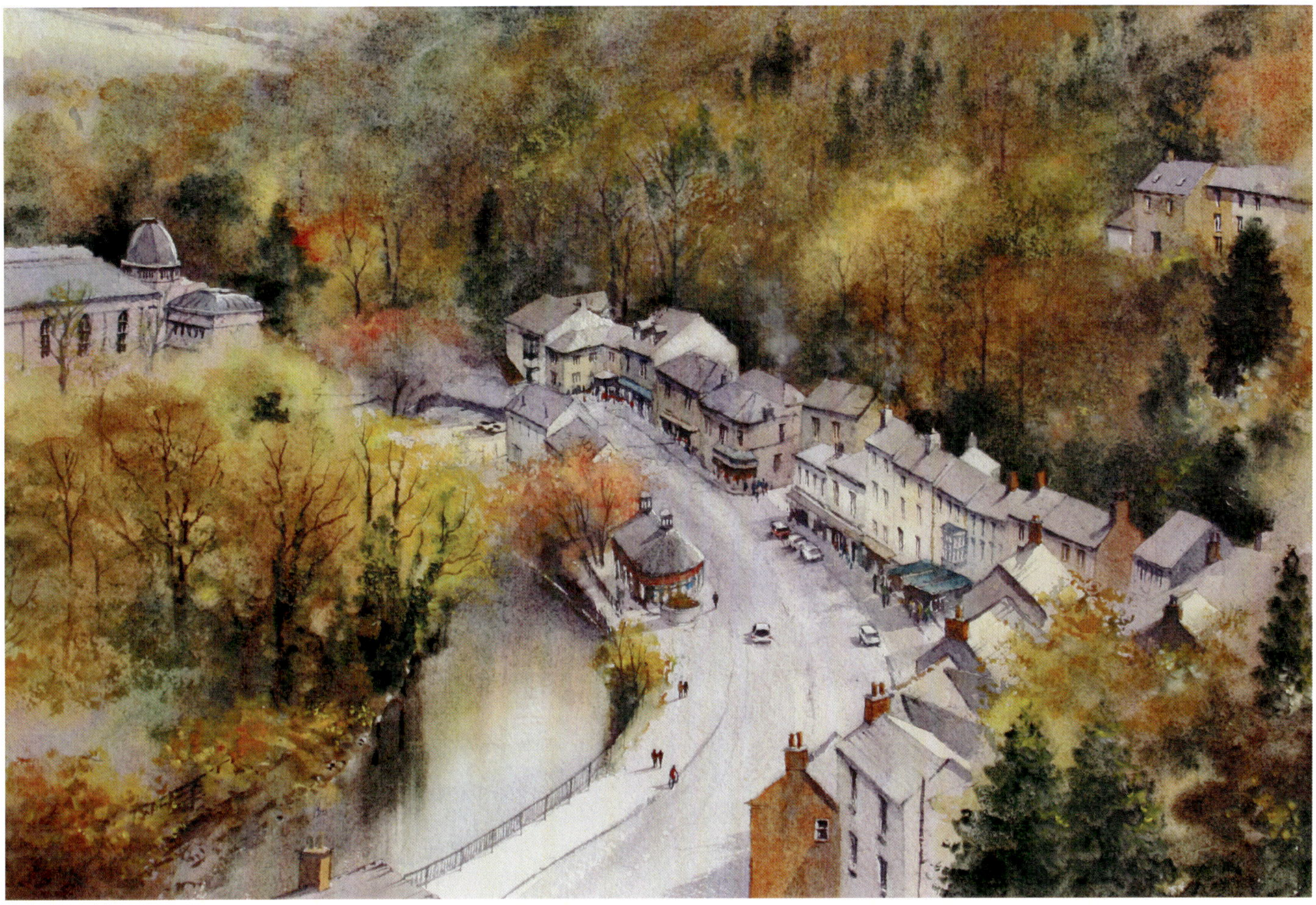

Looking down to Matlock Bath

As Matlock Bath is surrounded by high ground it is not difficult to get aerial views such as this one. Softer, less clearly defined forms of the autumn trees frame the harder edged shapes of the buildings and the road. The familiar shape of the Pavilion on the left indicates the continuing curve of the road even though it is obscured at this point by the trees.

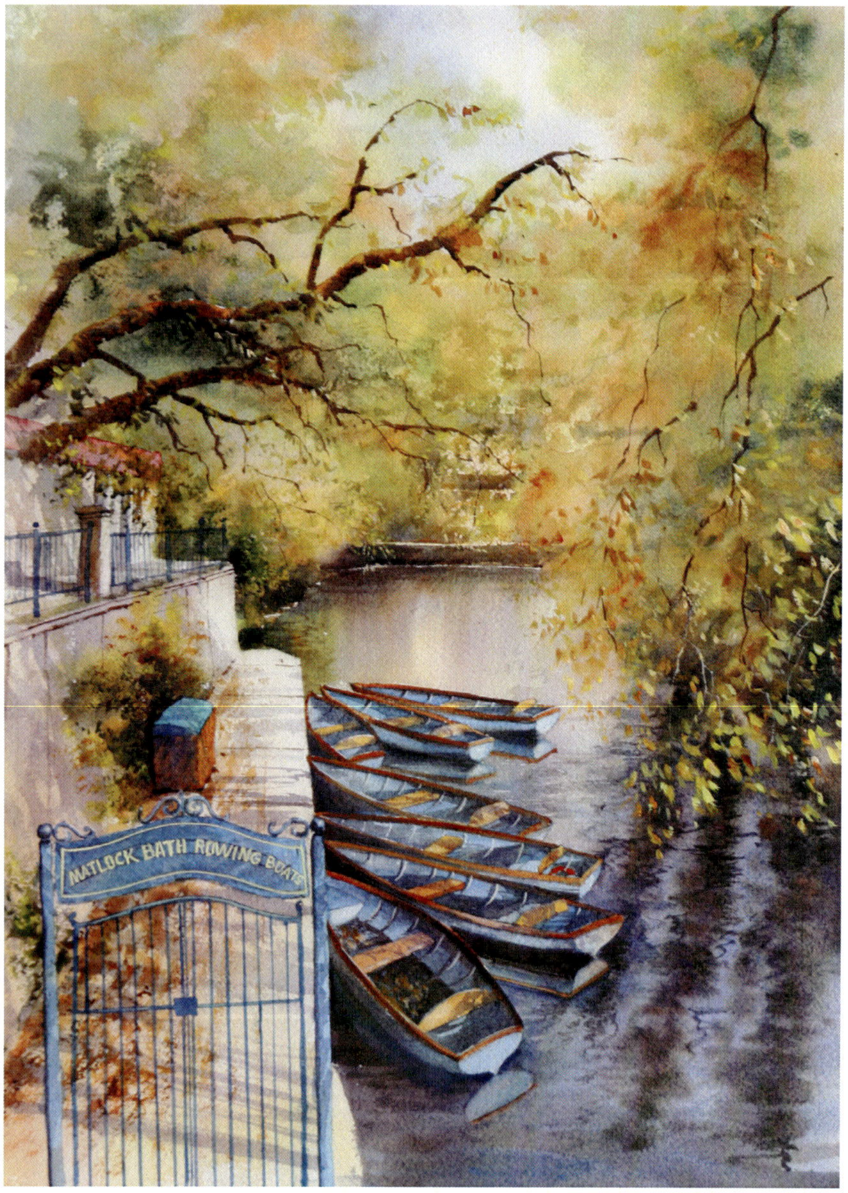

Rowing Boats, Matlock Bath

This scene is full of warm autumn colour. I have used the trees to frame and contain the image of the boats and reflections in the river. In this painting the impact of the colours is increased by using the opposites of yellow/orange against the different shades of blue. Painting from a high viewpoint allowed the interior detailing of the boats to be featured.

One of my favourite walks that again isn't too far from home is the five-mile stretch along the towpath of the Cromford Canal, from Cromford to Ambergate. I have painted many views along the way, although it is not suitable if wanting to see canal boats and barges, as it has been silted up for as long as I have been aware of it. Nevertheless it is rich with painting subjects and indeed has been declared a local nature reserve, it being a haven for water vole, grass snakes, little grebes, moorhen and coots.

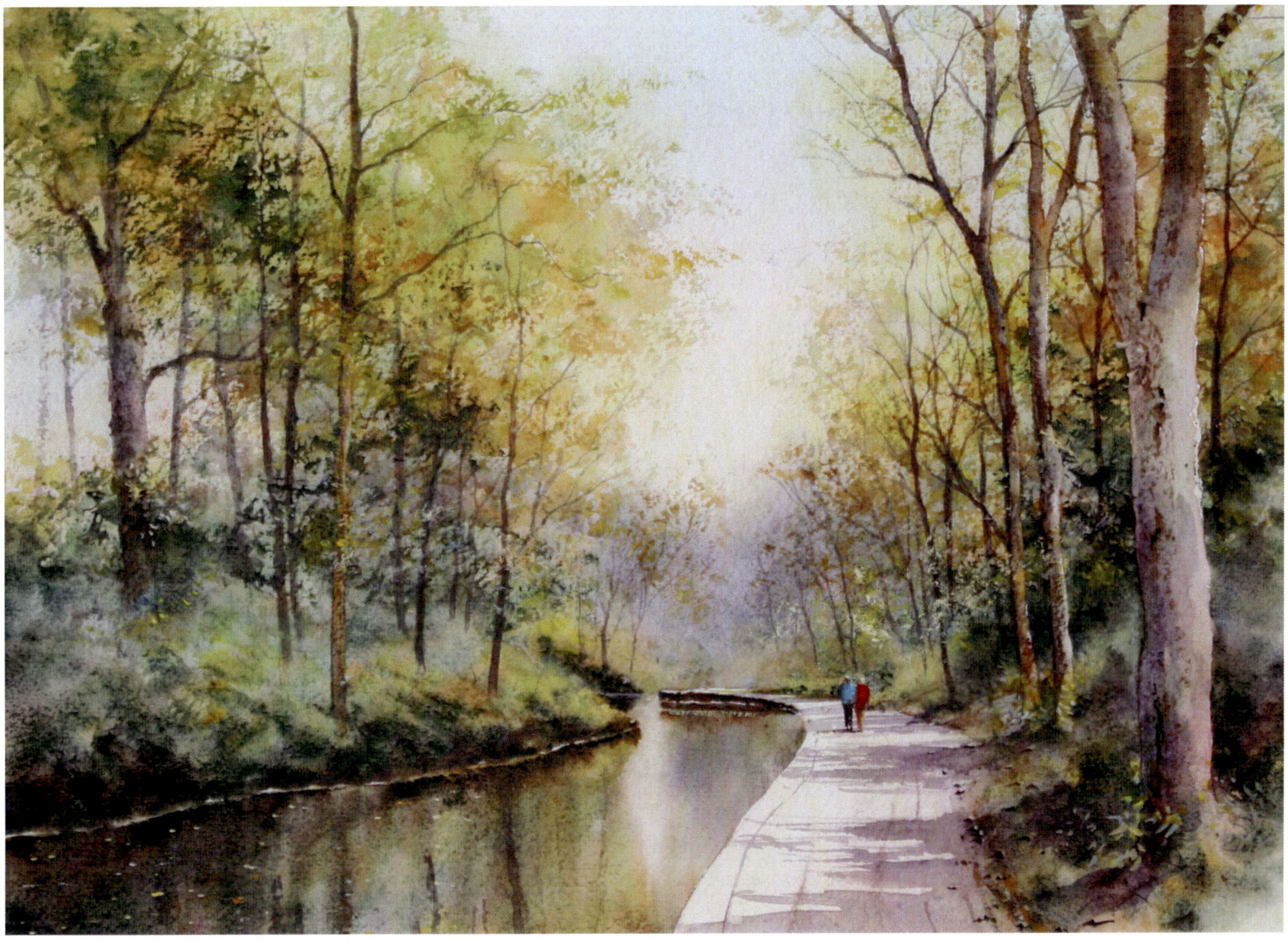

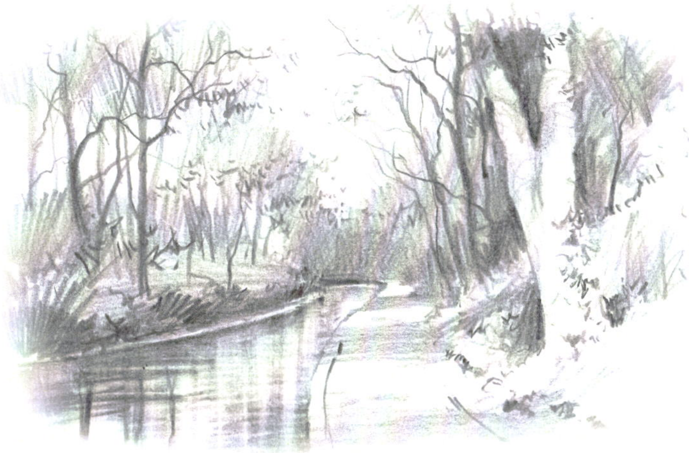

Cromford Canal

I love painting scenes like this where the initial stage consists of laying in a series of wet into wet washes, loosely forming the shapes of the foliage. In the second stage of the painting it was sharpened up using some dry-brushwork and some suggestions of detail.

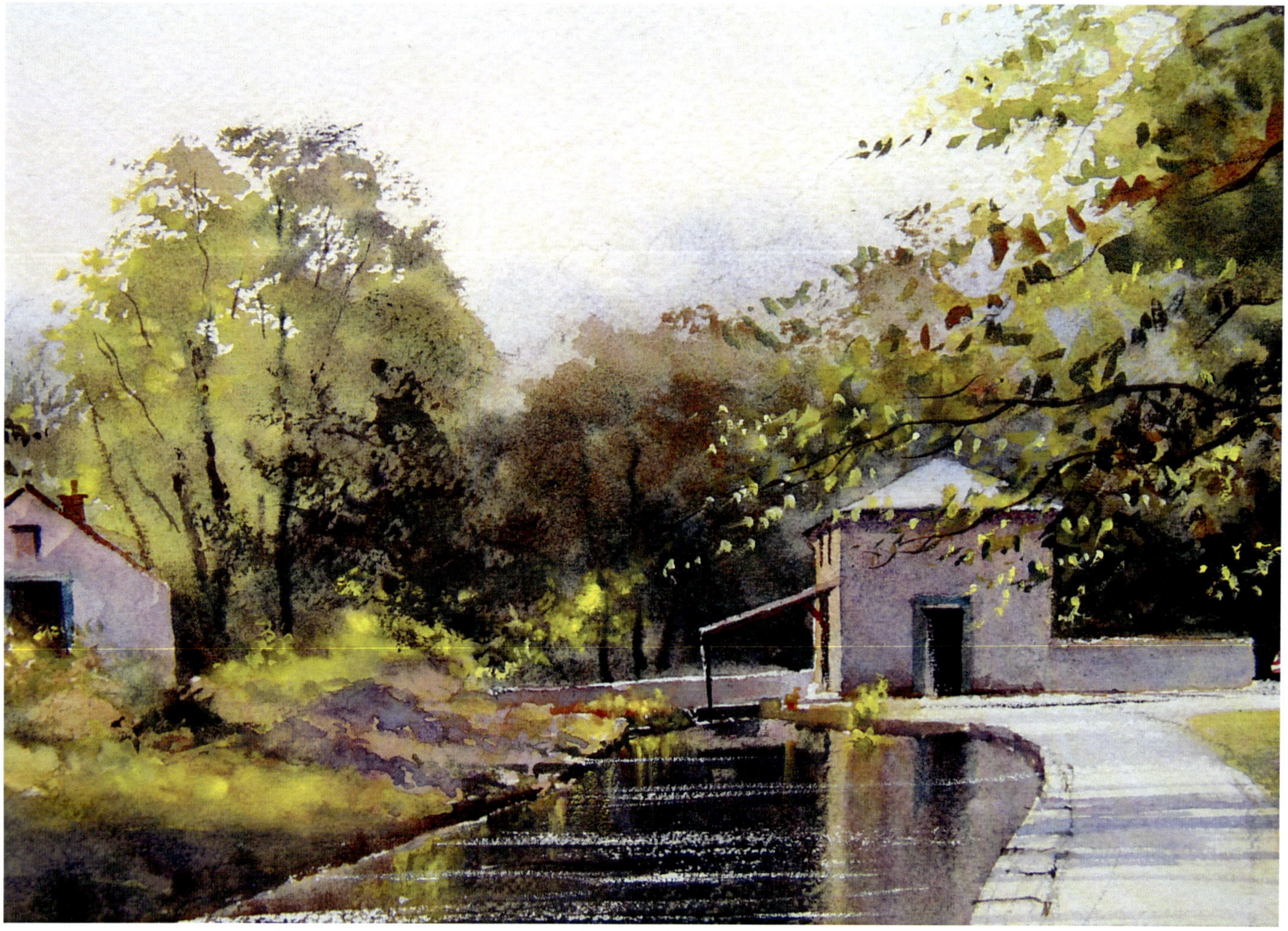

Wharf Shed, Cromford Canal

This is just a quick watercolour sketch depicting a summer evening. To me the most pleasing part of this scene is the sliver of warm sunlight on the side of the shed and the sloping roof of the lean to. Overleaf, is a larger, more considered painting of another wharf shed a couple of miles further along the towpath. I have tried to draw attention to the focal point of the building, with the two tarpaulins of contrasting manmade colours.

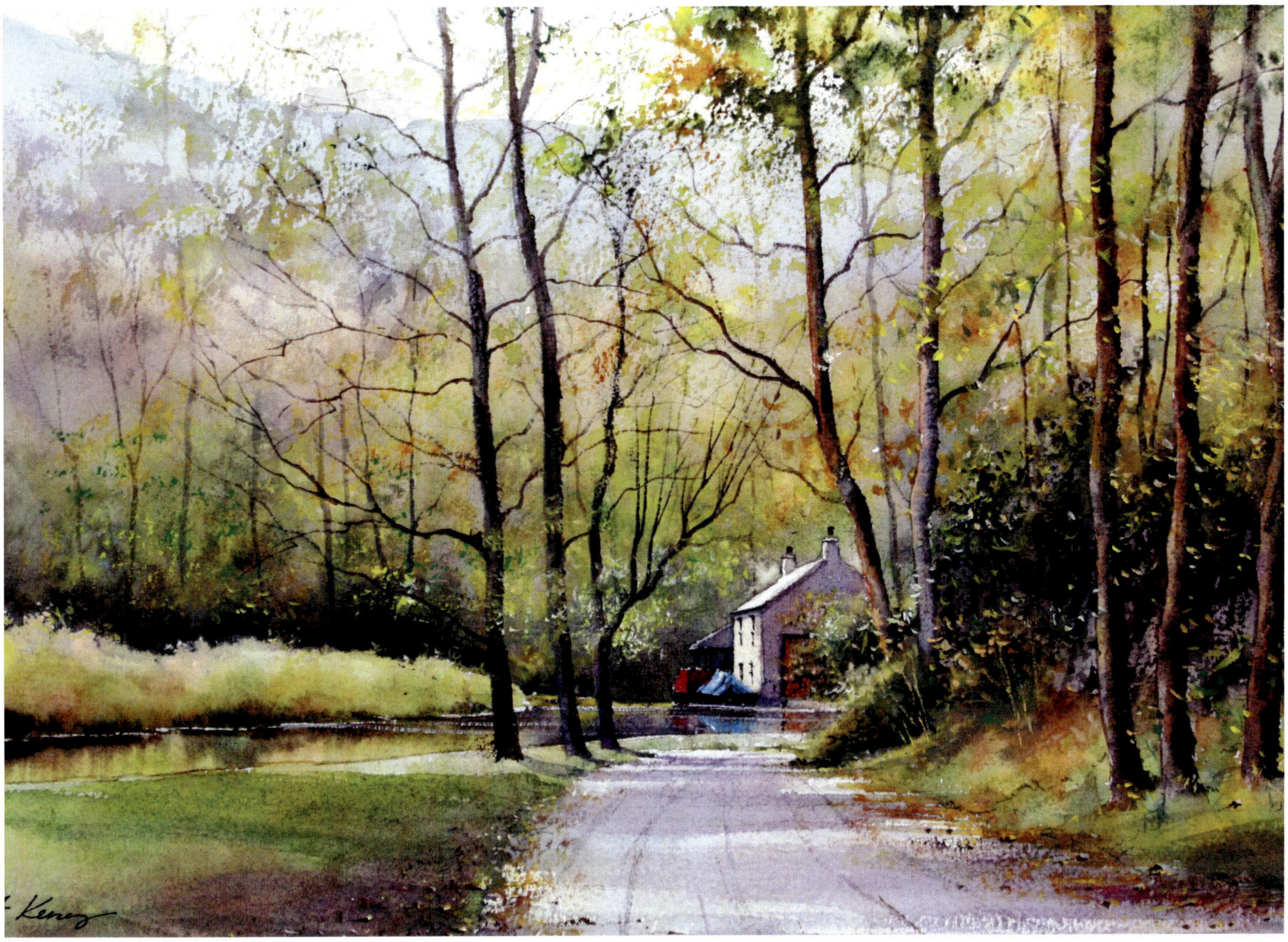

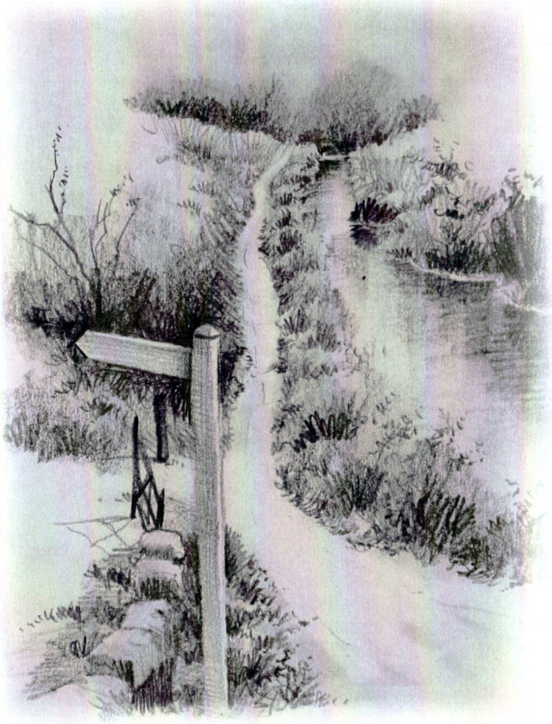

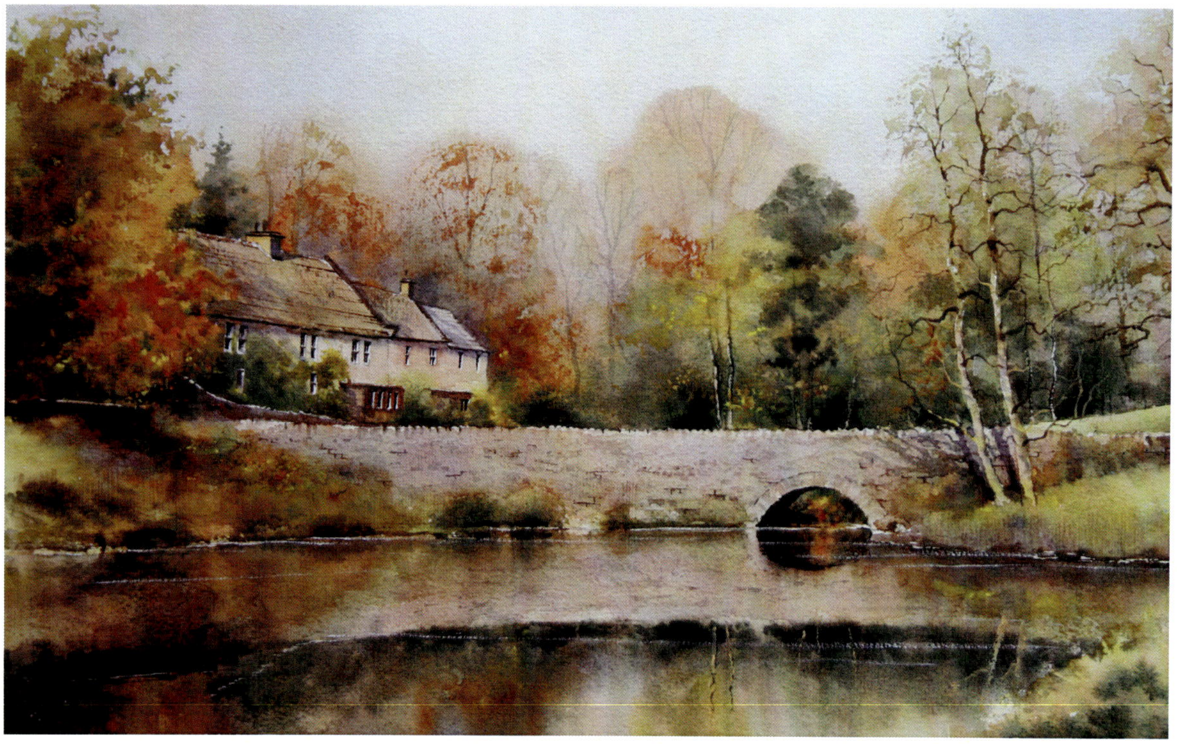

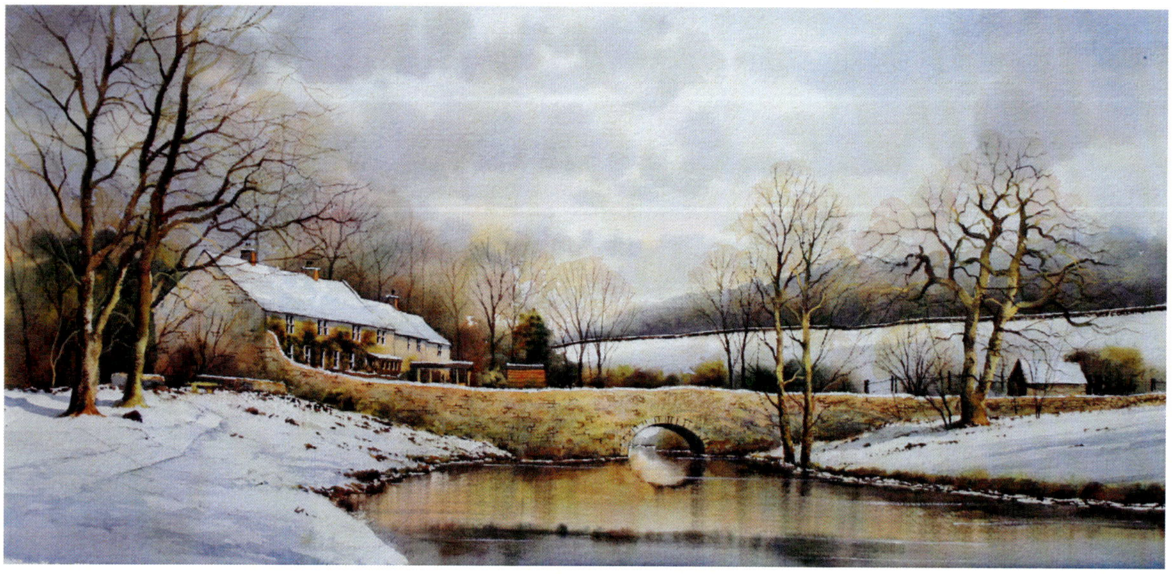

The Lumsdale Valley

Hidden away and not generally known to tourists, this little, narrow valley surrounds Bentley Brook, a fast-flowing, powerful stream that eventually joins the river Derwent. It was once a place of great industry, with mills, water wheels and factories that preceded the famous developments at Cromford. The remains of this industry are now in ruins, preserved by the Arkwright Society and I am particularly attracted to the way nature has been slowly reclaiming the valley, with the shells of the ruined buildings softened by the ever-encroaching trees and woodland.

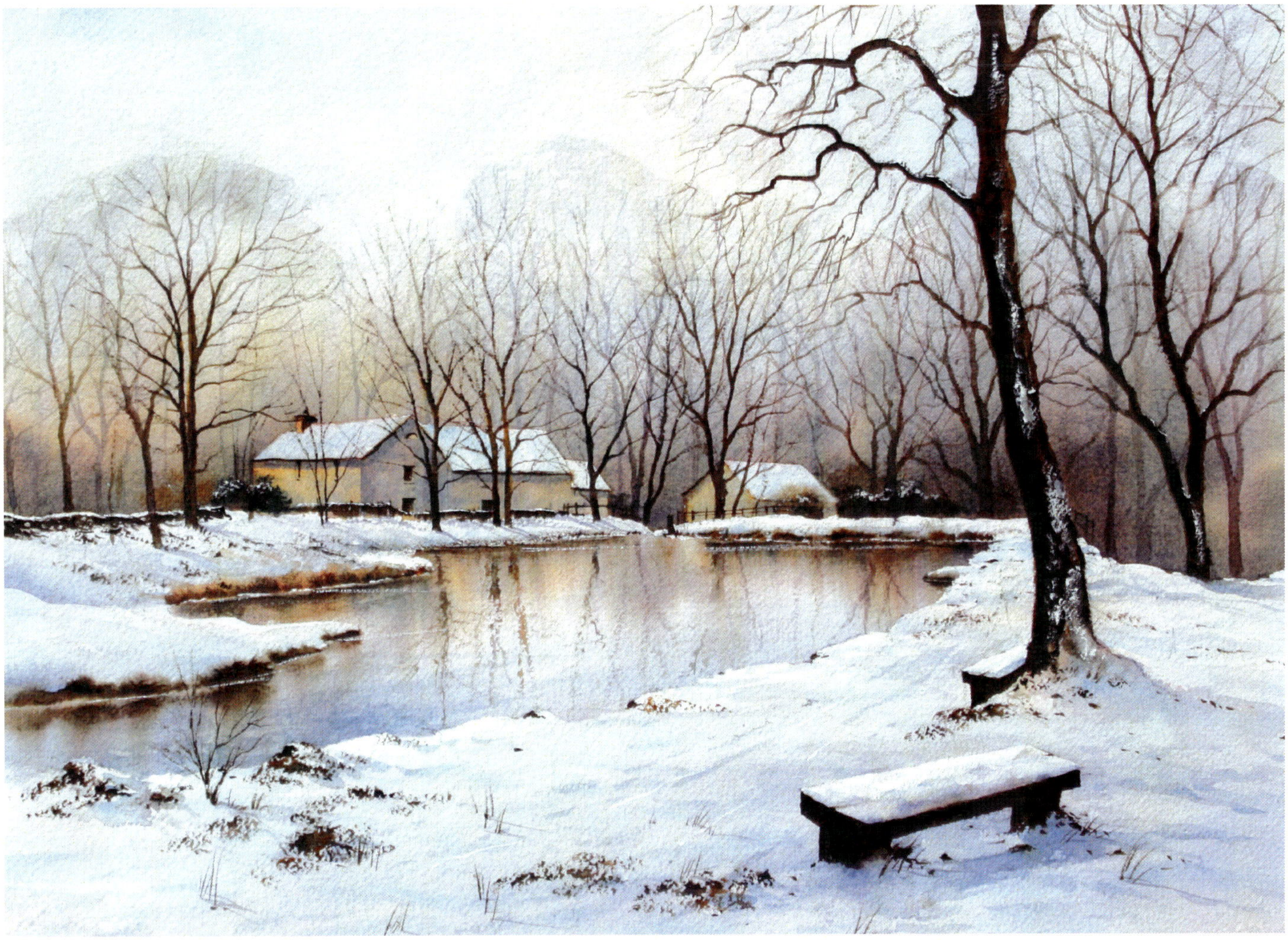

Upper Pond, Lumsdale

This is the same pond as on the previous page, but in the opposite direction, revisited in winter. I endeavoured here to get the still look of the water (essential for a millpond) by wetting the whole of the pond area with clean water, before repeating the exact colours of the sky, buildings and background, painting the same loose shapes directly beneath them in the pond. Then just before it dried, the colours were blurred with a few vertical downward strokes of a flat brush. The little bench gives a bit of foreground interest.

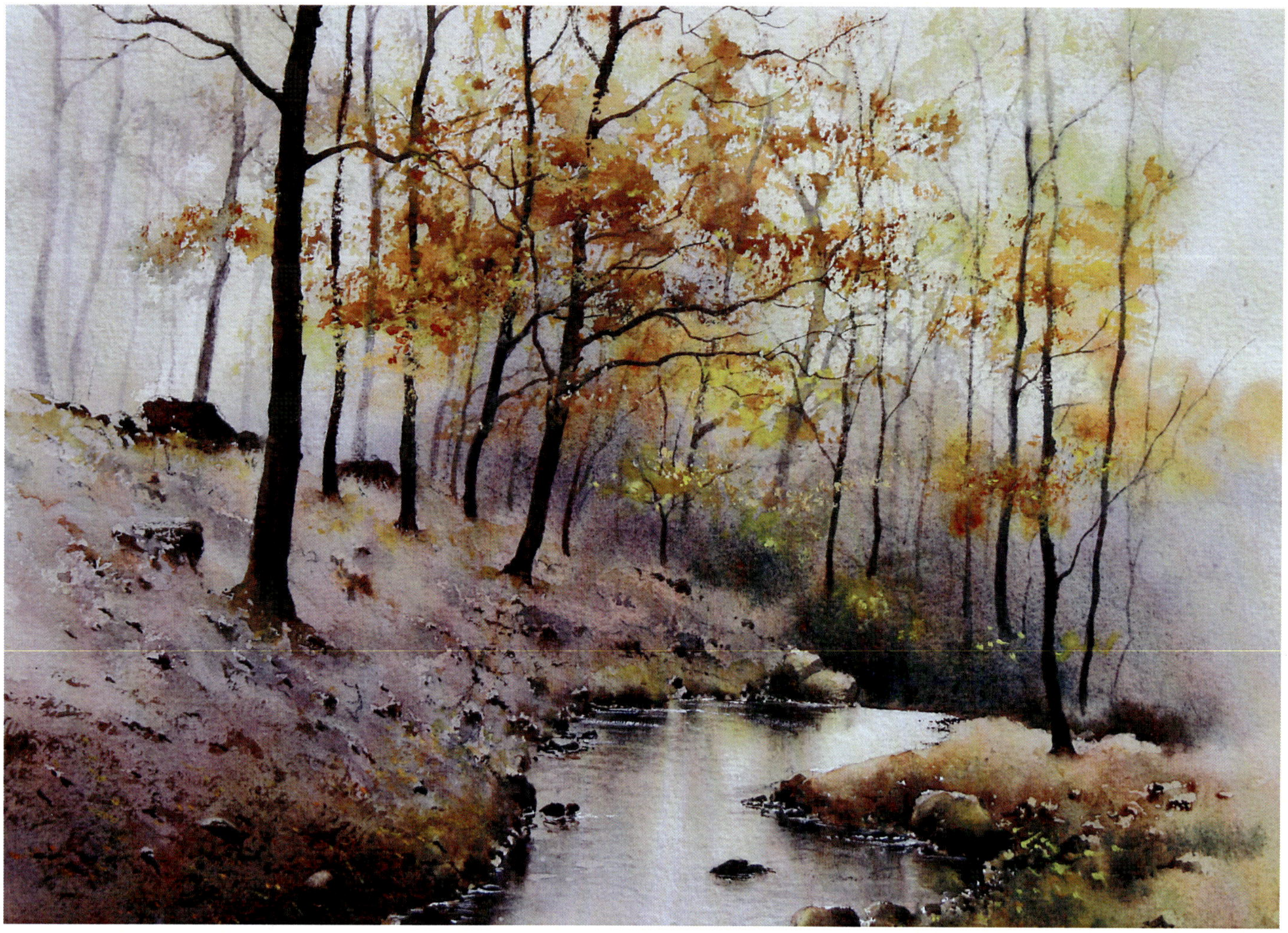

Bentley Brook, Lumsdale

This is quite late autumn, and while some of the russet colours linger, the skeletal forms of the trees remind of the approaching winter. The focal point of this scene is where the brook tips over the edge out of view, left as almost clean white paper, to contrast with the darks beyond.

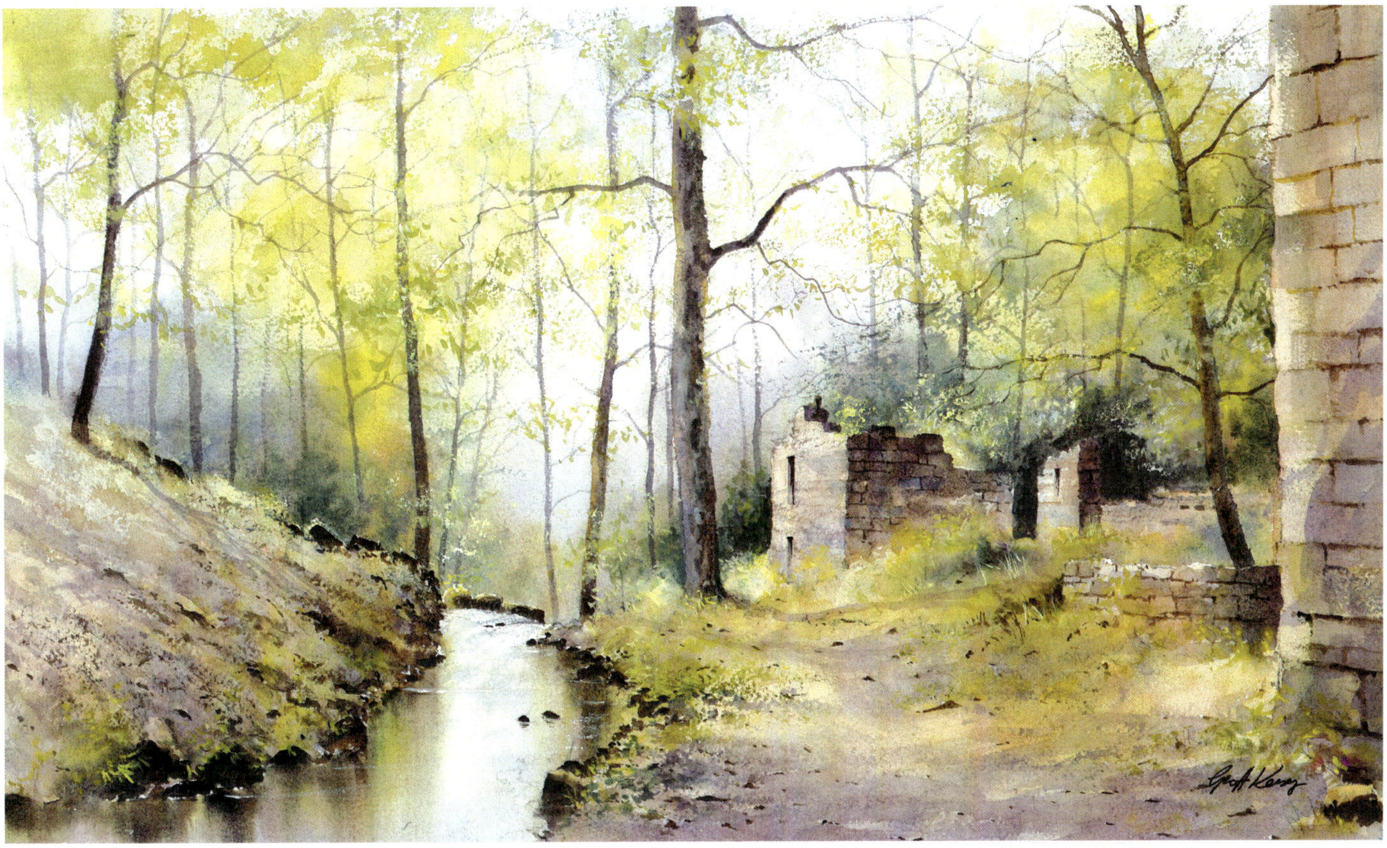

Mill Ruins, Lumsdale

Here I have tried to introduce plenty of colour into the stone-work, using raw sienna, rose madder and a few touches of cerulean blue to grey it in places. The shadow wash was cobalt blue with a touch of rose madder to tone in with the sky. The large tree is positioned rather centrally, and to compensate a wall on the far right is masked out to alter the composition. In the end, I decided to leave in this imperfection; it doesn't hurt to break the rules occasionally.

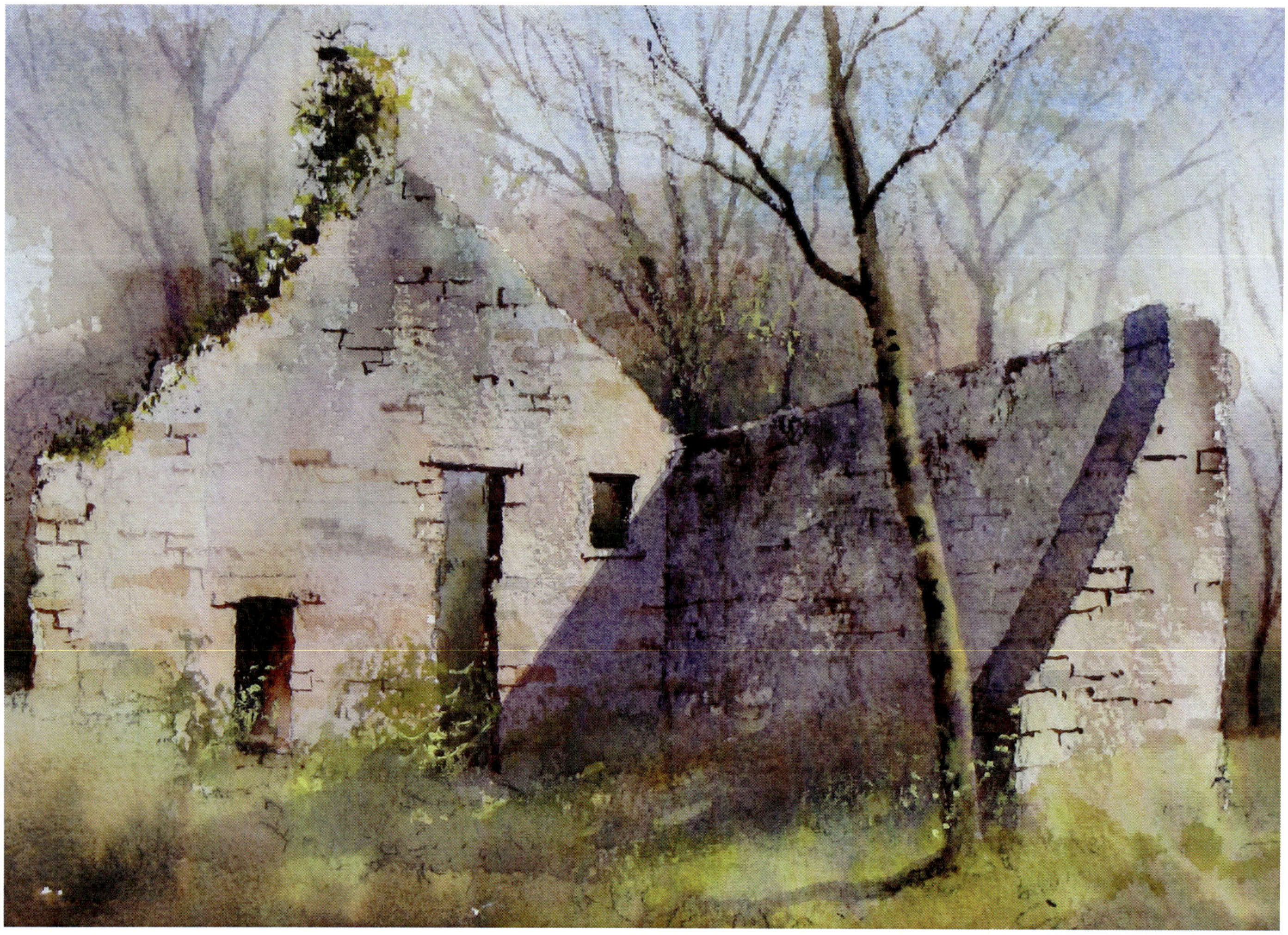

Old Paint Mill, Lumsdale

I produced this painting as part of an instructional DVD. The painting was done on camera, in the studio and had to take no longer than thirty-five minutes to complete, with an accompanying commentary. This is not the most relaxed way to paint, but it prevents overworking it.

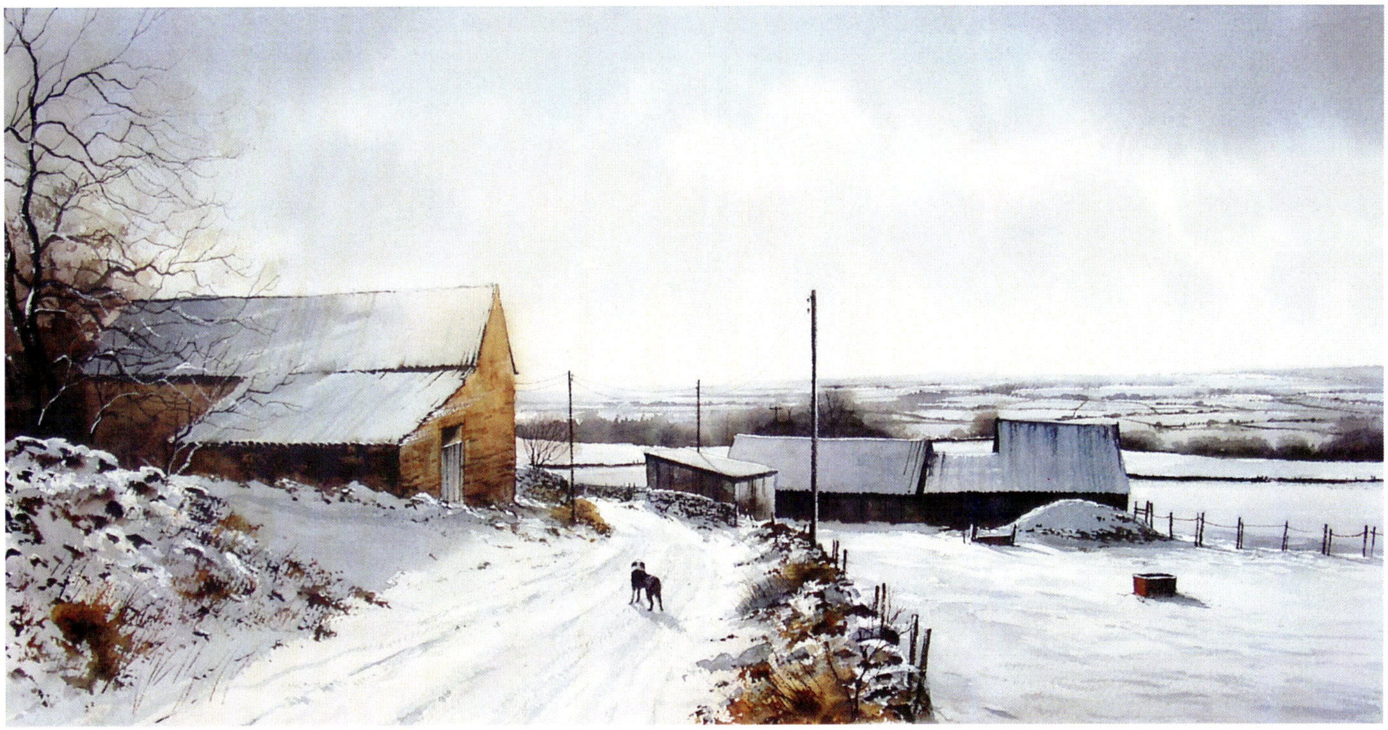

Woodside Farm

Looking down over Matlock Dale, these weathered old farm buildings made an excellent subject. Facing into the sun creates the silhouetted shapes and deep shadows. It's interesting how much difference the addition of the dog made to the composition. This scene was painted with just six colours, cobalt blue and neutral tint were used for the sky, plus a hint of vermillion for the wintery glow.

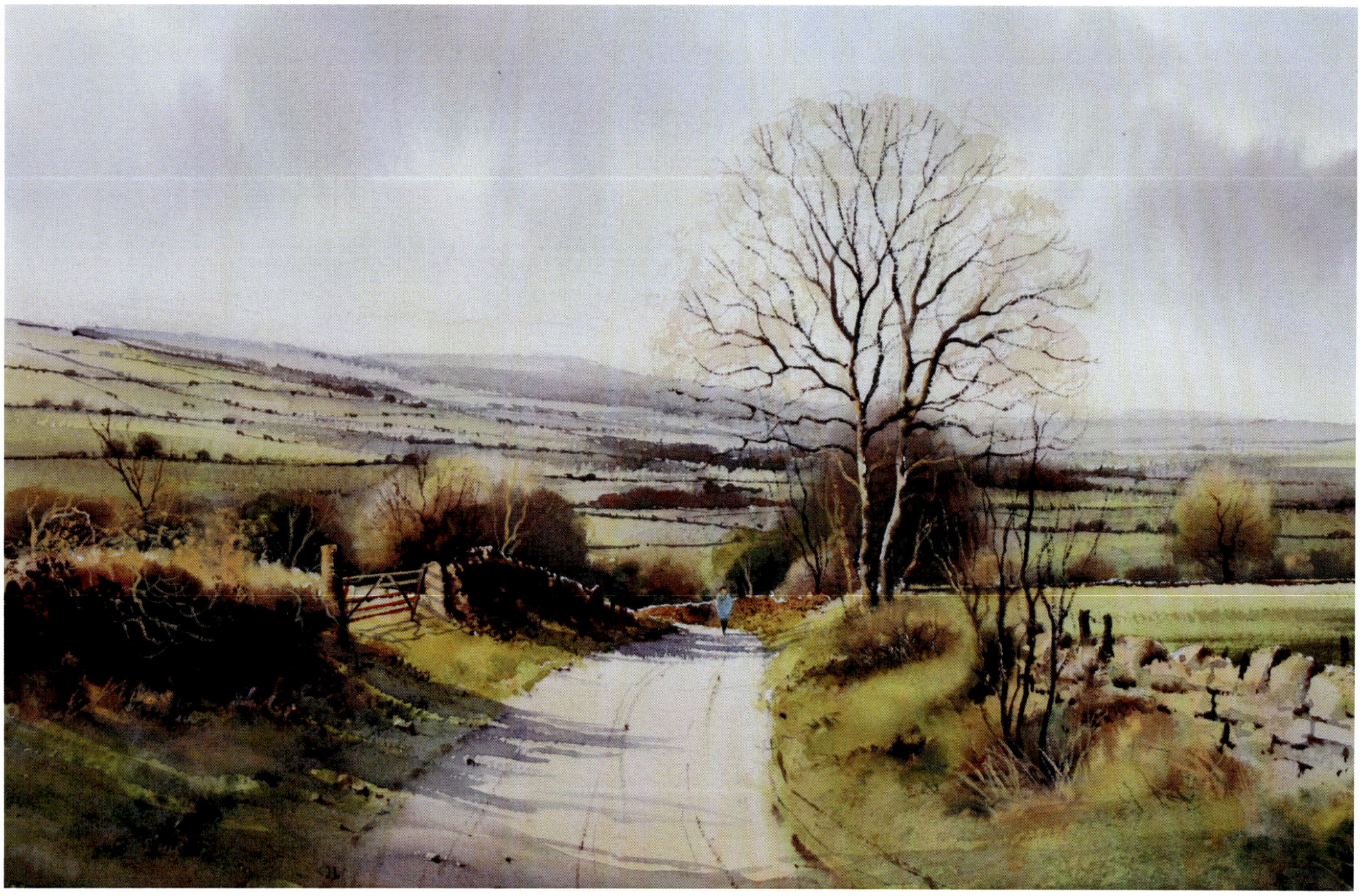

View over Matlock Dale

Here the shadows from the dry-stone wall on the left describe the slope of the bank and flatness of the lane. The gate gives an important break in the wall and the line of the shadows, providing some much needed variation.

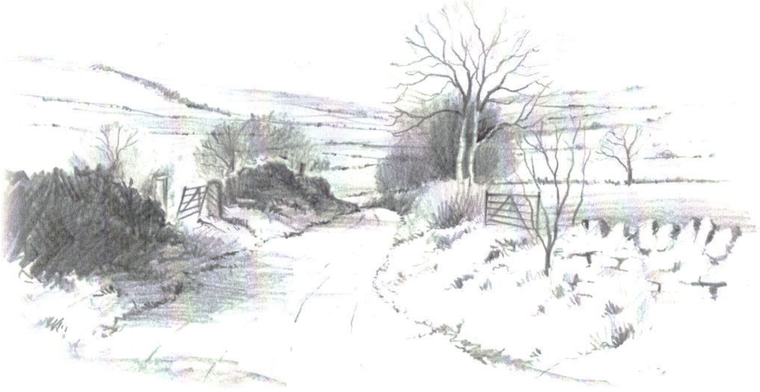

7 *Bakewell and Ashford in the Water*

Bakewell, known as the 'ancient capital of the Peak', is set in a beautiful location on the banks of the river Wye, with the river gently flowing through the centre and surrounded by excellent views. The name originates from 'Badkwell' meaning 'bath spring', as it grew up around twelve mineral springs, and it is believed people settled there as long ago as the Iron Age. Bakewell is the only market town in the National Park, the charter for a Monday Market – still held to this day – being granted in 1330.

There are many different types of event held throughout the year in Bakewell, one of the main ones being Bakewell's own agricultural show. This extremely busy show is held on the first Wednesday and Thursday in August and attracts visitors and exhibitors from throughout Britain and overseas. I once read that Bakewell is the most visited town of any national park in Europe; it certainly seems a very lively place with an eclectic mix of historic buildings, shops, cafés and restaurants attracting coach-loads of day trippers.

It would be remiss to talk of Bakewell without mentioning Bakewell Pudding. There are three bakeries selling the world famous Bakewell Pudding, each one claiming to have the original, secret recipe: regardless of whose claim is true, it is big business, with over 12,000 puddings selling each week during the summer season.

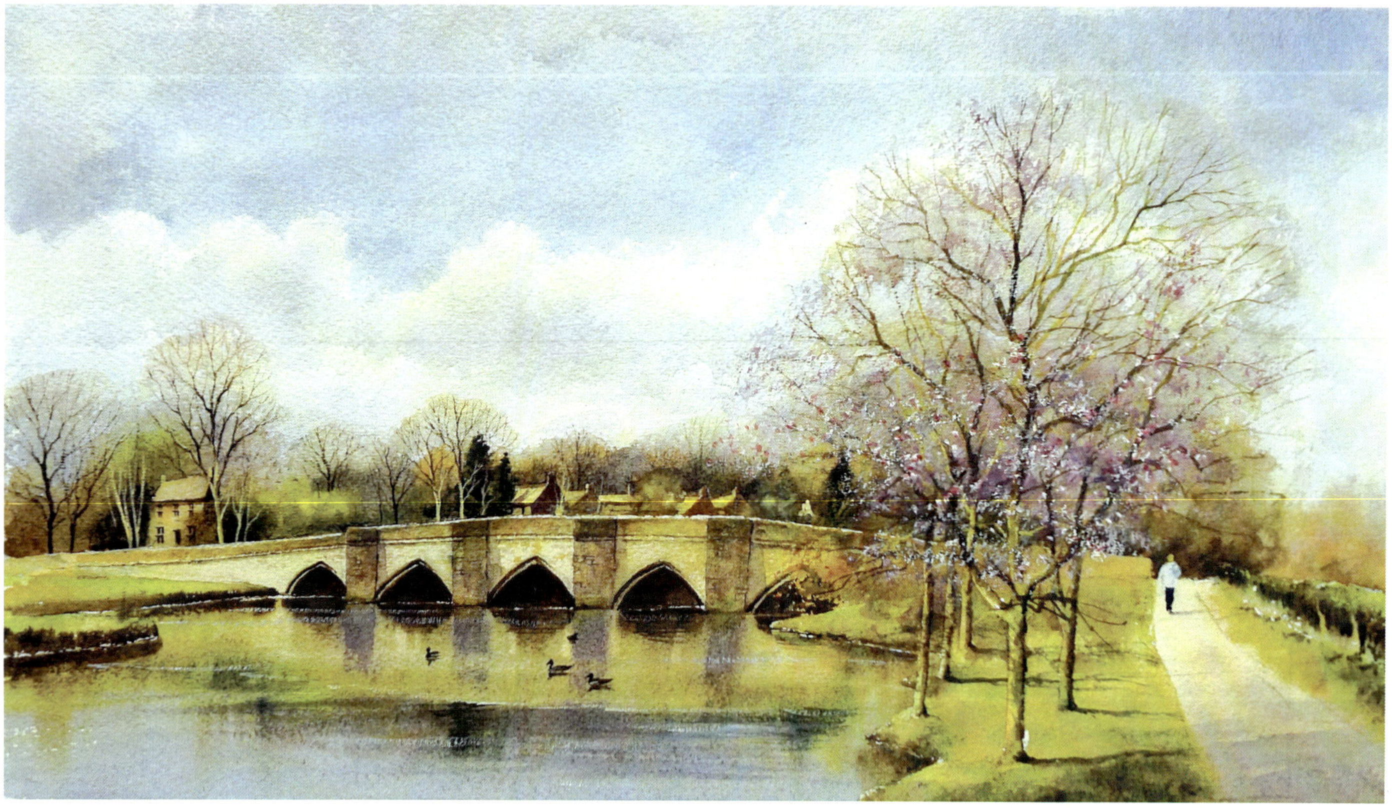

Bridge across the Wye, Bakewell

This beautiful packhorse bridge spans the River Wye, carrying the A619 to Chesterfield and Sheffield. Built around 1300 it has five gothic arches and triangular cornerstones over the buttresses. The bridge is tricky to paint just right and it is always worth taking a little time to do a preparatory sketch prior to tackling the painting. On the right is my sketch, which of course I had to draw again in outline onto the watercolour paper, ready to paint. By sketching the bridge twice before picking up a brush I had a better understanding of its structure, shape and proportions. This is always a good approach, especially when tackling a subject that is quite demanding to draw.

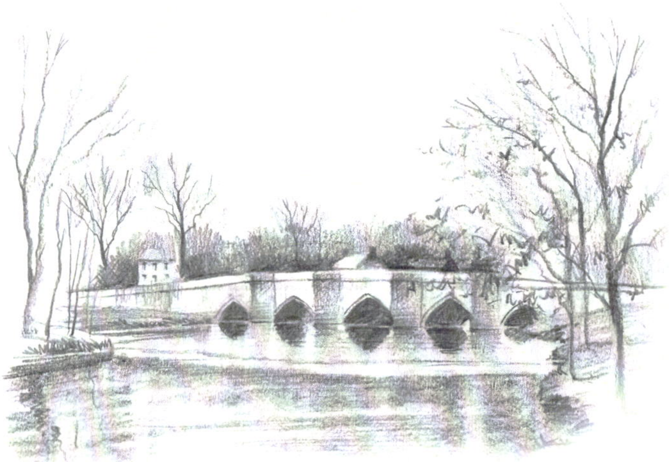

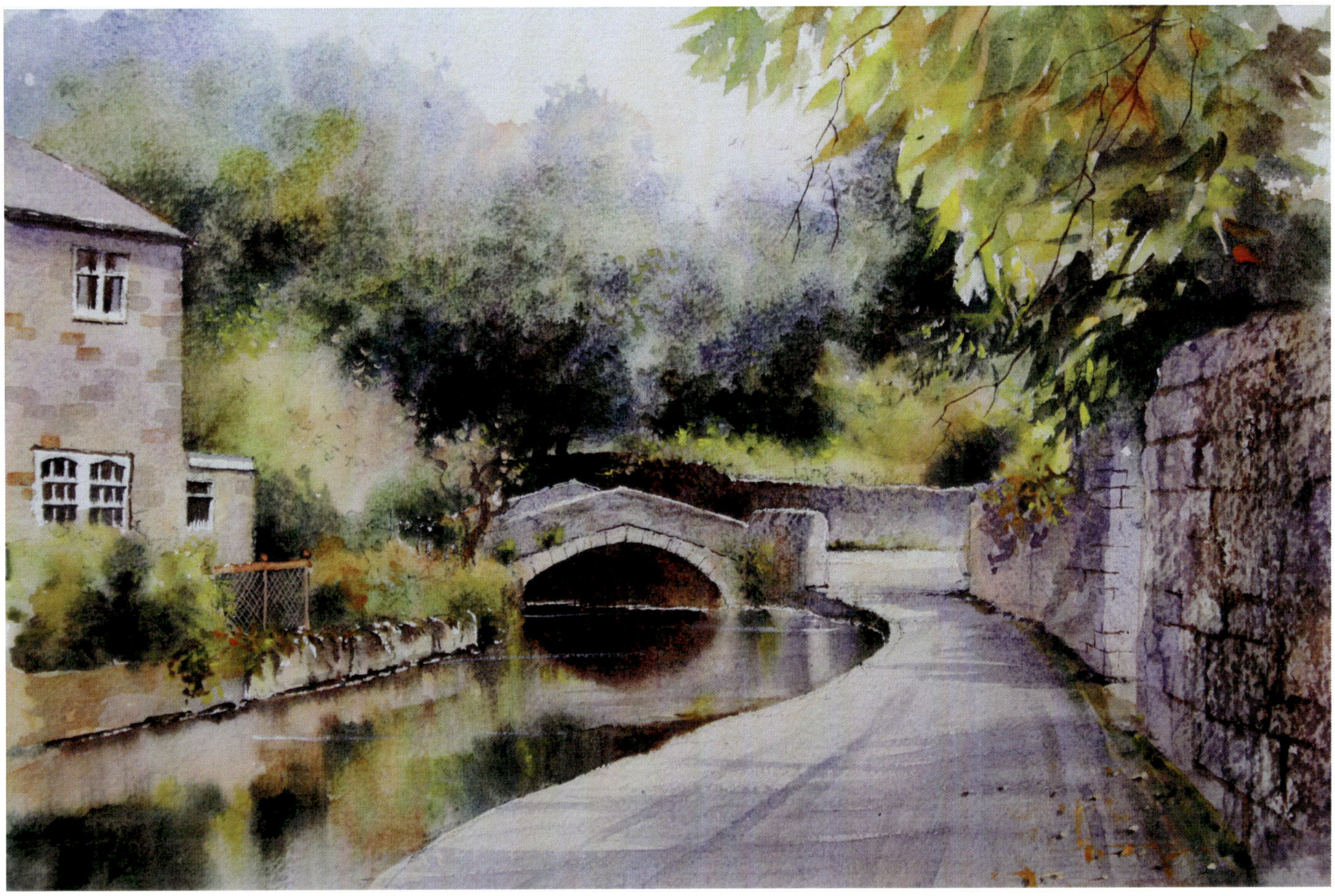

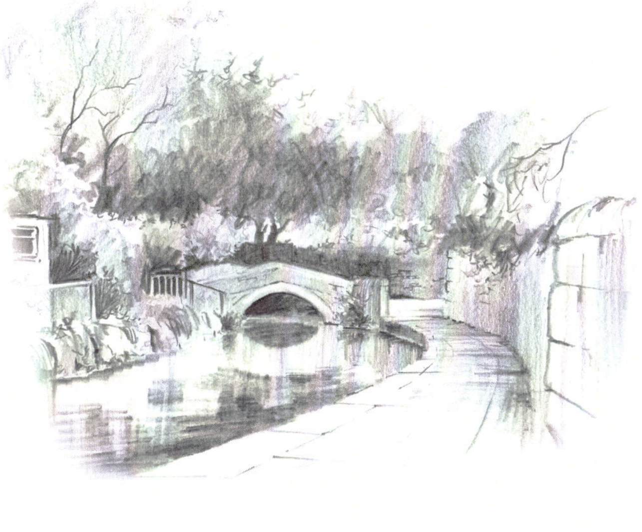

Milford, Bakewell

In a quiet part of town I came across this little scene of a much more humble bridge, but an excellent composition. To capture this bright October morning I explored the full range of tonal values by drawing the little 'value' sketch as seen opposite, before commencing the painting. I then repeated these rich tonal contrasts – but this time with colour – in the finished painting.

The dark trees behind the bridge team up with the dark shadows under the arch to push out the shape of the bridge. At the outset I masked out some of the leaf shapes in the overhanging tree at the top right so that later on I could drop in some bright washes, thus creating a rich contrast.

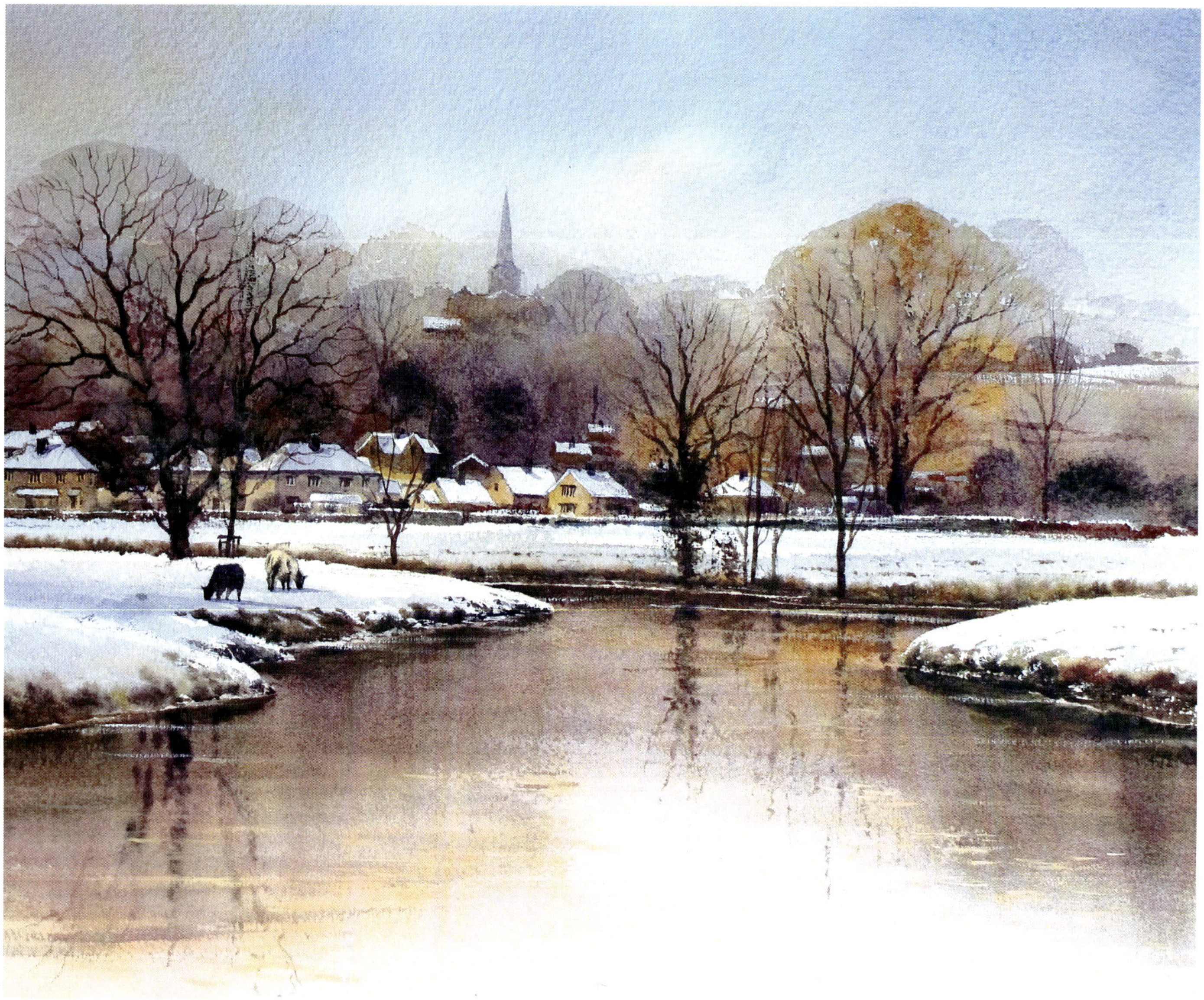

Bakewell across the Wye

I have a confession to make here! When actually stood at this viewpoint in Bakewell the tower of All Saints Church cannot be seen where painted on the distant hill. I moved it into the scene as I thought it lent an important focal point to the distance. Opinions vary as to whether or not this sort of inaccuracy should be employed, but I just claim it as 'artistic license'. However I made sure I accurately echoed the background colours in the river, to give the painting an overall harmony and continuity. In particular, the glimpses of snow-capped roofs stood out to me through the trees in this scene.

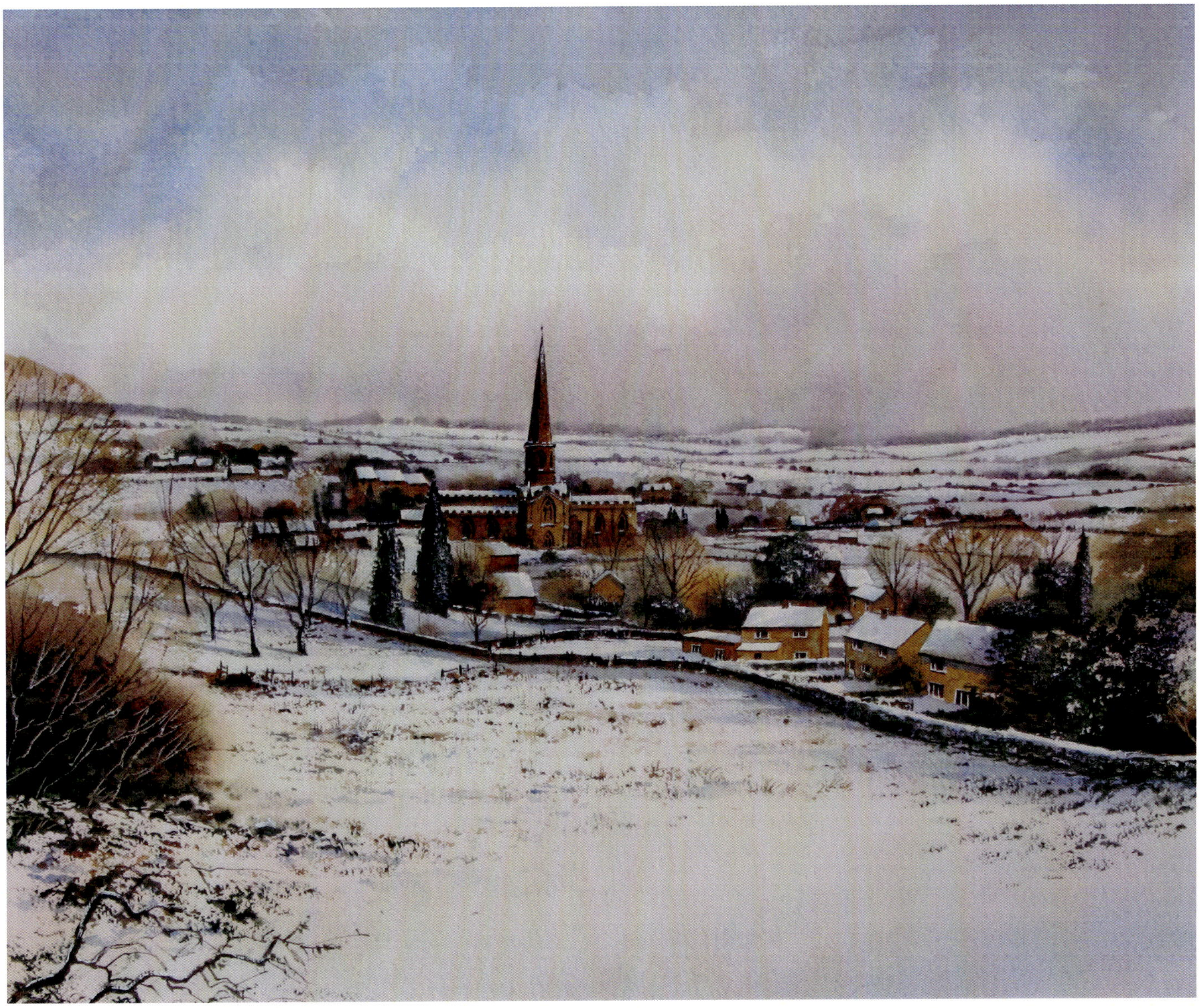

Bakewell in Winter

This view was painted from a farm gate on a steep, winding residential road that rises above Bakewell. The viewpoint affords this enchanting vista of All Saints Church, nestled in a cluster of houses, with gently undulating landscape, that is typical of Derbyshire, in the backdrop.

This scene was painted on a cold day that had the distinct feeling more snow would be on the way. I endeavoured to capture this by painting a cool sky of Cerulean and Cobalt blue, and echoed the colours in some of the rooftops and shadows. A cool grey added to the sky, created by adding a touch of Cadmium Red to the blue mixture, enhanced this feeling of 'more snow on the way'.

Some people find paintings like this can trigger feelings of nostalgia, while others comment that looking at it makes them shiver.

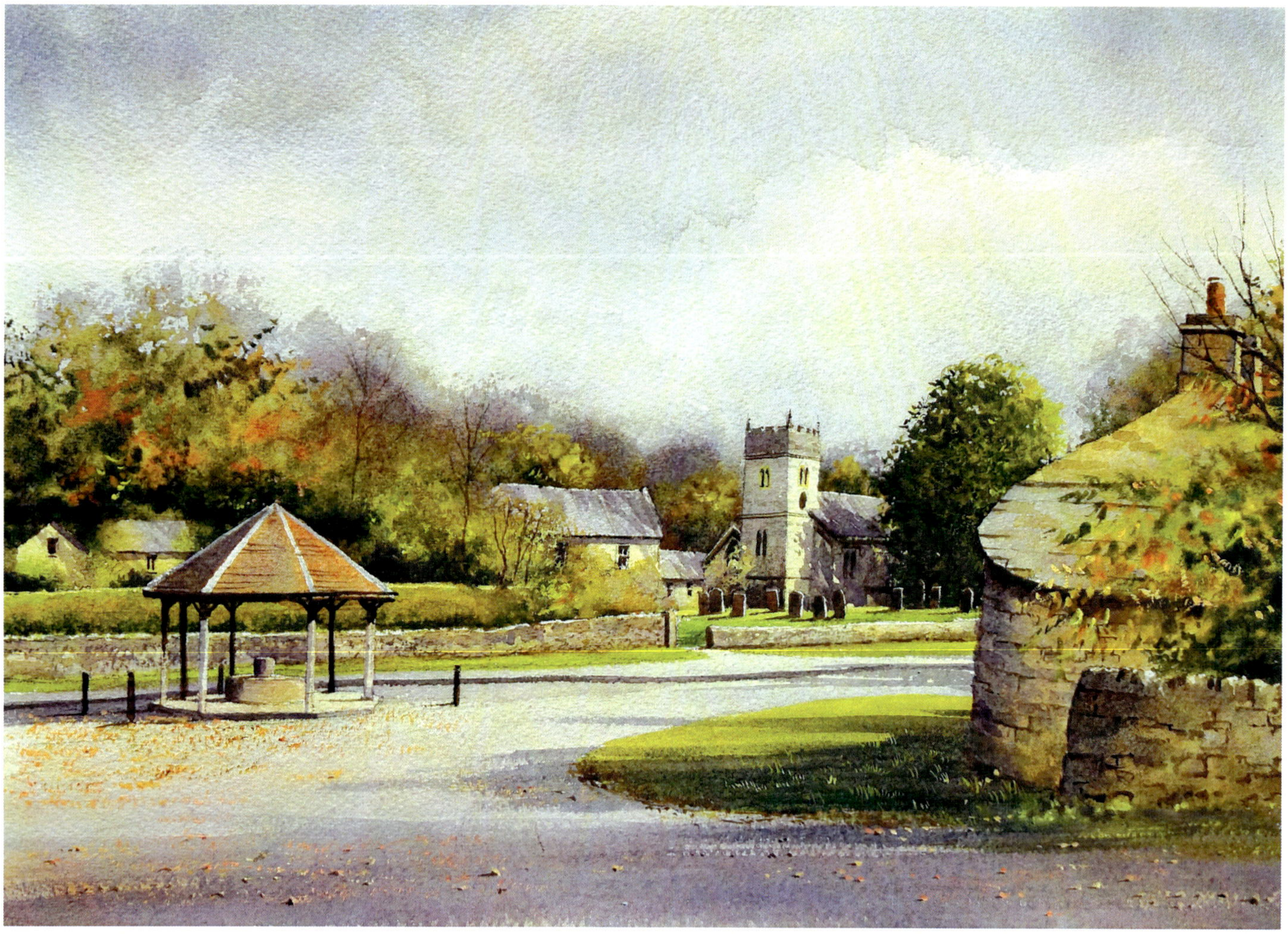

Ashford in the Water

Just 1.5 miles north-west of Bakewell lies the pretty village of Ashford in the Water. The village contains many old picturesque cottages, some of which were once owned by the Chatsworth estate. I am drawn time and again to the little market stand in the centre of the village, with the thirteenth-century Church of the Holy Trinity in the background. Again both these structures require careful drawing, to get the shapes to look convincing. The church features as a subject in one of my first instructional DVDs, *Improve your buildings in Watercolour*. It's good to think of this humble little church being carefully drawn and painted in other artists' studios.

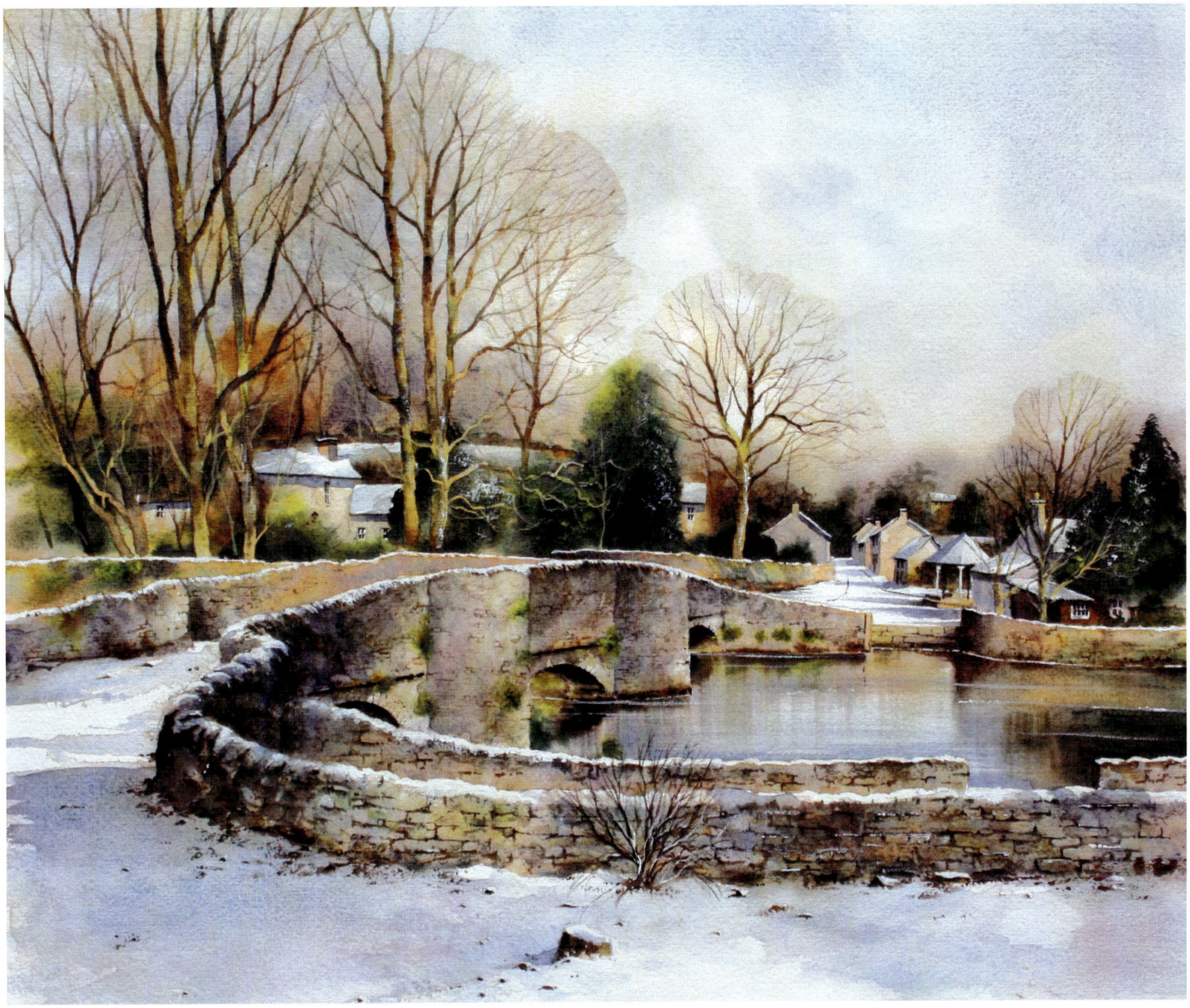

Sheepwash Bridge, Ashford in the Water

Arguably the main attraction to Ashford in the Water is the picturesque and ancient Sheepwash Bridge. It was originally a medieval packhorse bridge and until relatively recently, sheep were washed here prior to shearing. The lambs would be penned within the stone-walled pen at one side of the river, while the mothers would be thrown in at the other side. They would naturally swim across to their offspring, thus ensuring a good soaking. One of my earliest recollections of this bridge is being taken there as a child on one of our many day-trips from Sheffield, to watch the rainbow trout in the river below. The bridge is painted from a viewpoint further downstream on the opposite page.

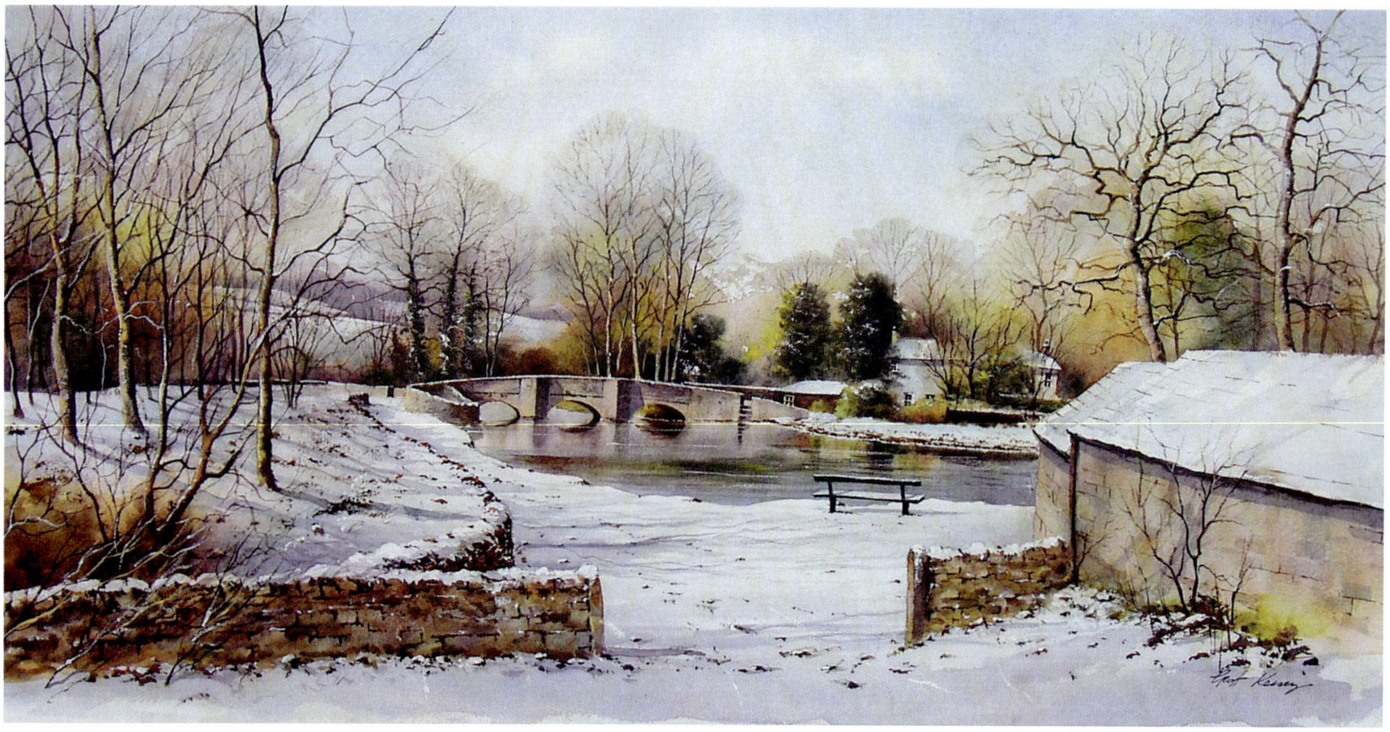

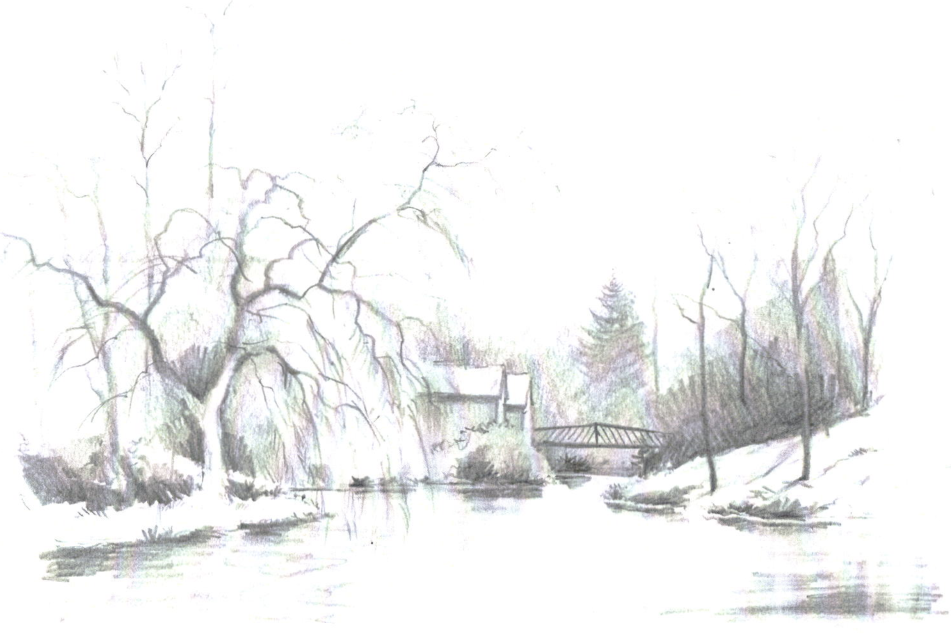

8 *Bradford Dale and Lathkildale*

The River Bradford runs from Middleton by Youlgrave to Alport where it meets the River Lathkil. Bradford Dale is quite short and like so many Peak District Dales has picturesque stretches of beautiful clear water, overhung by trees.

Alport is a small, quiet Peak District village, situated just off the main road. Named after the Portway road which ran through the settlement, the Saxon inhabitants of Alport added the prefix 'al' which means old. The stone houses with attractive gardens seen there today date back to the seventeenth and eighteenth centuries.

From Alport a five mile walk north through Lathkildale leads to Monyash, along one of the finest limestone dales, with plenty of inspiring scenery for painting. The River Lathkil is a famous trout fishing river, described by Izaak Walton as the 'purest and most transparent stream' he had seen.

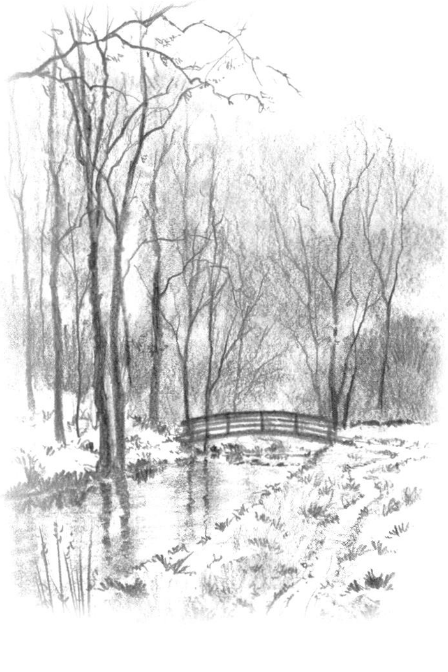

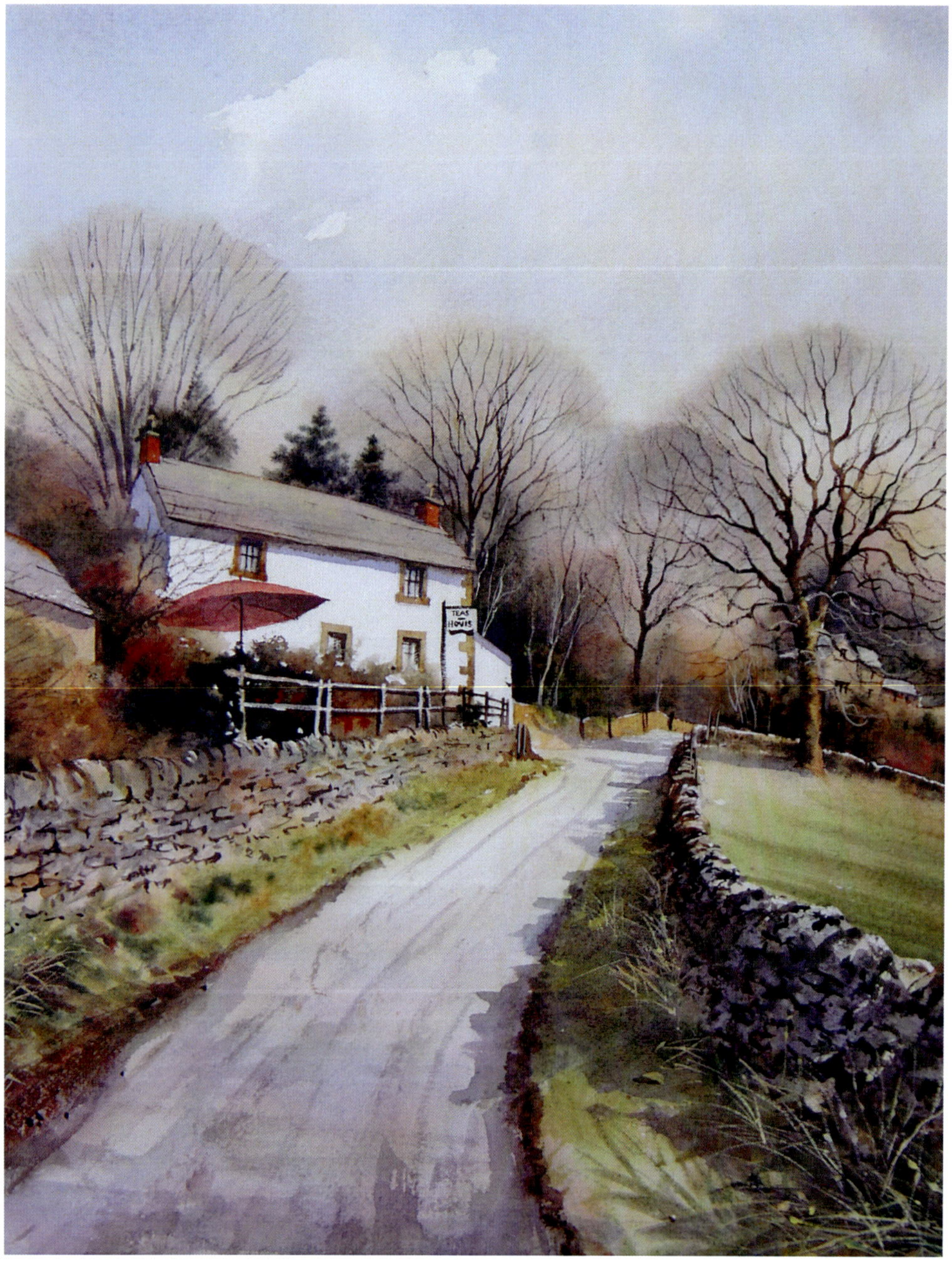

Hovis Café, Youlgrave

For many years this little café (now a private dwelling) made an excellent pit-stop and was very popular with walkers. I always called it the 'Hovis café' because of an old enamelled sign with the wording 'Teas Hovis' on it, hanging from a post in the garden. I did wonder if it was just me that had given it this name, but upon exhibiting the painting I soon found out many others had christened it with the same name.

I thought the juxtaposition of the red parasol and the whitewashed building made for an excellent focal point.

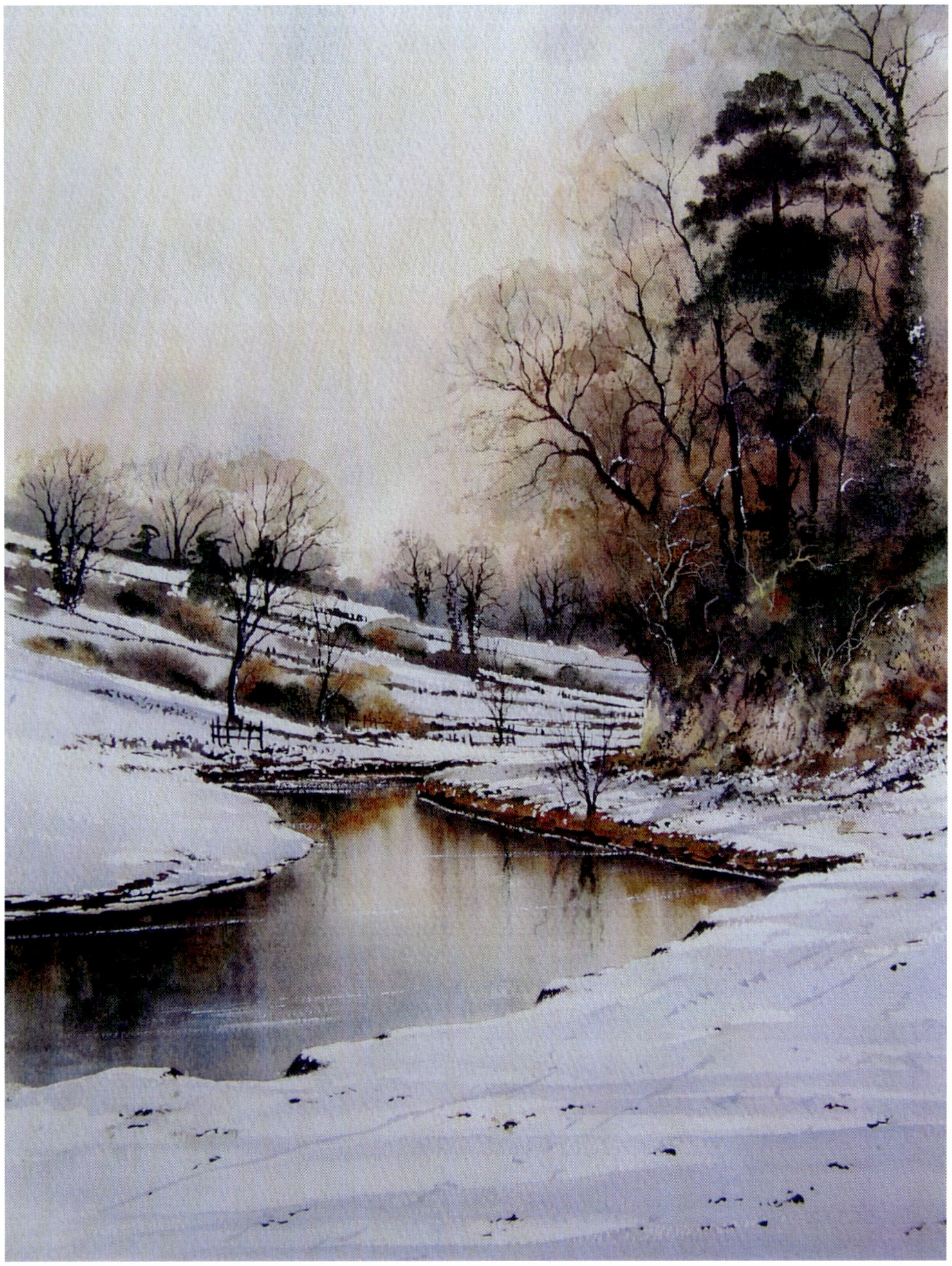

The River Bradford, Bradford Dale

On the approach to Alport, the path lead to this focal point, the slope of the distant hill also directs the viewer to the same place. In order to get the vertical reflections in the very slow-moving water, good use of masking fluid was made to keep the white of the banks clean.

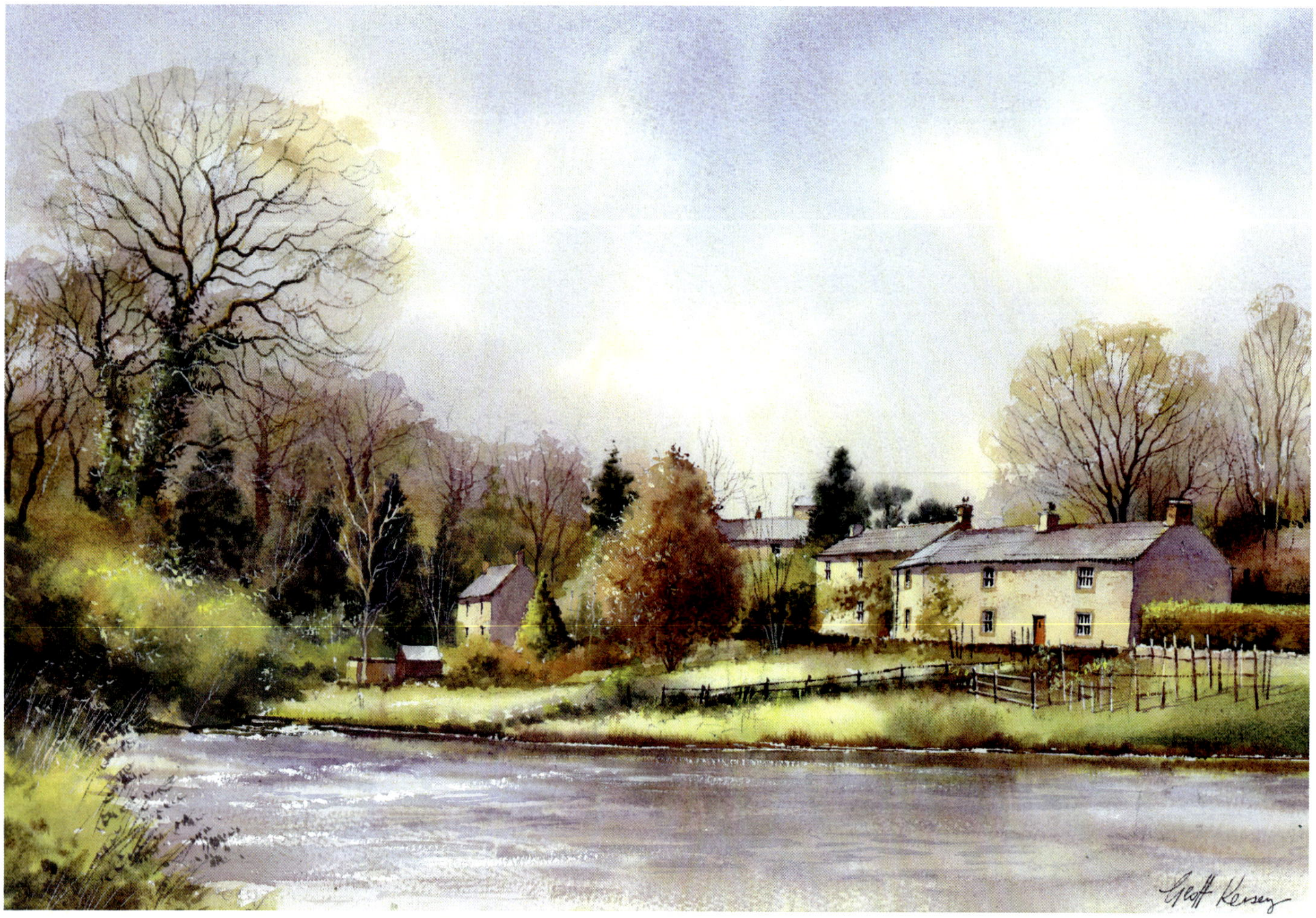

Alport

There's a strong sense of light in this painting, with the bright green on the gardens and the front of the cottages contrasted with the strong shadows on the two gables and under the eaves. Most of the trees were painted wet into wet to achieve the soft shapes of the foliage; particular attention was paid to the large coppery coloured one in the centre, using a red made from raw sienna and burnt sienna.

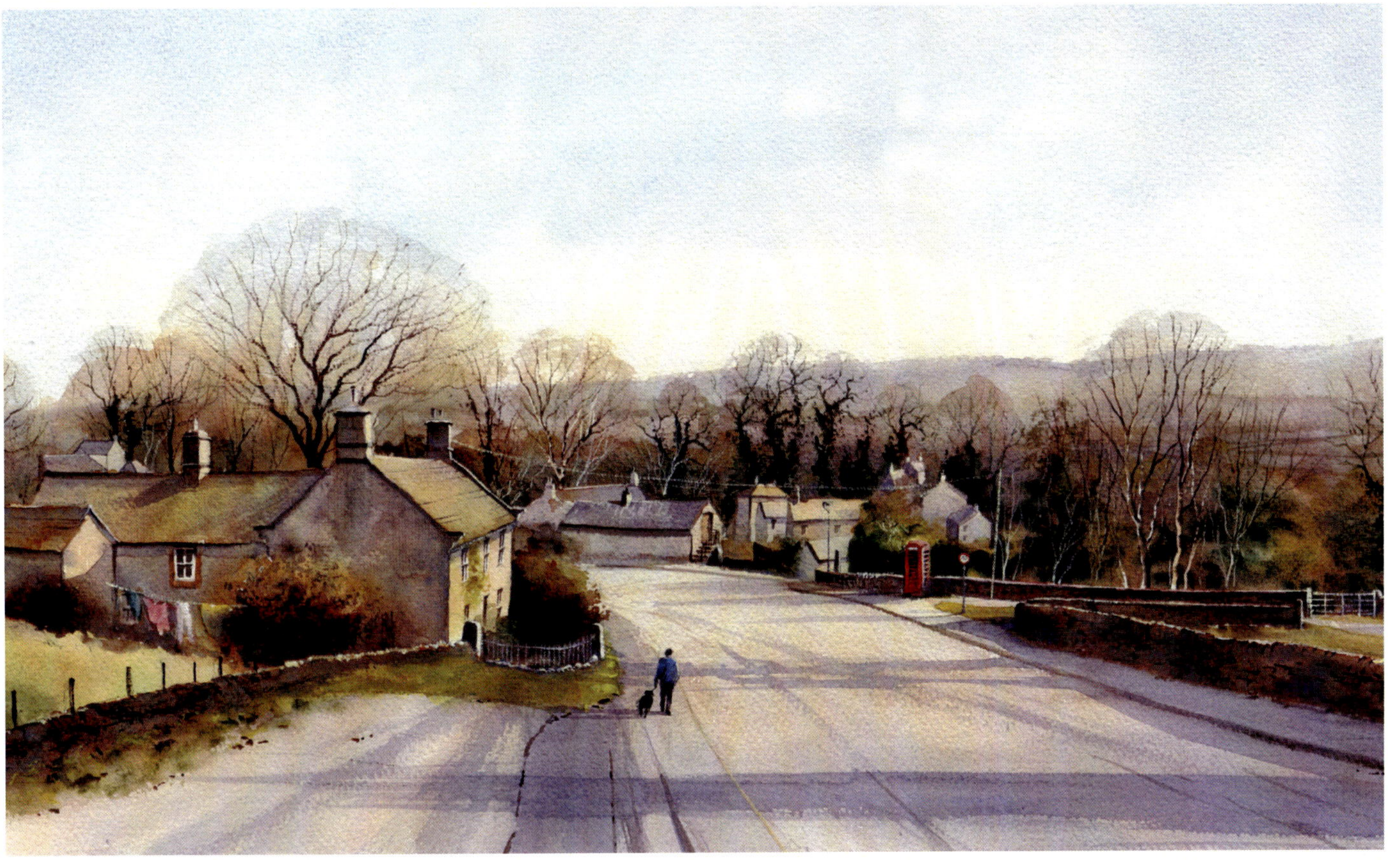

The Road to Alport, from Youlgrave

I chose a more panoramic format for this scene, with a strong, bright light on the road, highlighted by the dense trees and distant hills. It is often the observation of a few small details that make a painting, like the dog walker, the brightly coloured clothes on the washing line and the old-fashioned phone box in the middle distance.

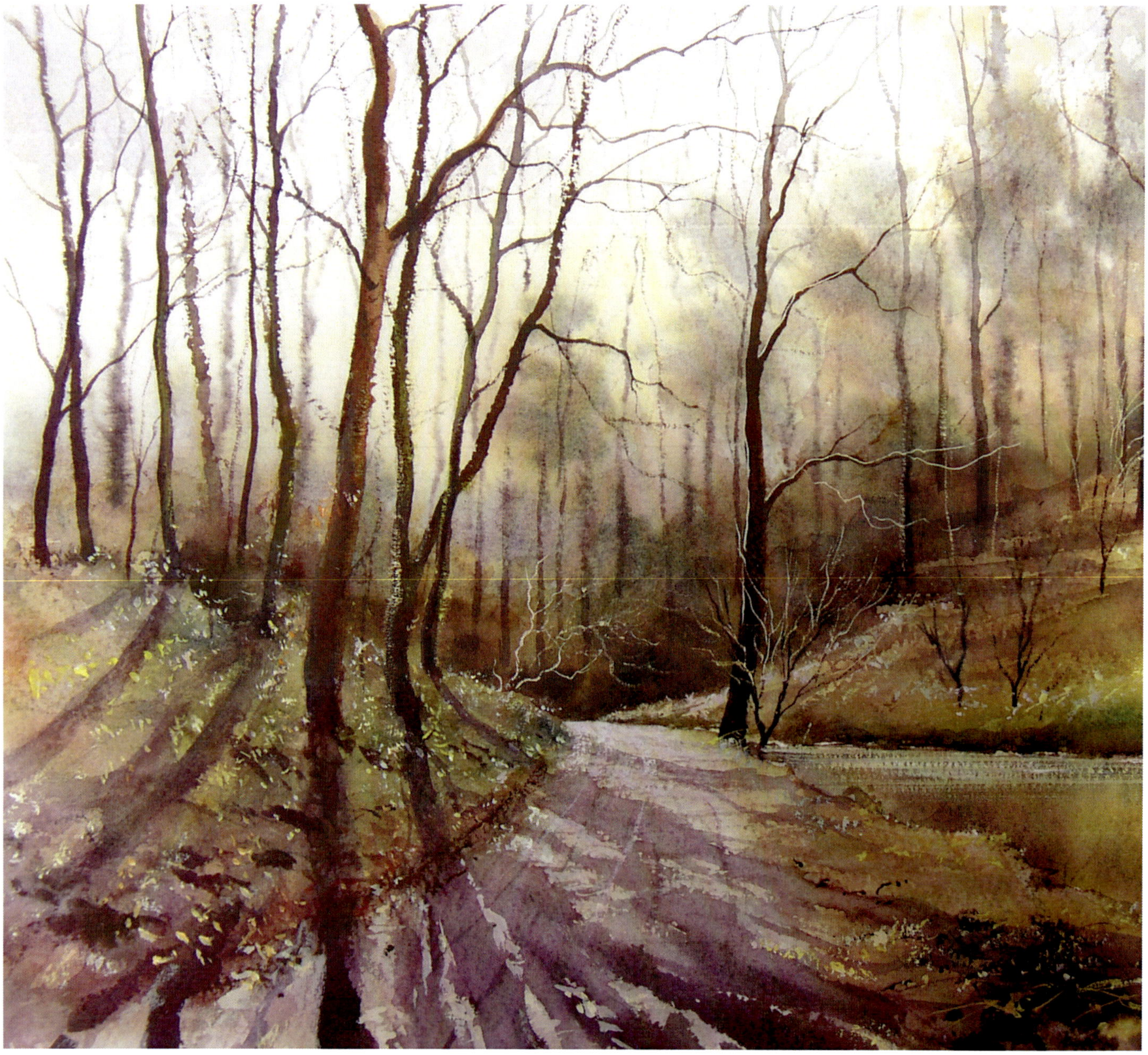

Looking into the light, Lathkildale

Every so often I enjoy painting a scene looking into the light or *contre jour*. This makes the trees almost silhouettes against the bright light behind them.

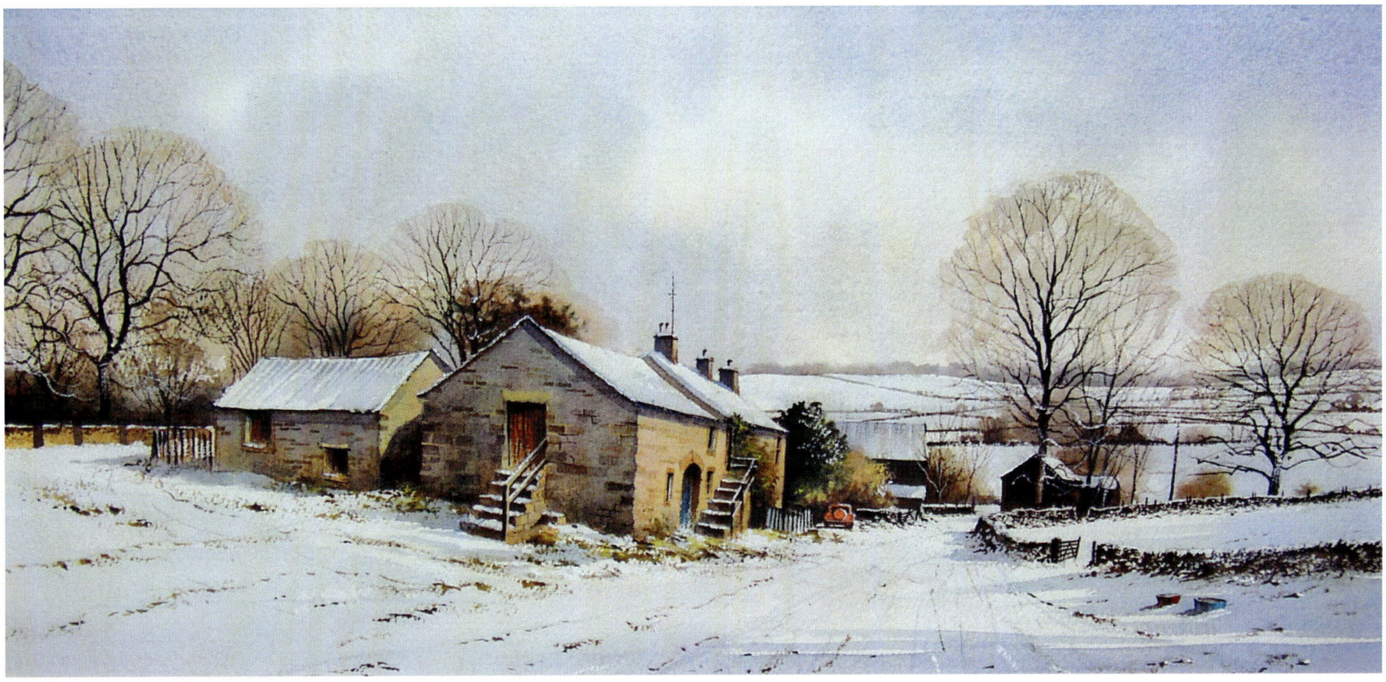

One Ash Grange, near Monyash

A perfect arrangement of weathered farm buildings; this scene is best painted in winter, above, or early spring, below, as in the height of summer the tree foliage gets in the way.

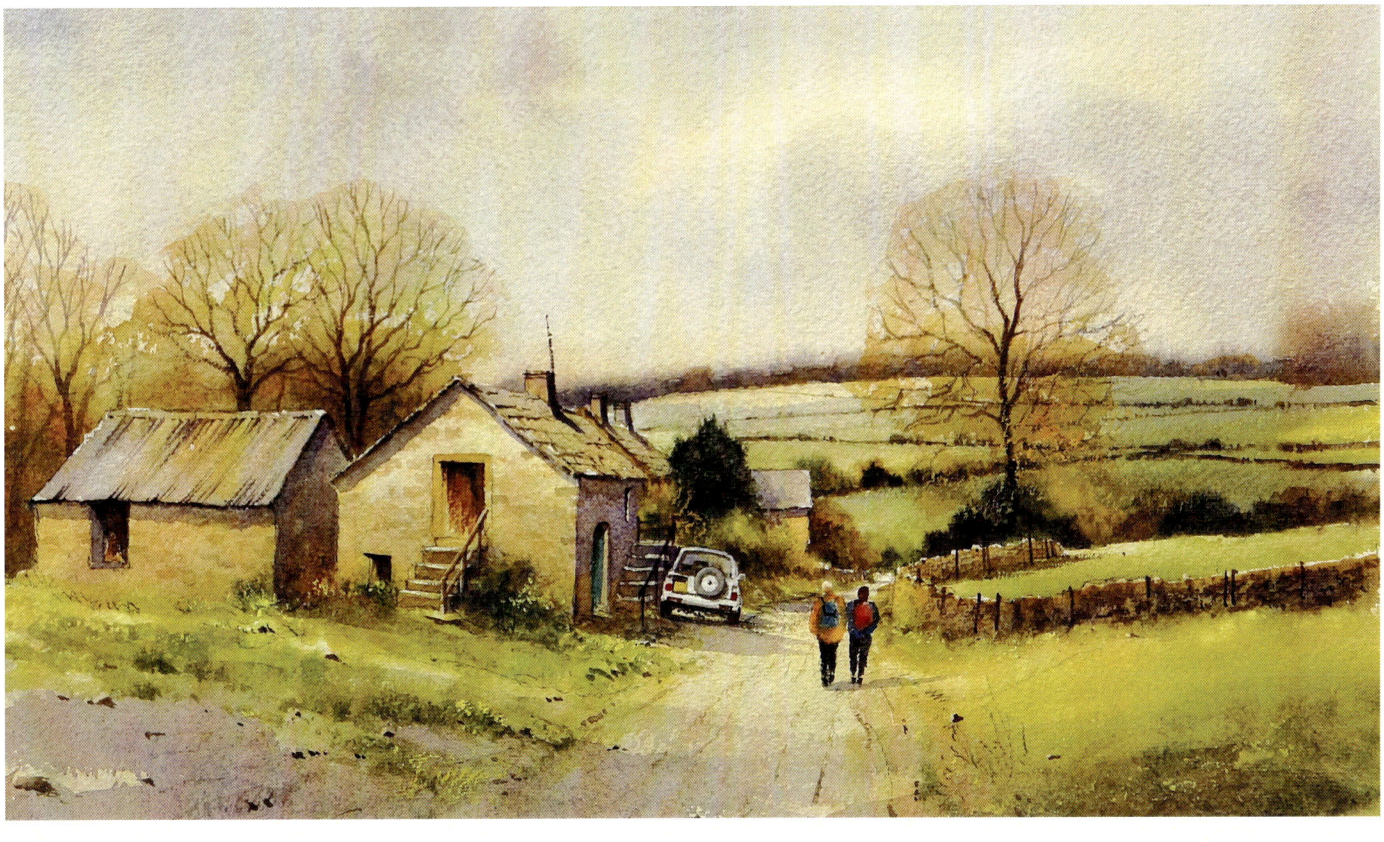

9 *Around Chatsworth*

When driving through Chatsworth Park and seeing the house for the first time, with its warm, honey coloured stone, set below a tree covered hillside and fronted by the River Derwent, it is understandable why it is arguably the premier tourist attraction of the area.

The original house was the work of Sir William Cavendish and his third wife Bess of Hardwick in the mid-sixteenth century. Sir William died in 1557, with the house only partly constructed, and Bess completed it. No trace of this house can still be seen, the present structure having been built between 1686 and 1707 with subsequent additions between 1790 and 1858.

The park was landscaped by the fourth Duke, who engaged Capability Brown to reshape the formal garden, giving it the more natural look seen today.

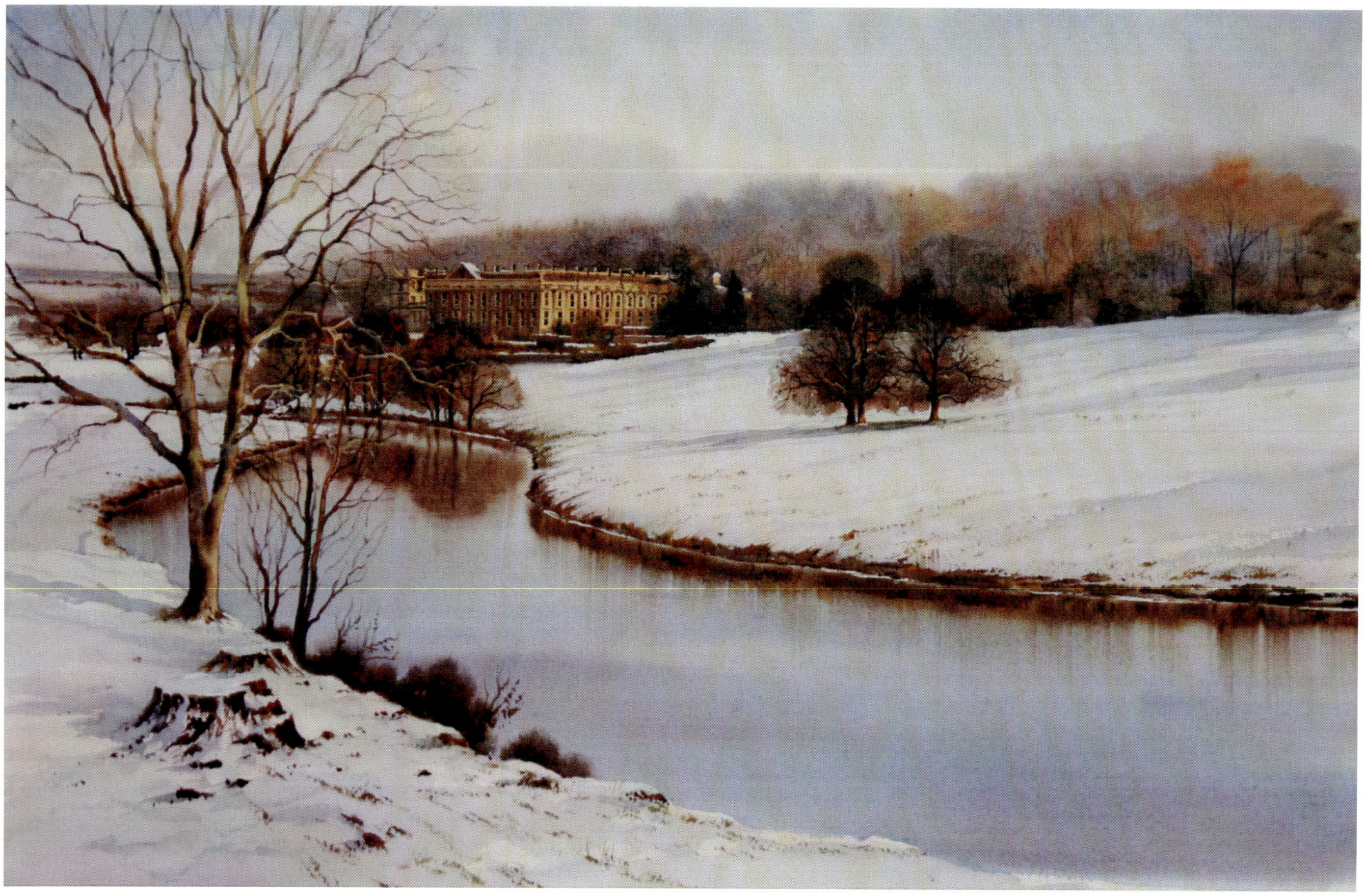

Chatsworth in Winter 1

My favourite view of the house, because it shows not just the attractive proportions of the building but the beauty of its setting. The size of the middle distance trees on the right-hand river bank are deliberately reduced, as they obscured the view of the house a little too much. I composed the picture with the house positioned a third of the way in from the left and a third of the way down from the top. The subject of composition can be quite involved, but thinking in 'thirds' generally prevents one from going far wrong.

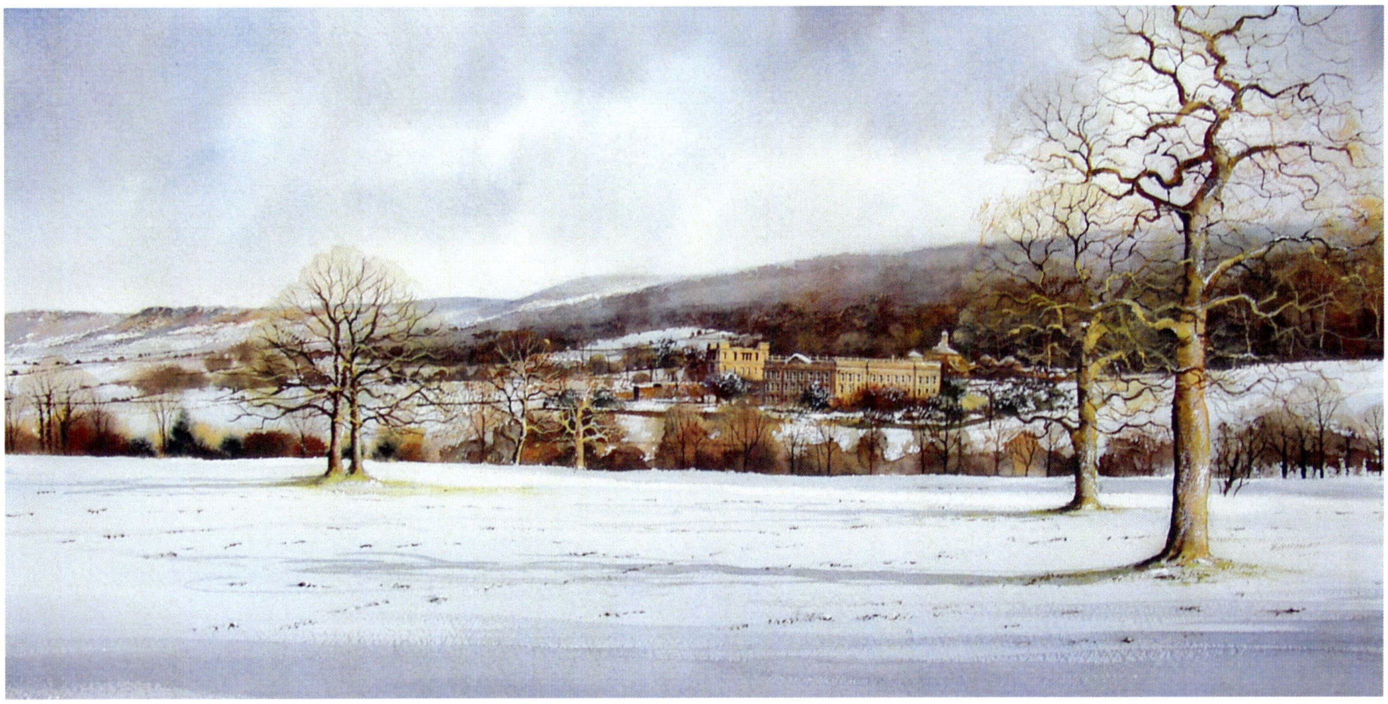

Chatsworth in Winter 2

A similar view of the house, but this time with the river hidden by the slope of the field. A few touches of neutral tint to the sky and shadows give it a colder appearance.

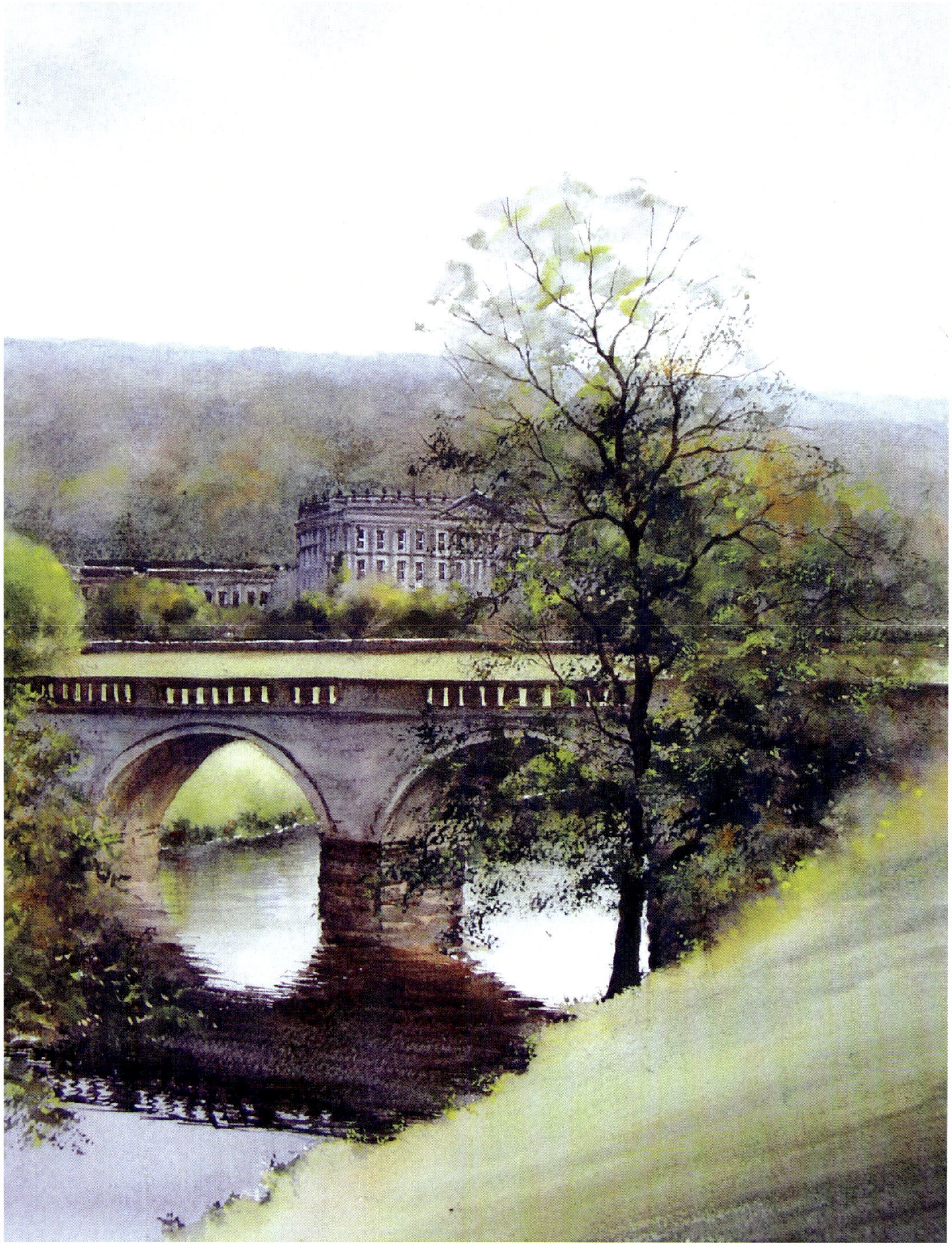

Chatsworth House from the Bridge

This is probably the view of Chatsworth most used on calendars and cards, probably because it is a perfect composition. The challenge with painting this scene is to avoid the house looking like it is hovering above the bridge, rather than in the middle distance. To achieve this shadow was used to cool the colour of the house, contrasted with the hint of warm reflected light under the arches of the bridge and in the reflections. It is a good rule of thumb that cool colours recede and warm colours appear nearer.

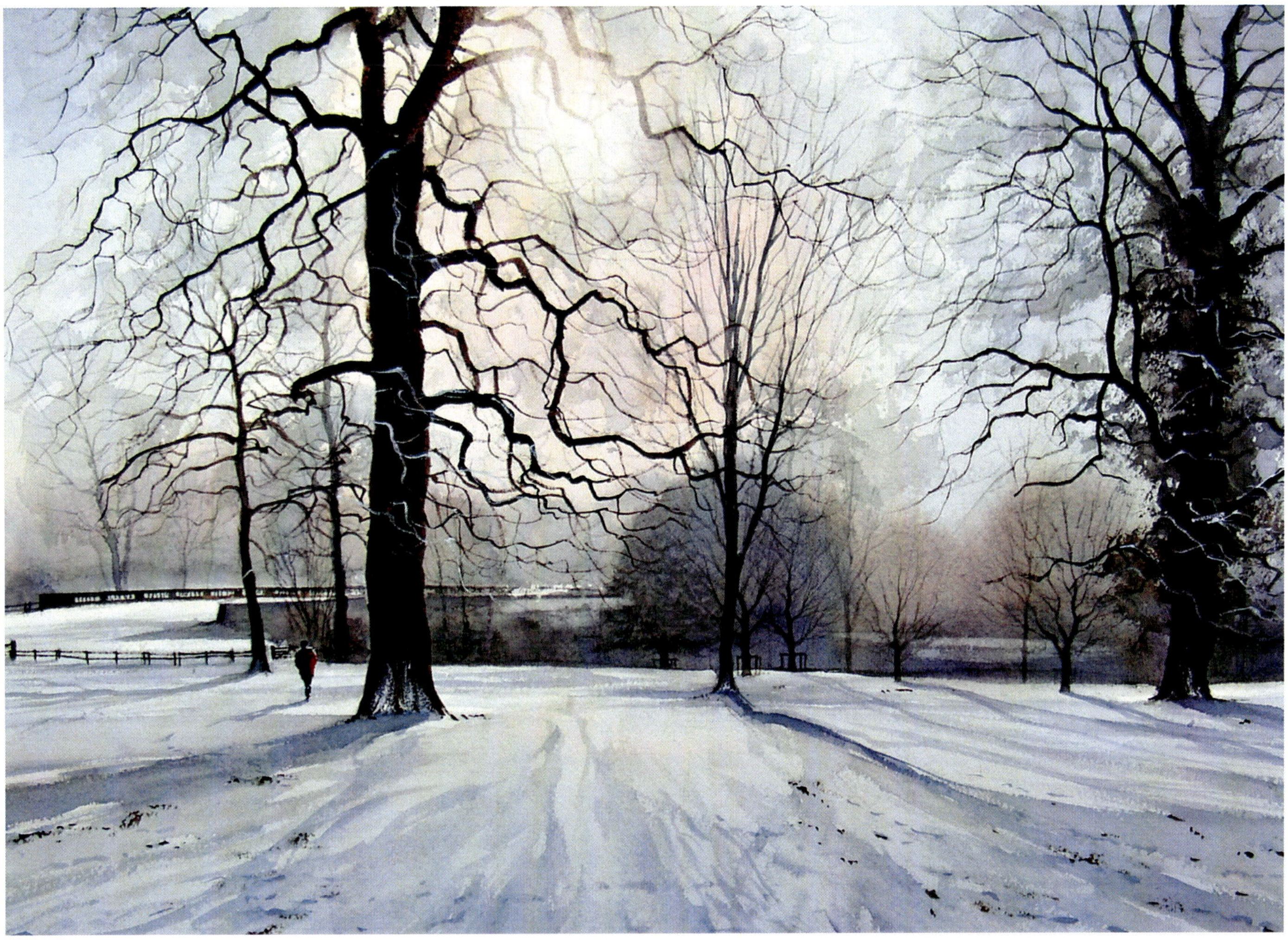

Winter Silhouettes, Chatsworth

In this view, giving us a glimpse of the bridge, I painted all the background wet into wet with light tones to provide a soft misty effect. In the top branches of the tree on the left the dry colour was brushed over with a stiff brush to wear some of it away, giving the impression of looking into the bright winter sunlight. The suggestions of thin, snow-covered branches in front of the trunks were painted with white gouache on a very fine brush.

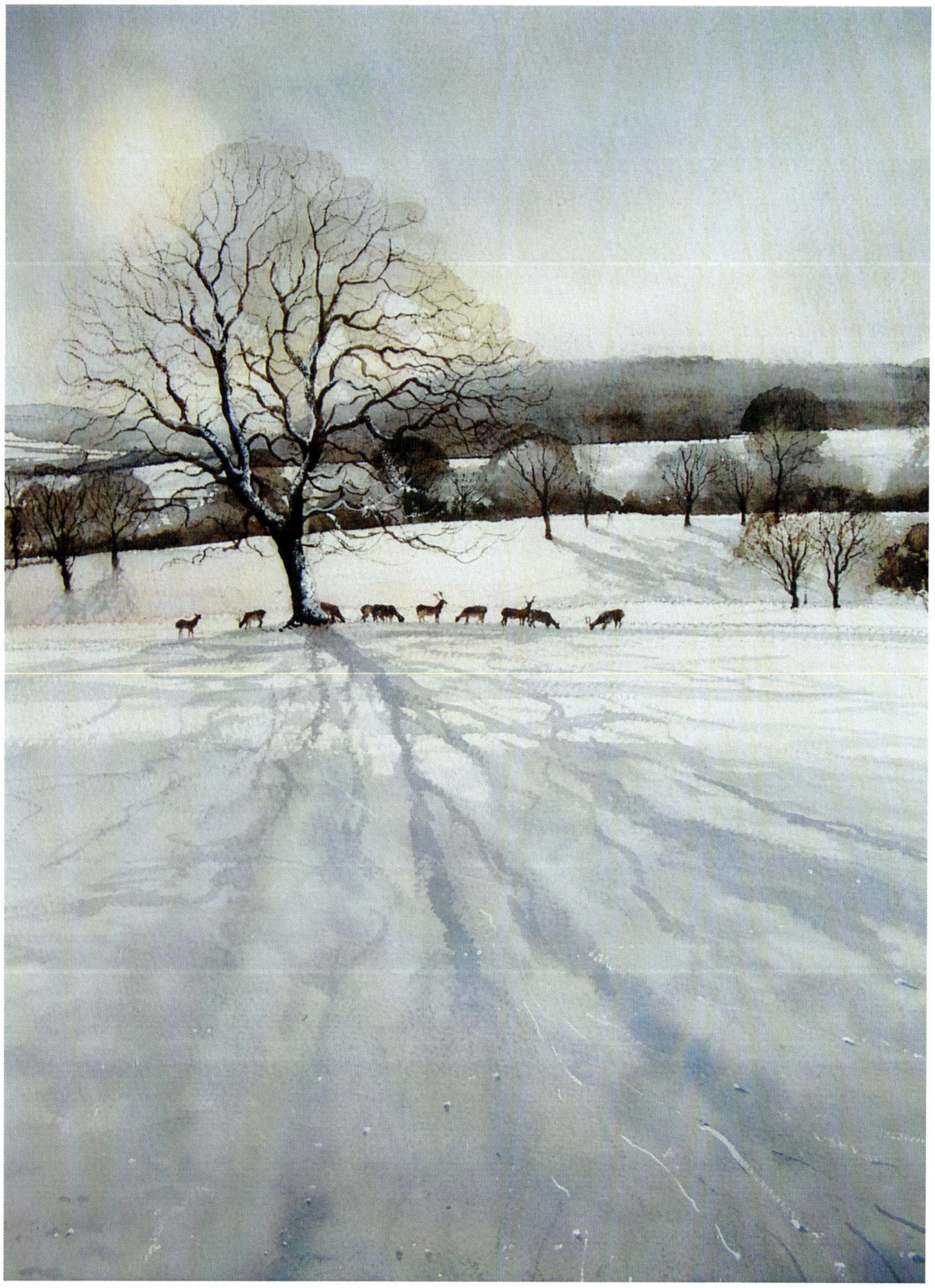

Deer in Chatsworth Park

In the above painting, a similar approach was taken as in *Winter Silhouettes* on the previous page. Facing into the sun again, a heard of grazing deer gather around the focal point, the perspective of the shadows leads the eye to this point.

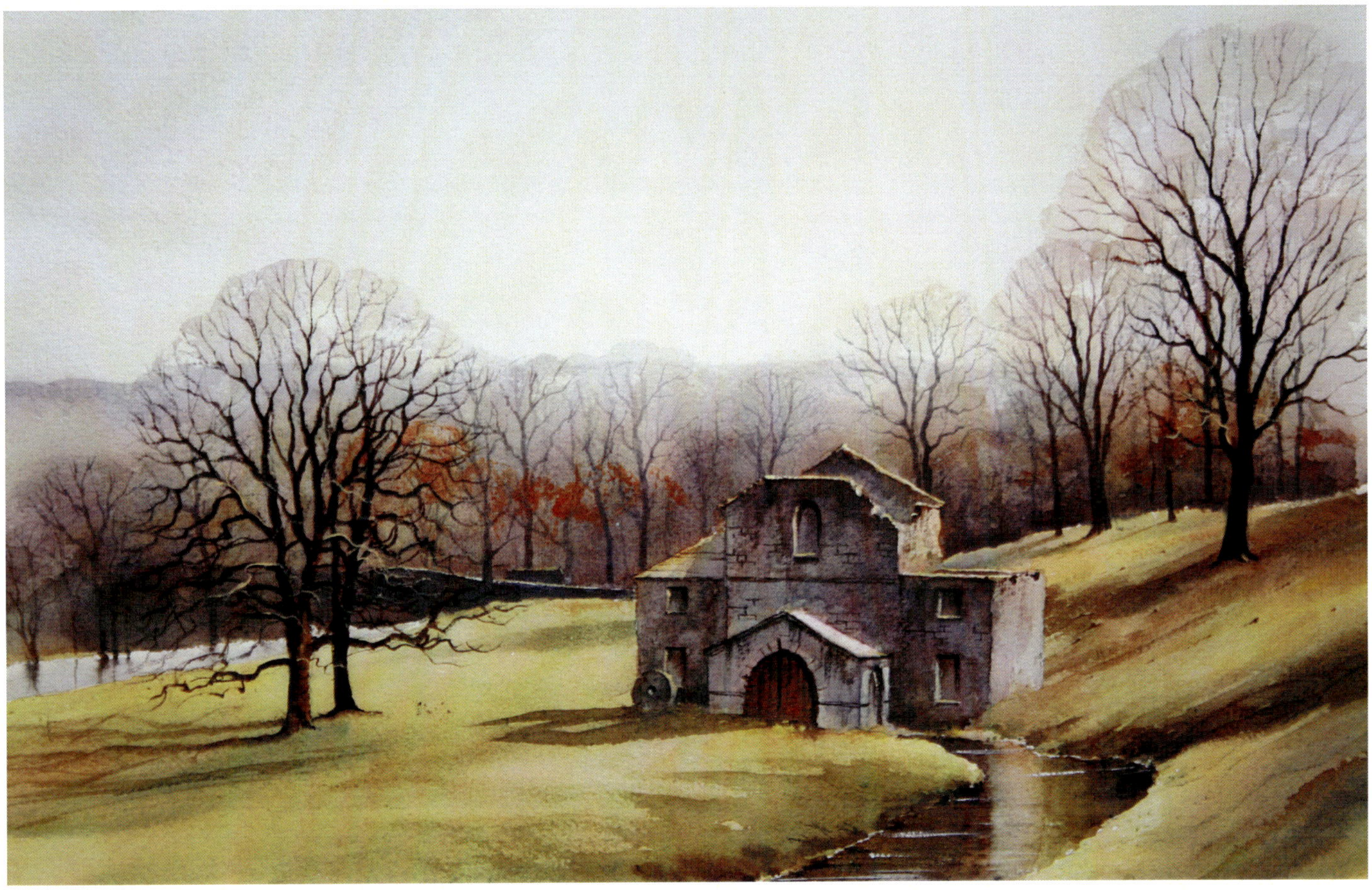

The Old Water Mill, Chatsworth

This ruined water mill built in 1760 is a symbol of Derbyshire's industrial heritage. It was badly damaged in 1962 when a couple of trees fell on it and there is a campaign to restore it, but to me, as a ruin it is a fascinating painting subject.

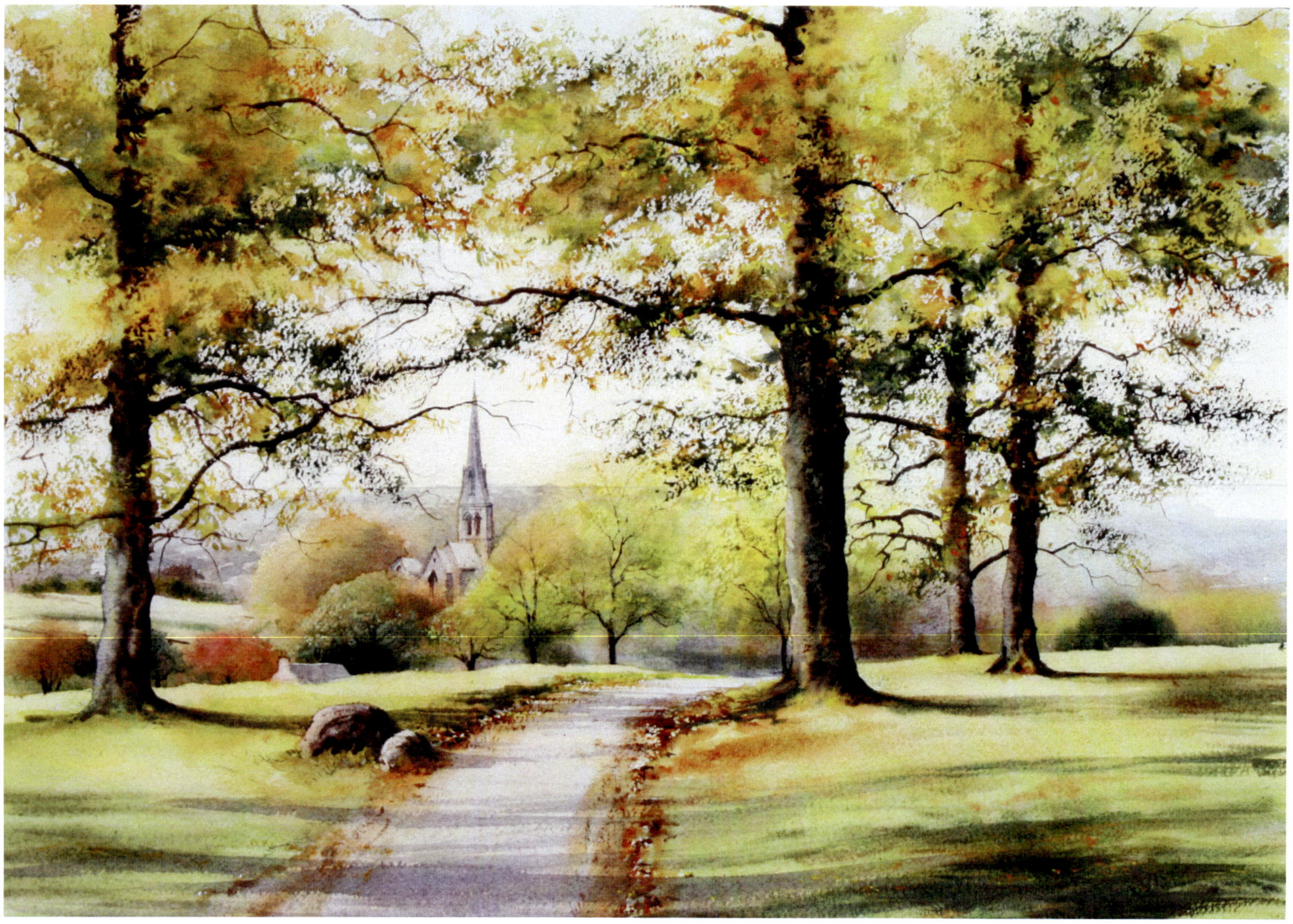

Looking towards Edensor

Edensor (pronounced 'Ensor') is the nearest village to Chatsworth House and much of it belongs to the Duke of Devonshire. The village was originally immediately below Chatsworth, close to the River Derwent, but the Dukes had it moved out of sight over a hill, apart from one cottage whose tenant didn't want to move, which still stands in Chatsworth Park.

In the churchyard of Edensor's St Peter's Church are the graves of Joseph Paxton and U.S. President John F. Kennedy's sister Kathleen Kennedy, who was married to the tenth Duke's eldest son. Kennedy visited the grave during his presidency.

In early autumn, with plenty of foliage on the trees, all that can be seen of Edensor is the church, whereas when the landscape is opened up in winter *(overleaf in Edensor, Chatsworth)* there is a much clearer impression of the shape of the village.

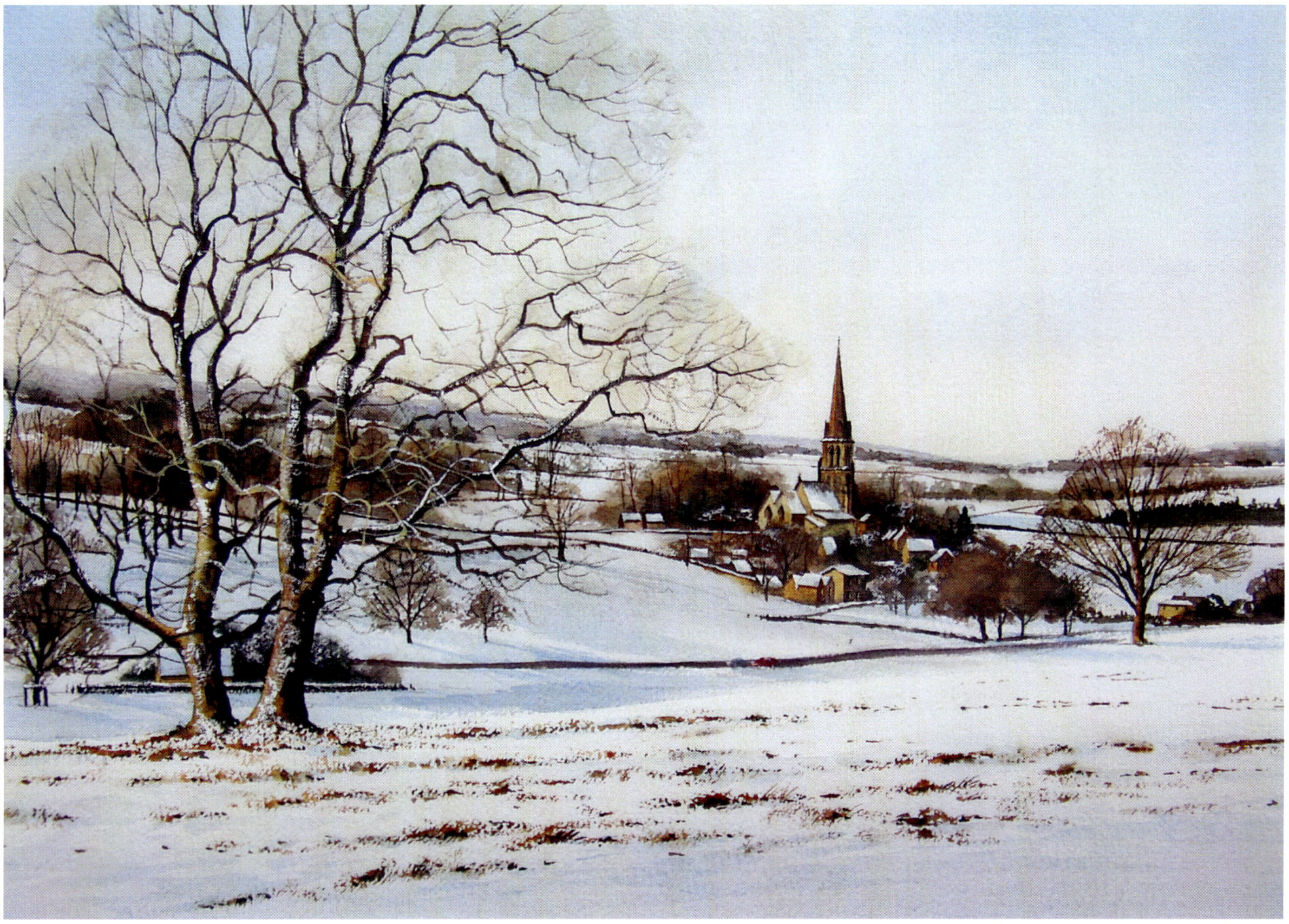

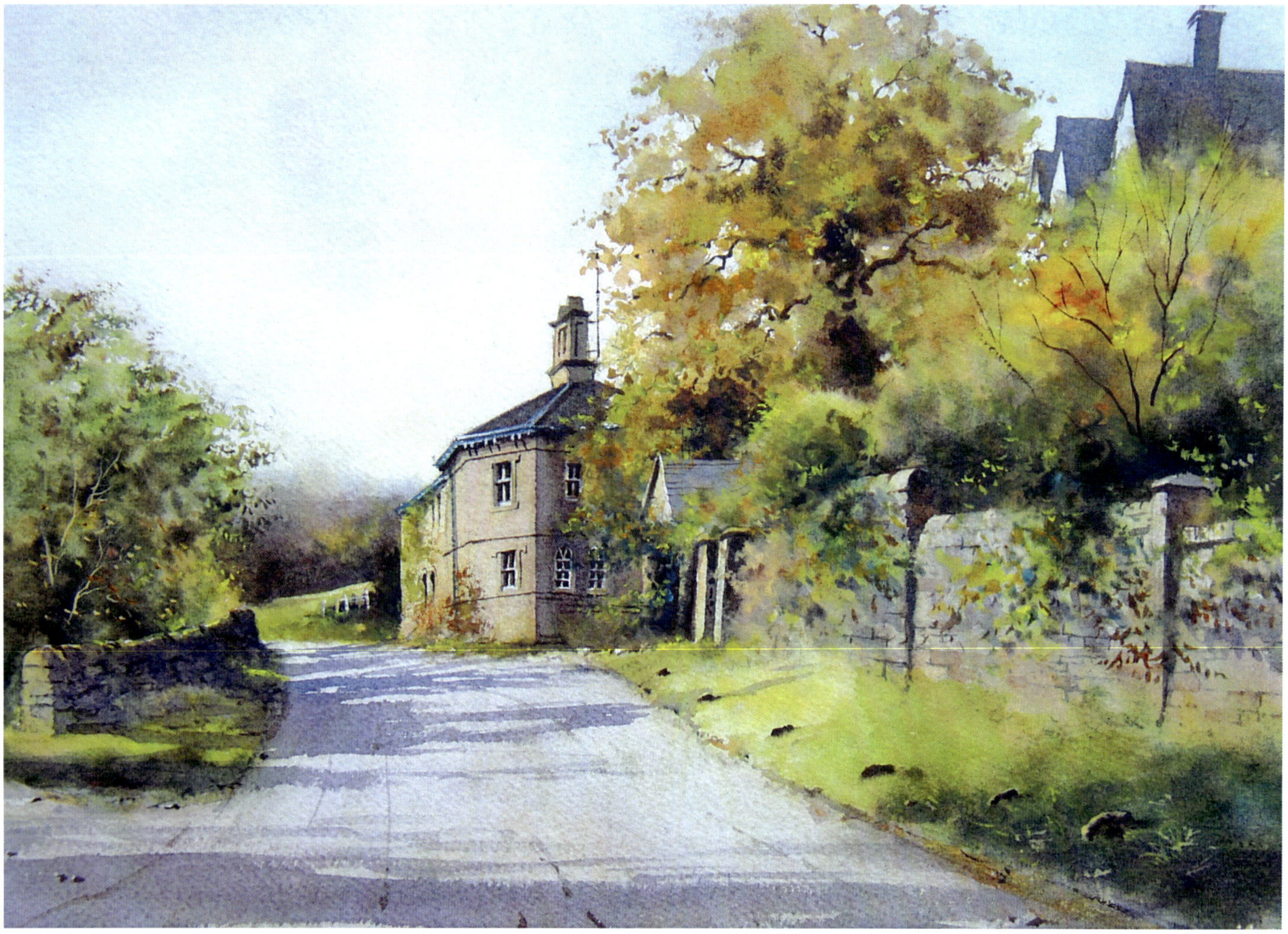

Edensor, Chatsworth

In these scenes – again one in autumn and one in winter – we are looking up the lane going out of Edensor. This makes a good walk, eventually leading to Ball Cross, from where a descent can be made into Bakewell. I particularly like the unusual octagonal shape of the cottage with the three arched windows.

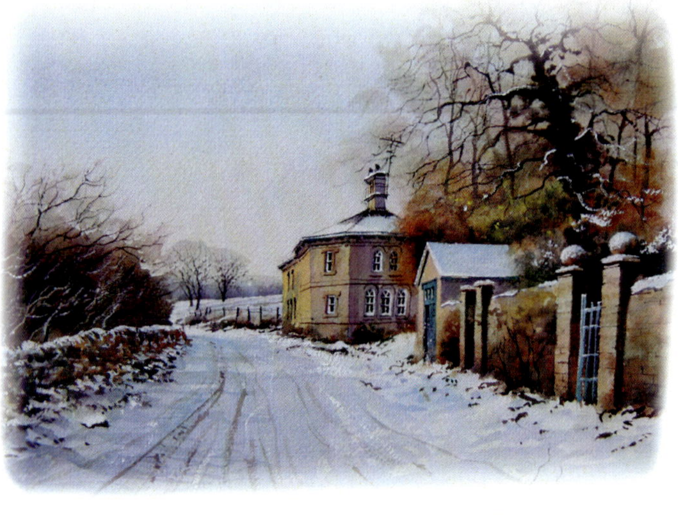

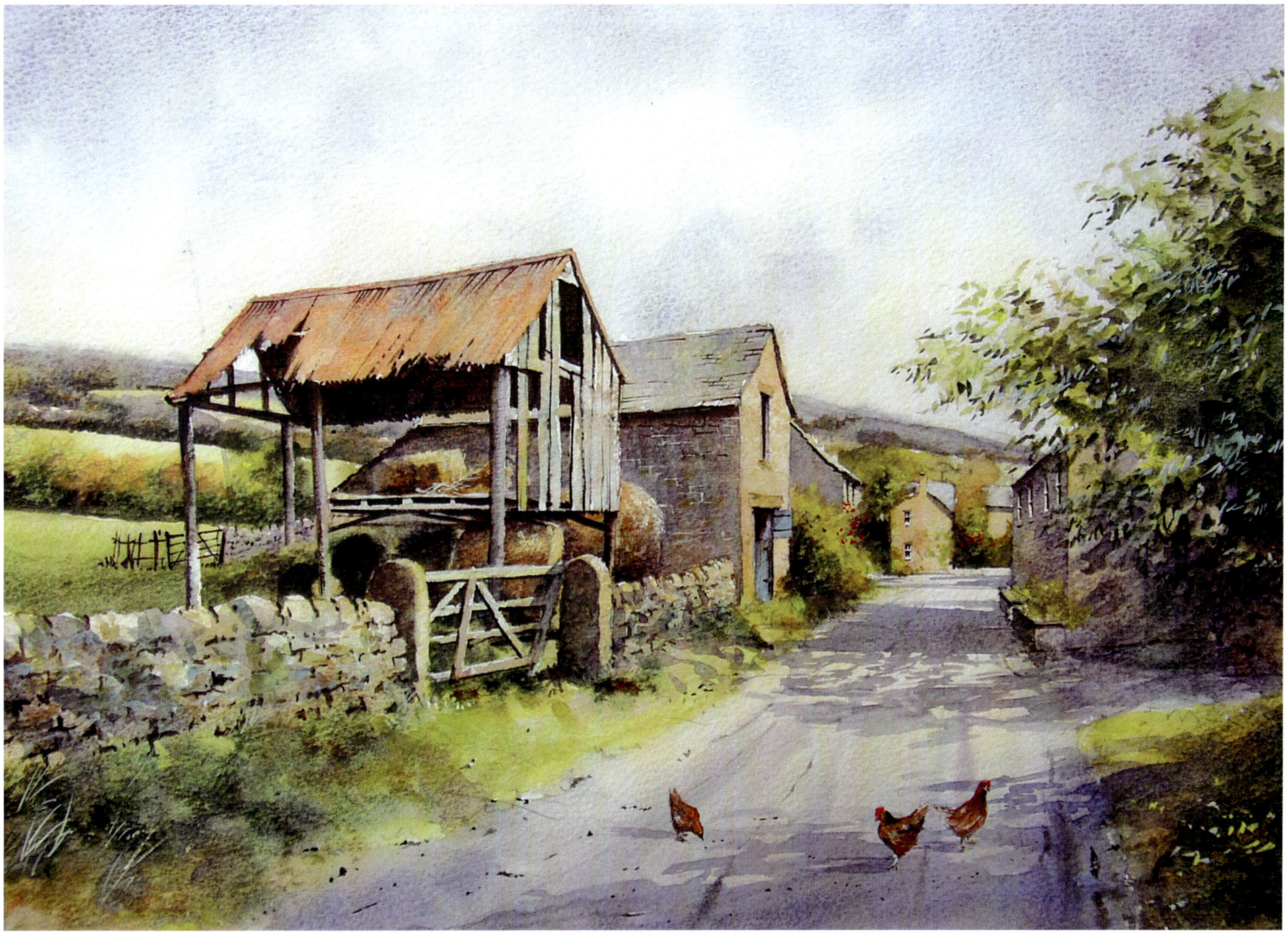

Pig Lane Beeley

Beeley is a small village just off the B6012 between Chatsworth and Rowsley. It has been part of the Chatsworth estate since the eighteenth century, although a lot of the houses are now privately owned. In this scene I was drawn to the rusting corrugated roof of the foreground barn, along with the gaps in the rotting timbers, and the haphazard way the gate leans between the stone posts.

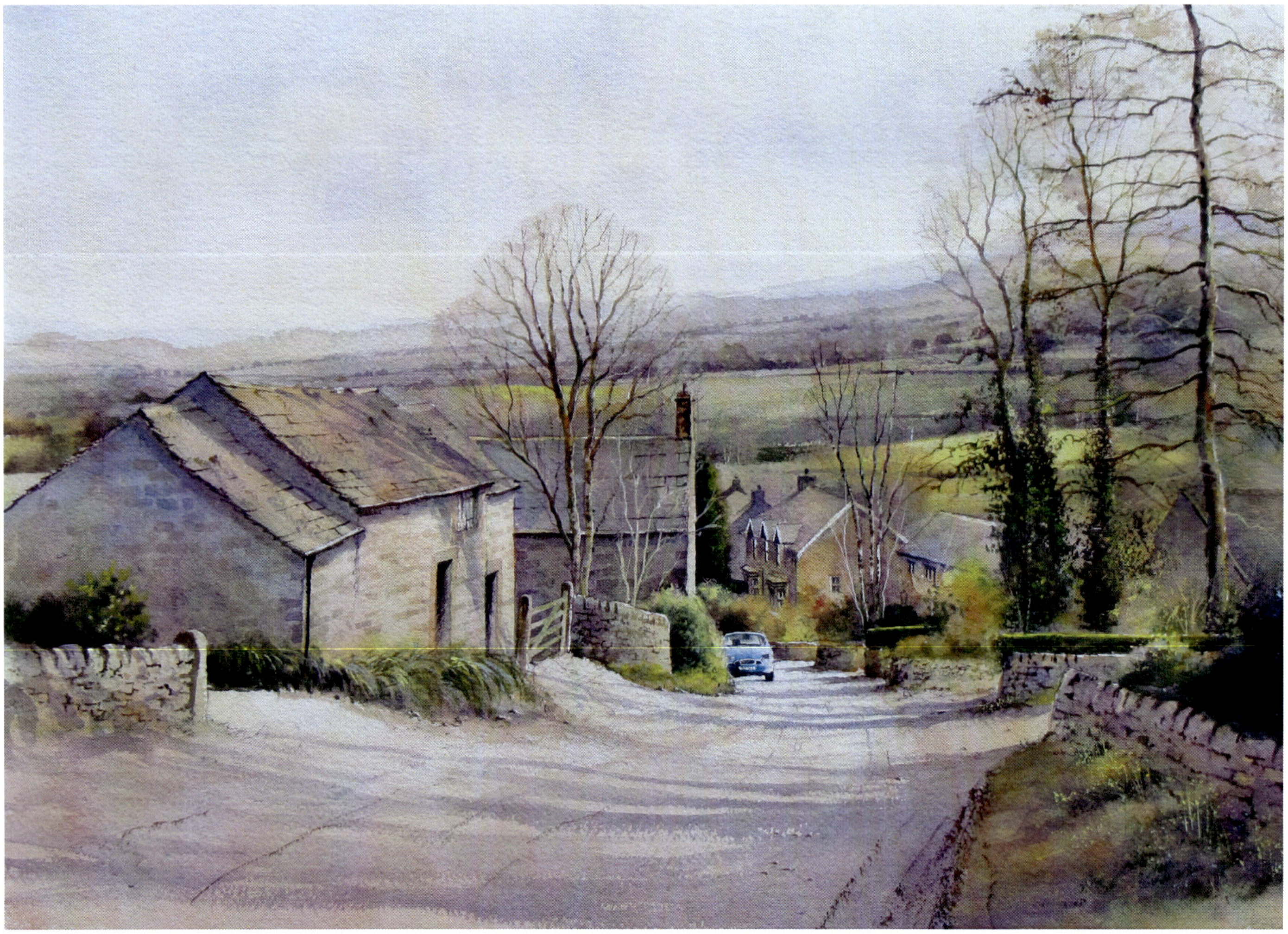

Looking Down to Rowsley

The little village of Rowsley is split into two parts, divided by the A6 Matlock to Bakewell Road. The view here is on the Chatsworth side of the road; a view I have painted a few times. The cool greys in the distant hills were used to create a 'far away' look, before gradually changing to the rich meadow greens in the middle distance, contrasted with sweeps of cloud shadow. The car and foreground buildings are a lot sharper, adding to the sense of distance.

10 *Castleton*

High above the attractive village of Castleton stand the imposing ruins of Peveril Castle, one of England's earliest Norman fortresses, the keep having been built in 1176. A day in Castleton wouldn't be complete without a climb to this prominent Peak District landmark to enjoy the panoramic views over the Hope Valley.

In addition to the castle there are another two main features of interest: Cave Dale and Peak Cavern. Cave Dale is a collapsed cavern, the very bottom part being covered by a natural arch until around 200 years ago. Peak Cavern, which has a very impressive entrance, was once used by a family of rope makers who built their cottages within the cave entrance. It is open to visitors from April to October, but it is well worth walking to it even when closed.

Surrounding the village square are some excellent old houses and cottages, including several pubs. Along the main road are several shops selling jewellery and objets d'art made from Blue John, a local variety of fluorspar known for its beautiful colouring.

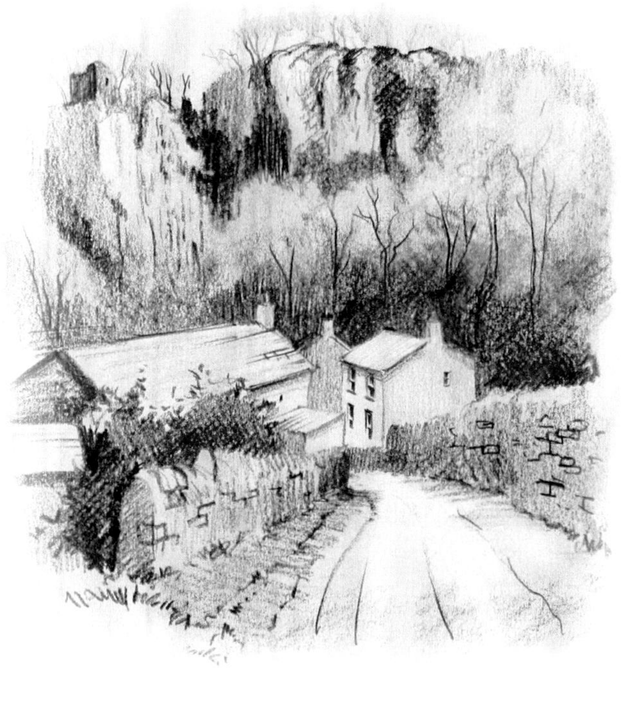

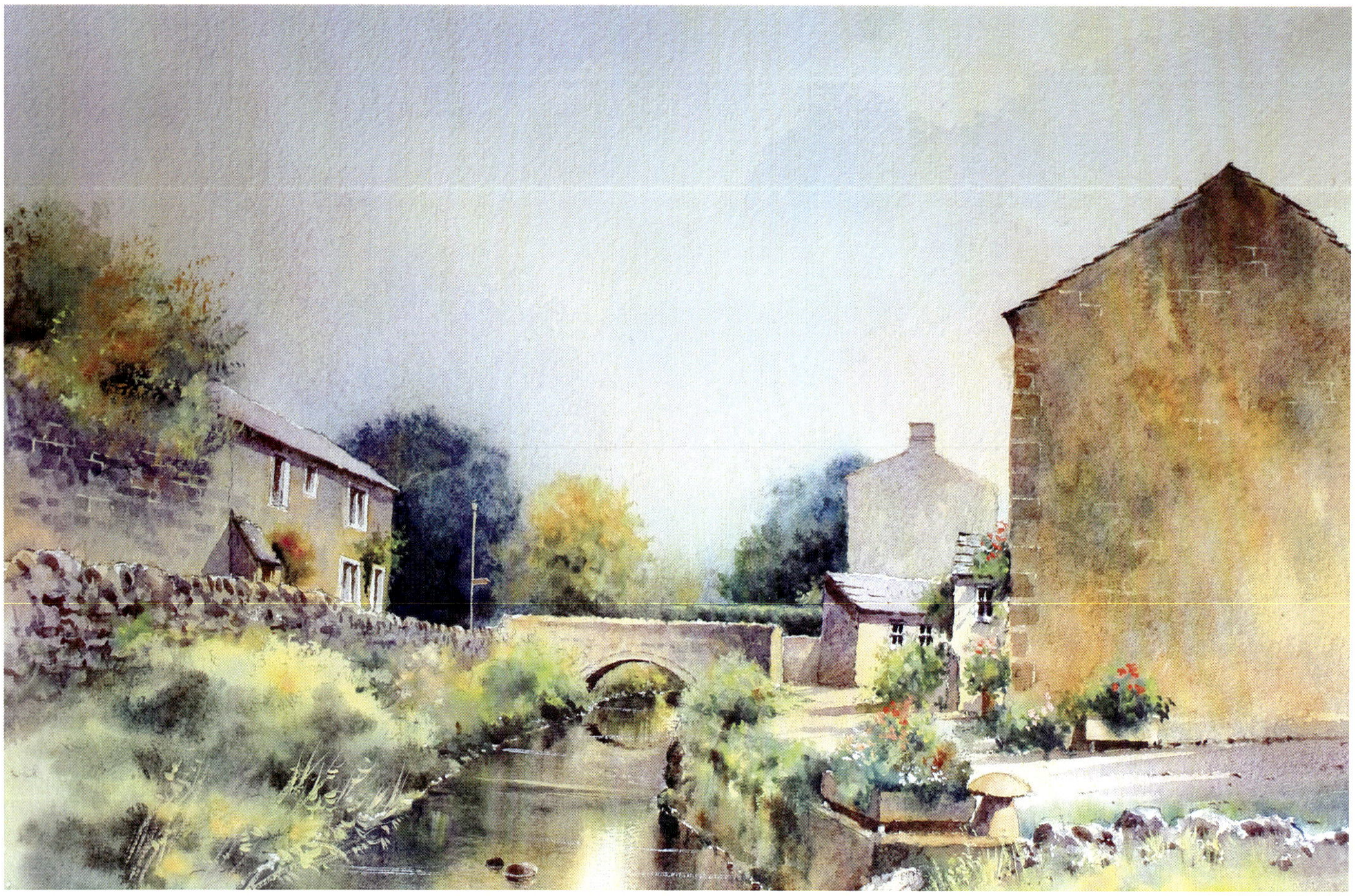

Peak Cavern Walk

Although not the traditional view of Peak Cavern walk favoured by artists and photographers alike and adorning many a calendar, I like this scene, taken from the opposite direction looking towards the little footbridge. The assortment of pots and planters on the right gave an excuse to add a few splashes of colour. The water that sustains this little river flowing through the village has travelled underground from caverns on Winnats Pass and is known as 'Peak Holes Water'.

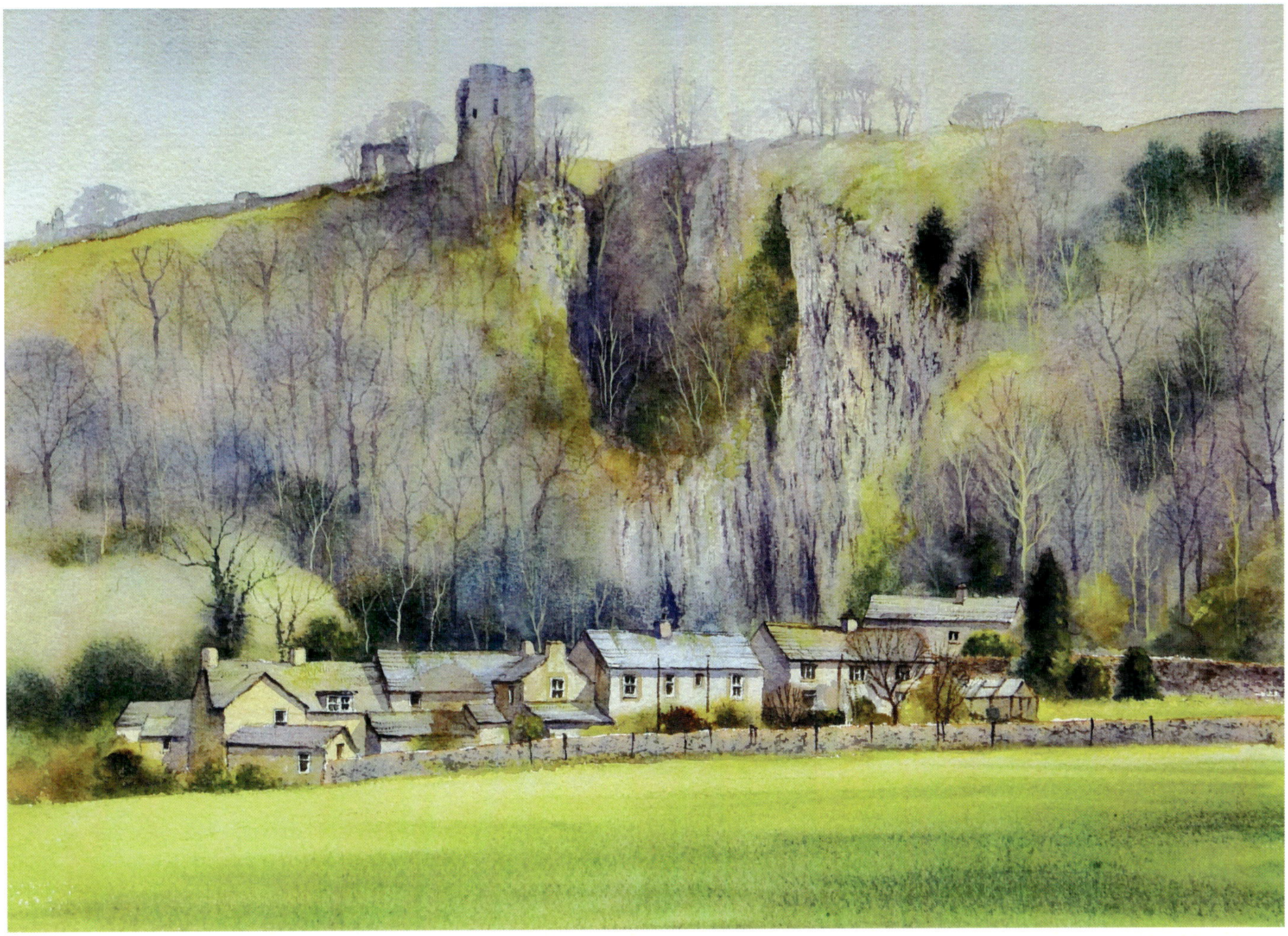

Peak Cavern Entrance, below Peveril Castle

The view of this steep, almost sheer drop, with houses and cottages nestling at its foot, is on the road out of Castleton towards Winnats Pass. The challenge with a scene like this is to contrast the rough texture of the rock face with the softer shapes of the masses of trees. I was particularly drawn to the almost silhouetted shape of Peveril Castle, perched on top, overlooking the scene.

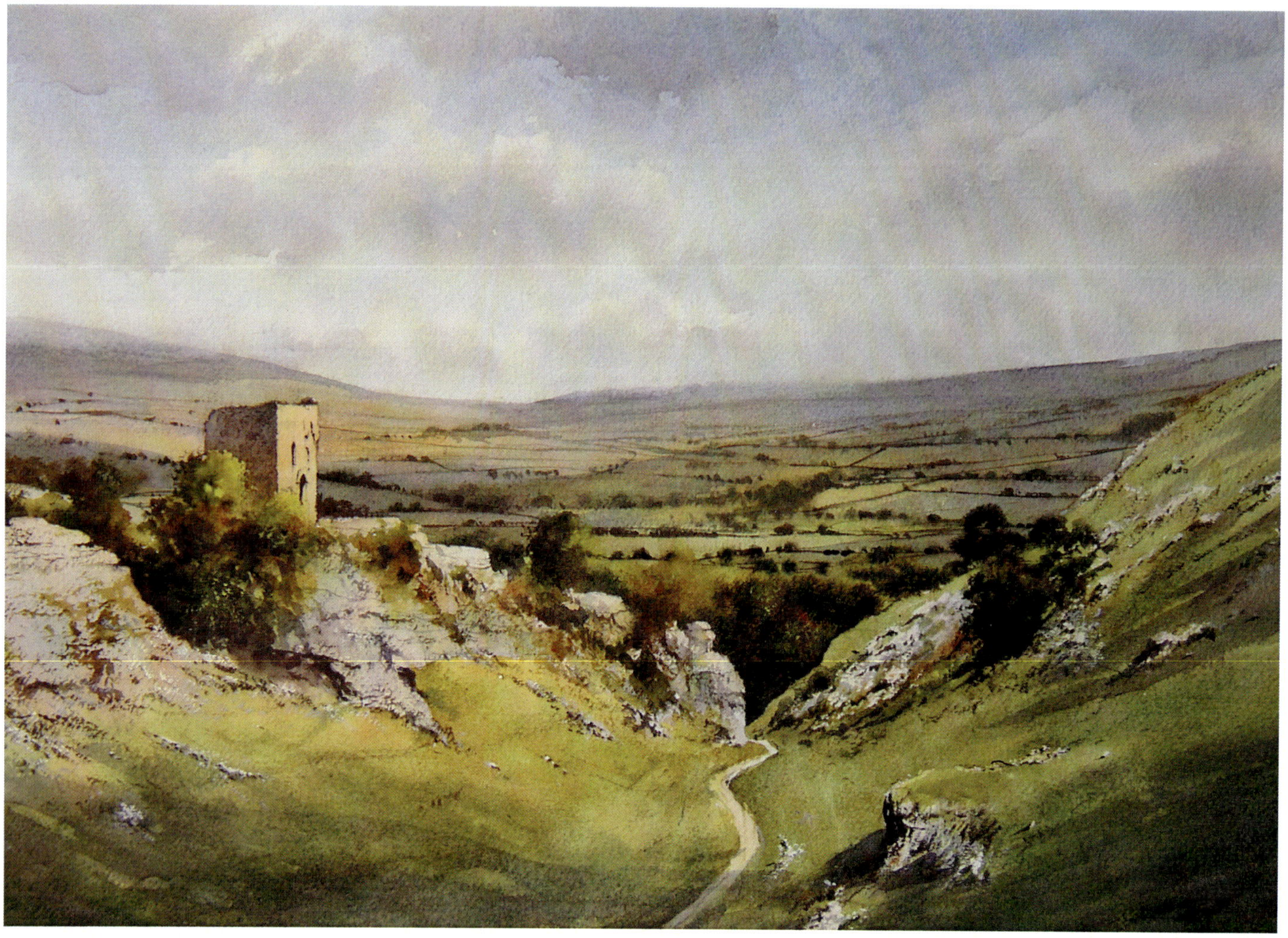

Cave Dale on the Limestone Way

The Limestone Way is a waymarked long distance footpath that goes from south of the village of Castleton, through dramatic dales and rolling landscape to Rocester, on the banks of the River Dove. At this point it passes very close to Peveril Castle with a stunning panoramic view of the Hope Valley.

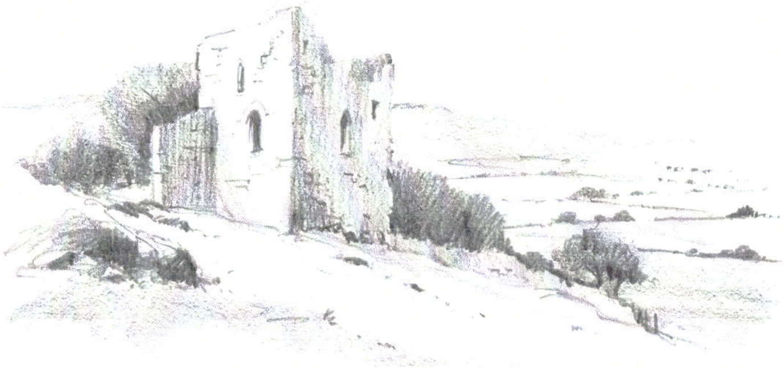

This composition uses the winding footpath as a device to lead into the scene, before taking a dramatic drop out of view in the middle distance. The placement of the dark trees in this area provides an important contrast to the bright light on the rocks immediately to the left of the gap.